GARTH ENNIS

RUSS BRAUN

JIMMY'S BASTARDS™

VOLUME 2

WHAT DID YOU JUST SAY?

JOHN KALISZ

ROB STEEN

ANDY CLARKE

AFTERSHOCK™

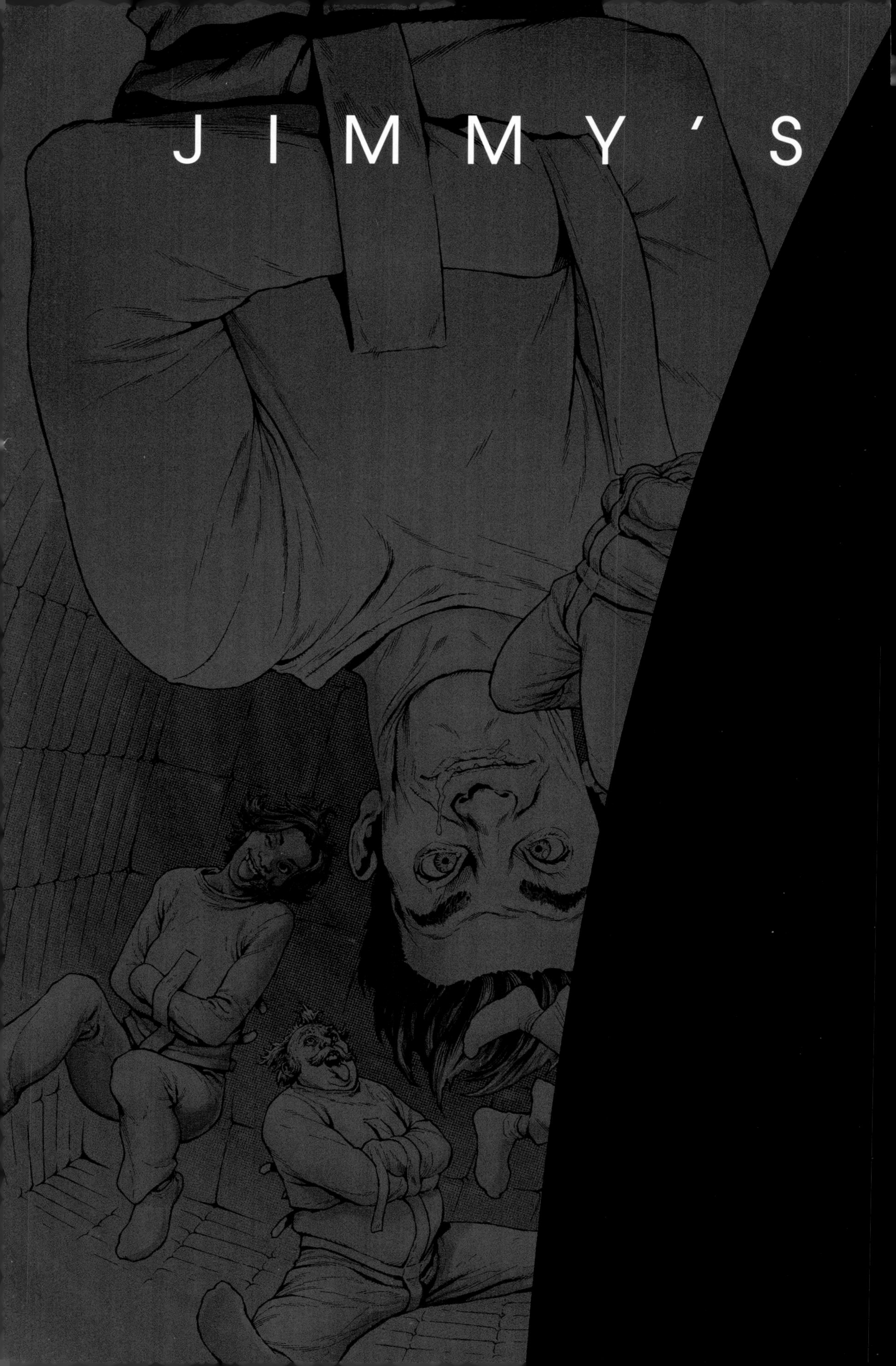
JIMMY'S

B A S T A R D S
V O L U M E   2
W H A T   D I D   Y O U   J U S T   S A Y ?

GARTH ENNIS co-creator & writer

RUSS BRAUN co-creator & artist

JOHN KALISZ colorist

ROB STEEN letterer

ANDY CLARKE w/ **JOSE VILLARRUBIA** original covers

JOHN J. HILL logo designer

COREY BREEN book designer

MIKE MARTS editor

AFTERSHOCK

MIKE MARTS - Editor-in-Chief • JOE PRUETT - Publisher/ Chief Creative Officer • LEE KRAMER - President
JON KRAMER - Chief Executive Officer • STEVE ROTTERDAM - SVP, Sales & Marketing • LISA Y. WU - Retailer/Fan Relations Manager
CHRISTINA HARRINGTON - Managing Editor • JAY BEHLING - Chief Financial Officer • JAWAD QURESHI - SVP, Investor Relations
AARON MARION - Publicist • CHRIS LA TORRE - Sales Associate • KIM PAGNOTTA - Sales Associate • LISA MOODY - Finance
CHARLES PRITCHETT - Comics Production • COREY BREEN - Collections Production • TEDDY LEO - Editorial Assistant
SIMON WHITE - Proofreader

AfterShock Trade Dress and Interior Design by JOHN J. HILL • AfterShock Logo Design by COMICRAFT
Publicity: contact AARON MARION (aaron@publichausagency.com) & RYAN CROY (ryan@publichausagency.com) at PUBLICHAUS
Special thanks to: IRA KURGAN, STEPHAN NILSON, JULIE PIFHER and SARAH PRUETT

AFTERSHOCKCOMICS.COM Follow us on social media

JIMMY'S BASTARDS ™

6

THE LAUGHING ACADEMY

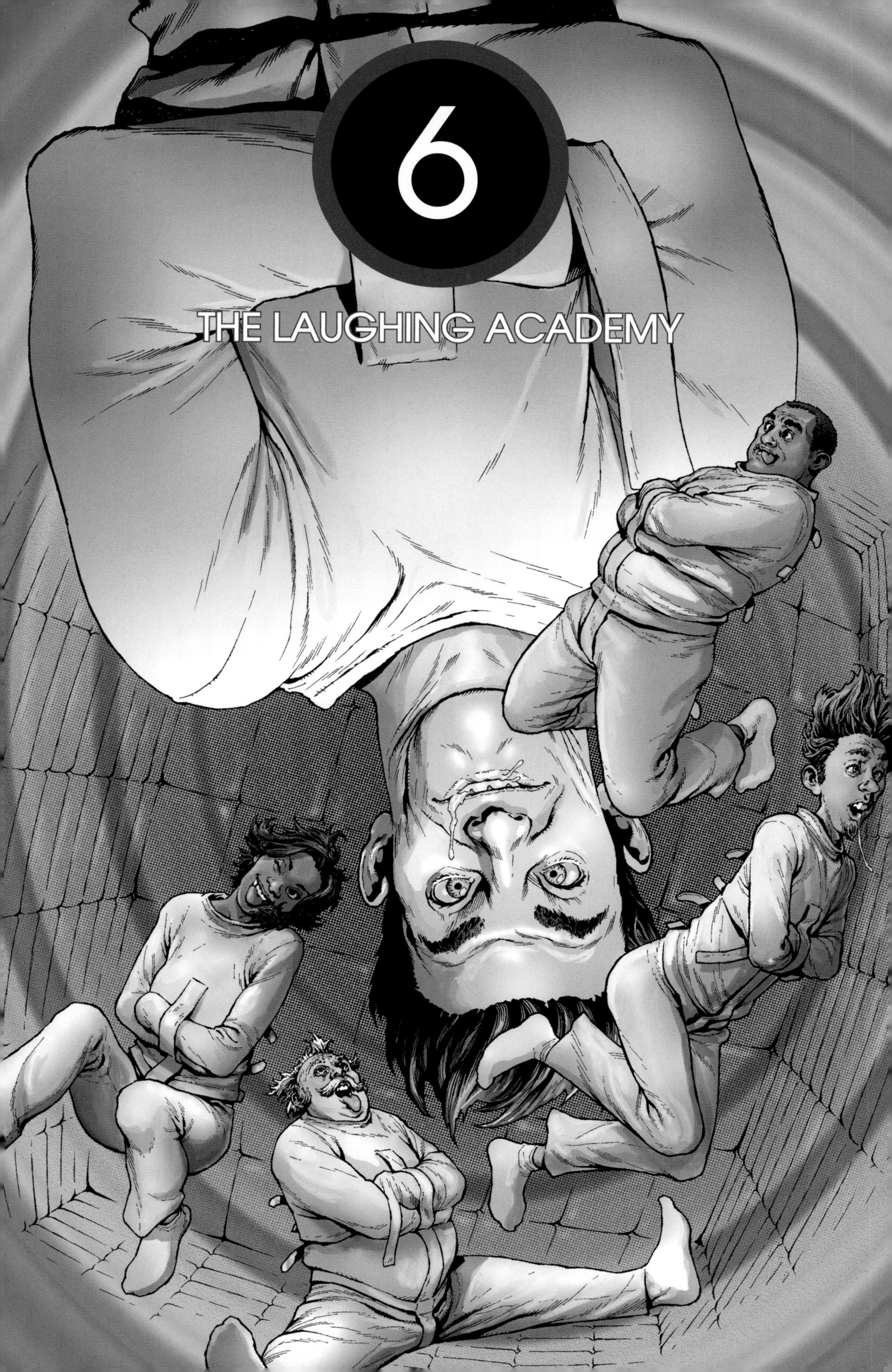

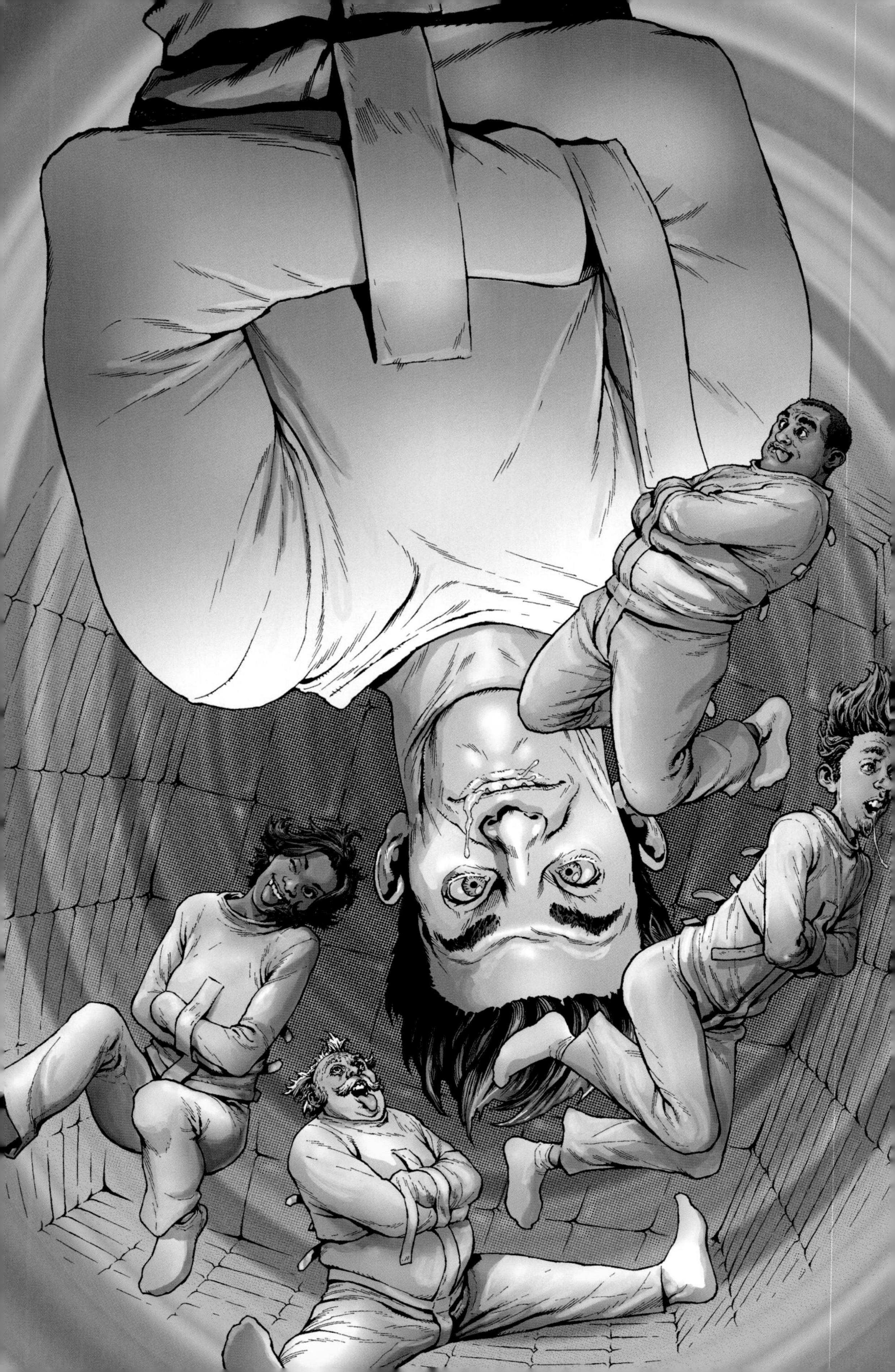

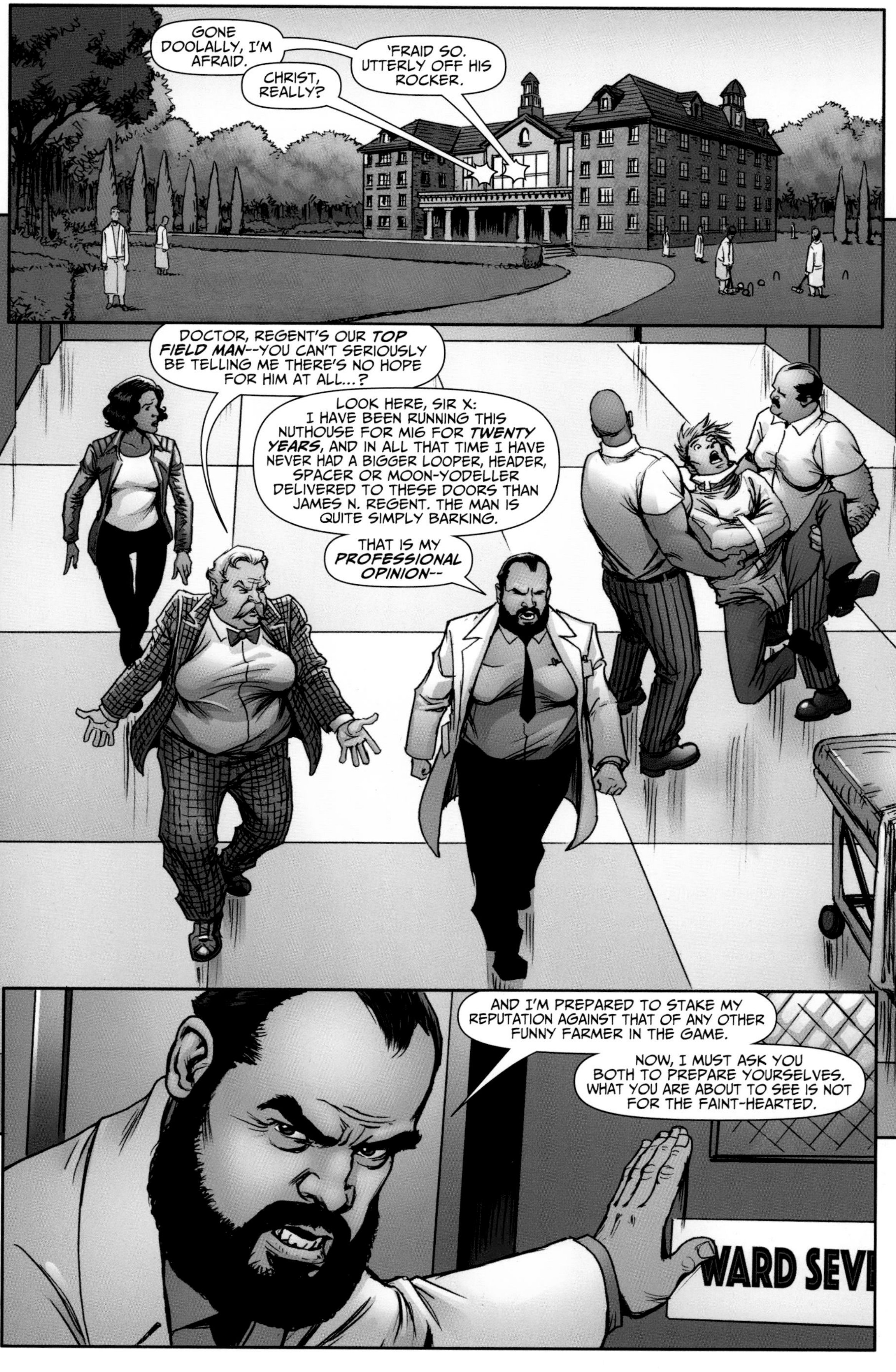
GONE DOOLALLY, I'M AFRAID.
CHRIST, REALLY?
'FRAID SO. UTTERLY OFF HIS ROCKER.
DOCTOR, REGENT'S OUR TOP FIELD MAN--YOU CAN'T SERIOUSLY BE TELLING ME THERE'S NO HOPE FOR HIM AT ALL...?
LOOK HERE, SIR X: I HAVE BEEN RUNNING THIS NUTHOUSE FOR MI6 FOR TWENTY YEARS, AND IN ALL THAT TIME I HAVE NEVER HAD A BIGGER LOOPER, HEADER, SPACER OR MOON-YODELLER DELIVERED TO THESE DOORS THAN JAMES N. REGENT. THE MAN IS QUITE SIMPLY BARKING.
THAT IS MY PROFESSIONAL OPINION--
AND I'M PREPARED TO STAKE MY REPUTATION AGAINST THAT OF ANY OTHER FUNNY FARMER IN THE GAME.
NOW, I MUST ASK YOU BOTH TO PREPARE YOURSELVES. WHAT YOU ARE ABOUT TO SEE IS NOT FOR THE FAINT-HEARTED.
WARD SEVE

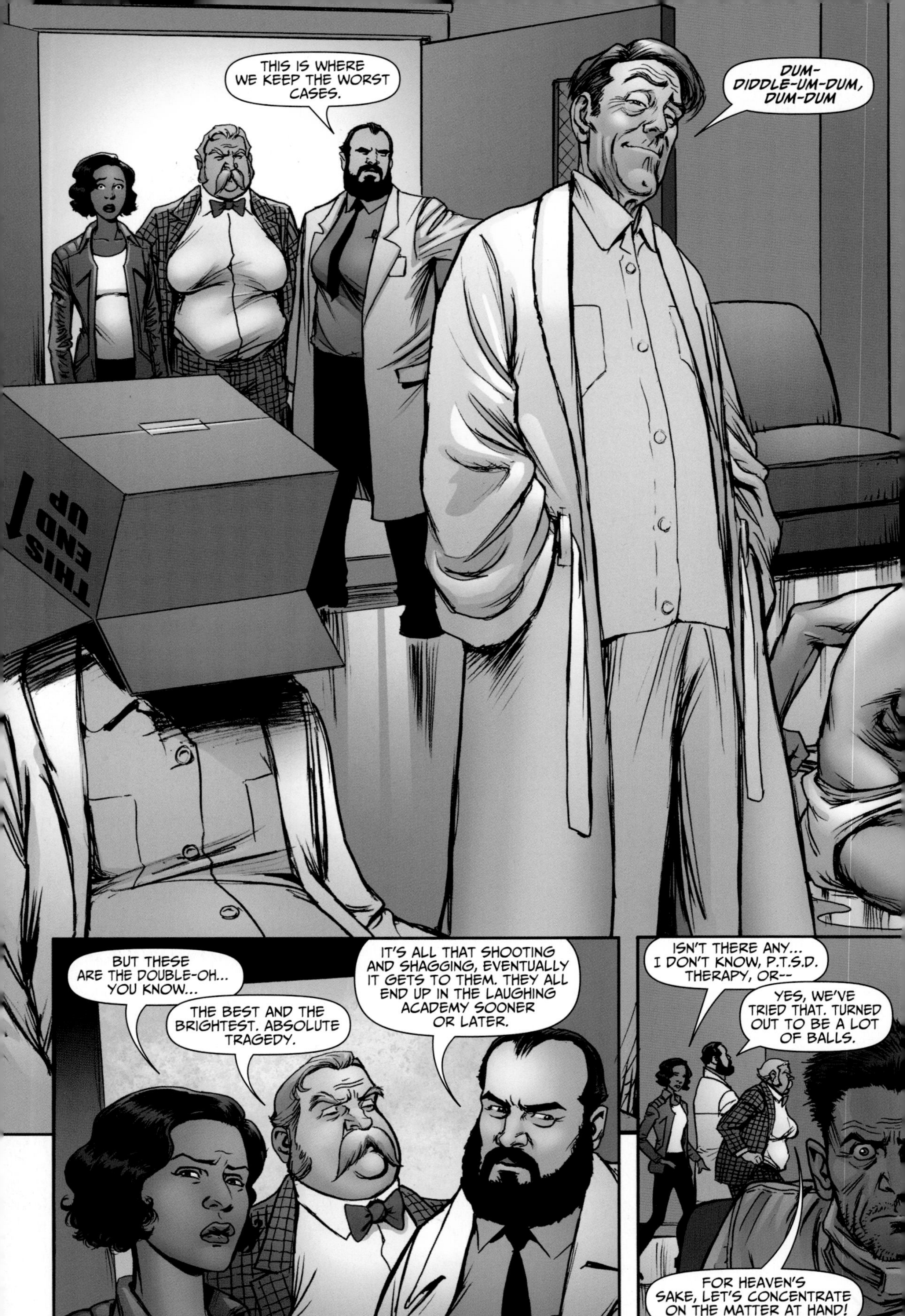
THIS IS WHERE WE KEEP THE WORST CASES.
DUM-DIDDLE-UM-DUM, DUM-DUM
THIS END UP
BUT THESE ARE THE DOUBLE-OH... YOU KNOW...
THE BEST AND THE BRIGHTEST. ABSOLUTE TRAGEDY.
IT'S ALL THAT SHOOTING AND SHAGGING, EVENTUALLY IT GETS TO THEM. THEY ALL END UP IN THE LAUGHING ACADEMY SOONER OR LATER.
ISN'T THERE ANY... I DON'T KNOW, P.T.S.D. THERAPY, OR--
YES, WE'VE TRIED THAT. TURNED OUT TO BE A LOT OF BALLS.
FOR HEAVEN'S SAKE, LET'S CONCENTRATE ON THE MATTER AT HAND!

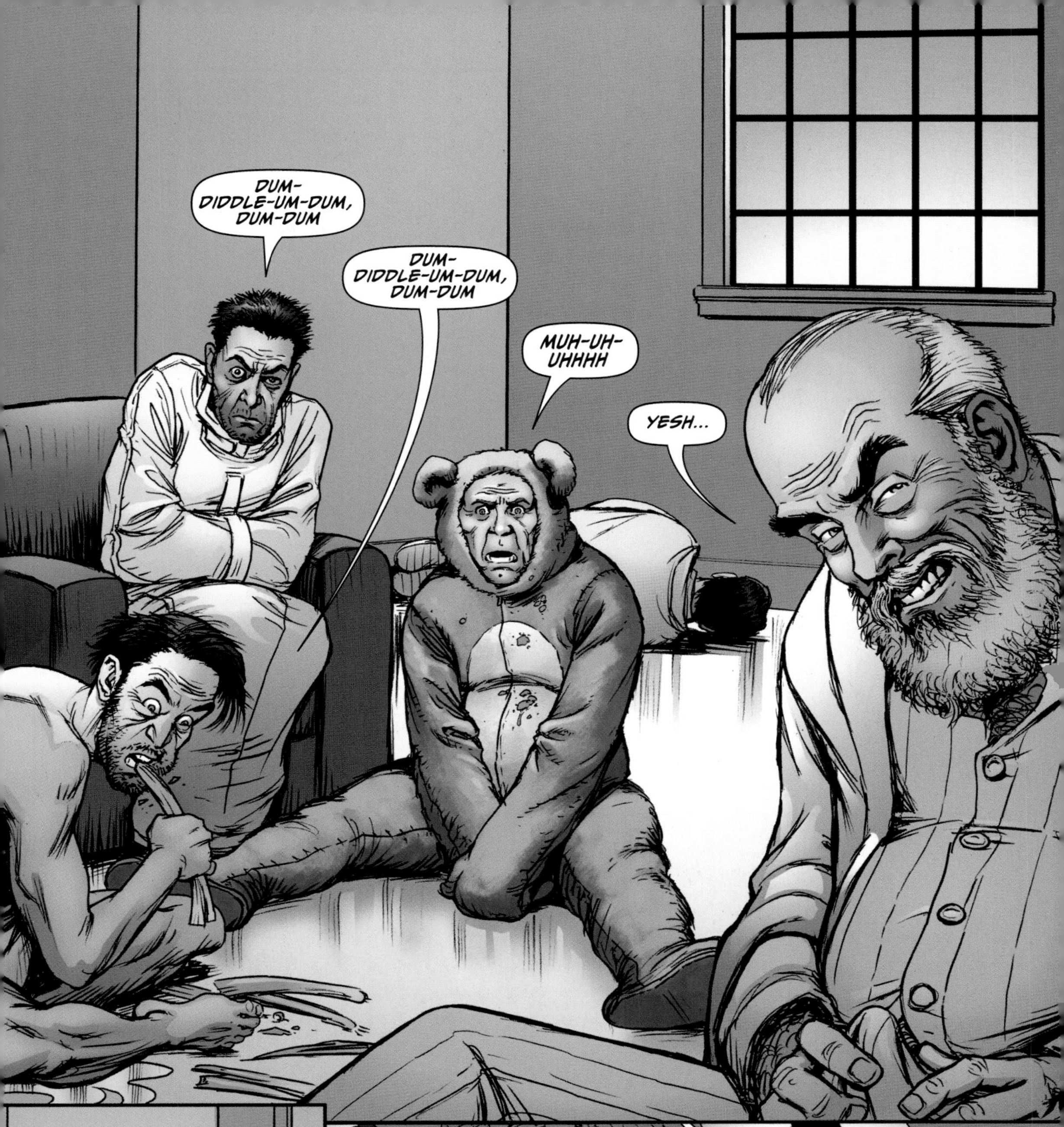
DUM-
DIDDLE-UM-DUM,
DUM-DUM
DUM-
DIDDLE-UM-DUM,
DUM-DUM
MUH-UH-
UHHHH
YESH...
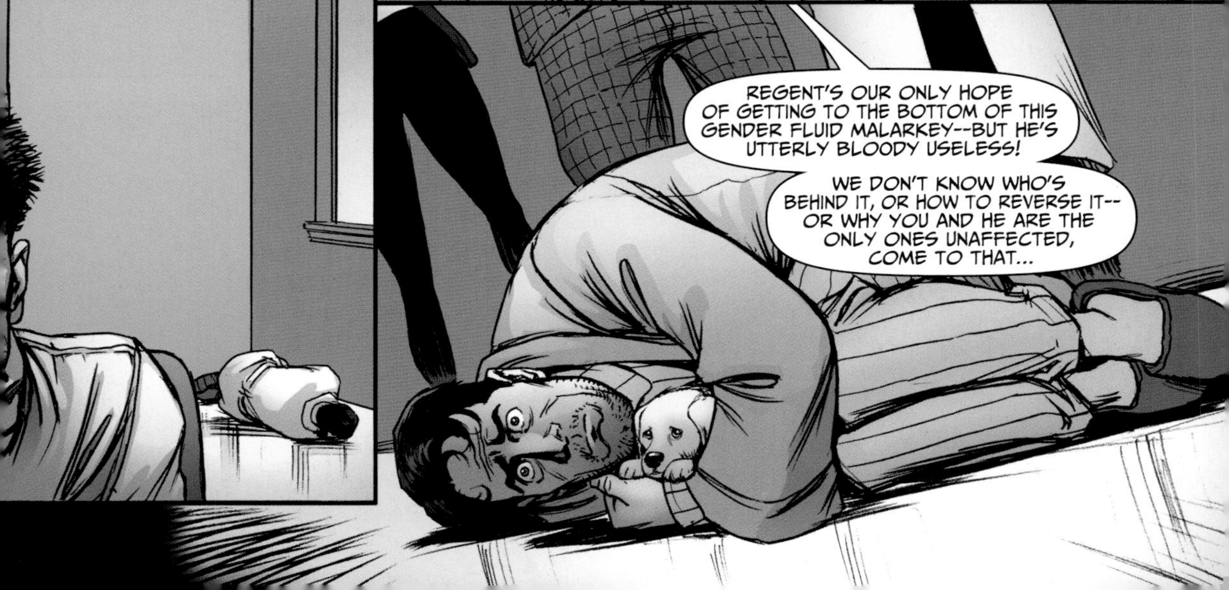
REGENT'S OUR ONLY HOPE OF GETTING TO THE BOTTOM OF THIS GENDER FLUID MALARKEY--BUT HE'S UTTERLY BLOODY USELESS!
WE DON'T KNOW WHO'S BEHIND IT, OR HOW TO REVERSE IT--OR WHY YOU AND HE ARE THE ONLY ONES UNAFFECTED, COME TO THAT...

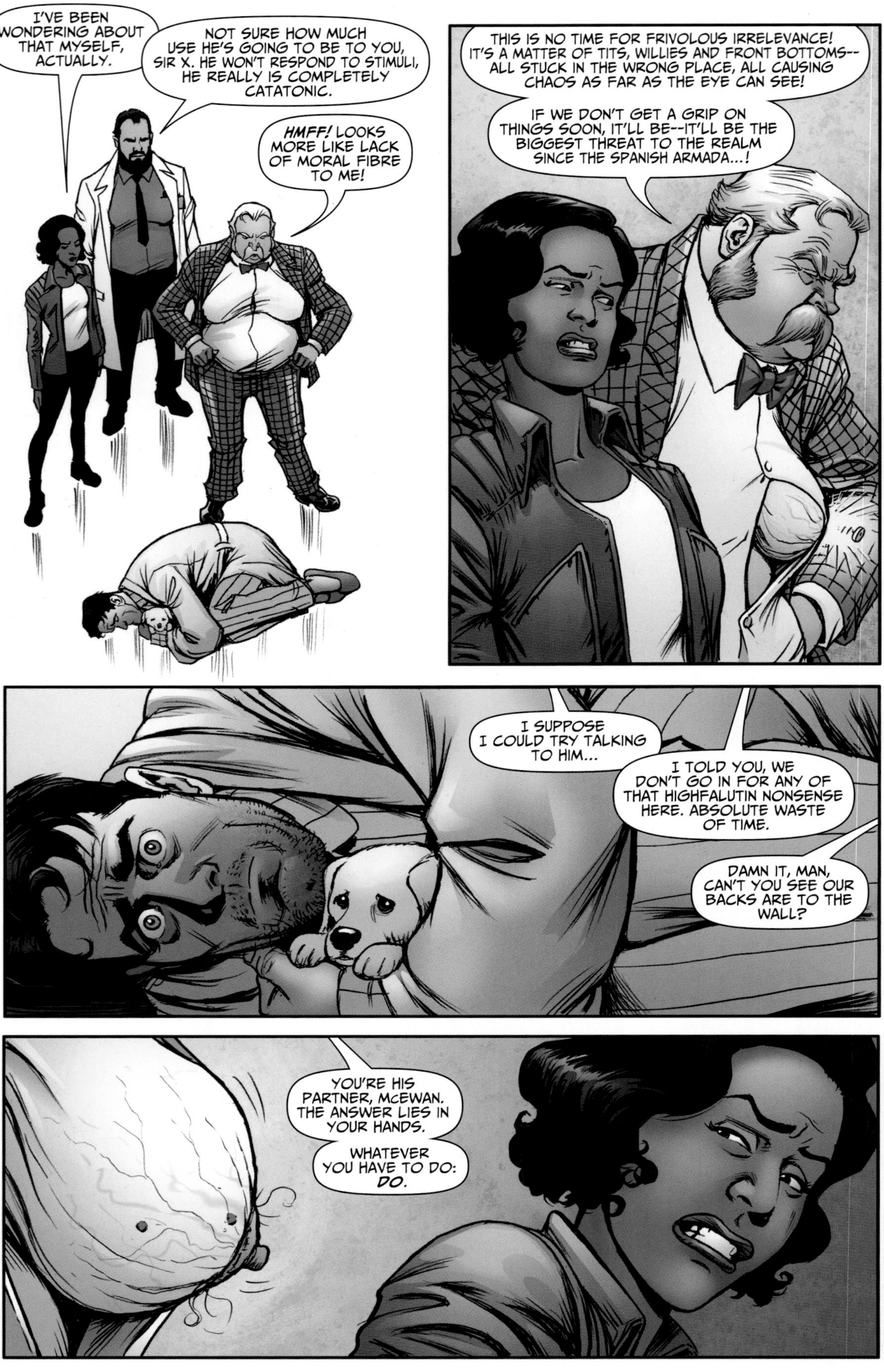
I'VE BEEN WONDERING ABOUT THAT MYSELF, ACTUALLY.
NOT SURE HOW MUCH USE HE'S GOING TO BE TO YOU, SIR X. HE WON'T RESPOND TO STIMULI, HE REALLY IS COMPLETELY CATATONIC.
HMFF! LOOKS MORE LIKE LACK OF MORAL FIBRE TO ME!
THIS IS NO TIME FOR FRIVOLOUS IRRELEVANCE! IT'S A MATTER OF TITS, WILLIES AND FRONT BOTTOMS-- ALL STUCK IN THE WRONG PLACE, ALL CAUSING CHAOS AS FAR AS THE EYE CAN SEE!
IF WE DON'T GET A GRIP ON THINGS SOON, IT'LL BE--IT'LL BE THE BIGGEST THREAT TO THE REALM SINCE THE SPANISH ARMADA...!
I SUPPOSE I COULD TRY TALKING TO HIM...
I TOLD YOU, WE DON'T GO IN FOR ANY OF THAT HIGHFALUTIN NONSENSE HERE. ABSOLUTE WASTE OF TIME.
DAMN IT, MAN, CAN'T YOU SEE OUR BACKS ARE TO THE WALL?
YOU'RE HIS PARTNER, McEWAN. THE ANSWER LIES IN YOUR HANDS.
WHATEVER YOU HAVE TO DO: DO.

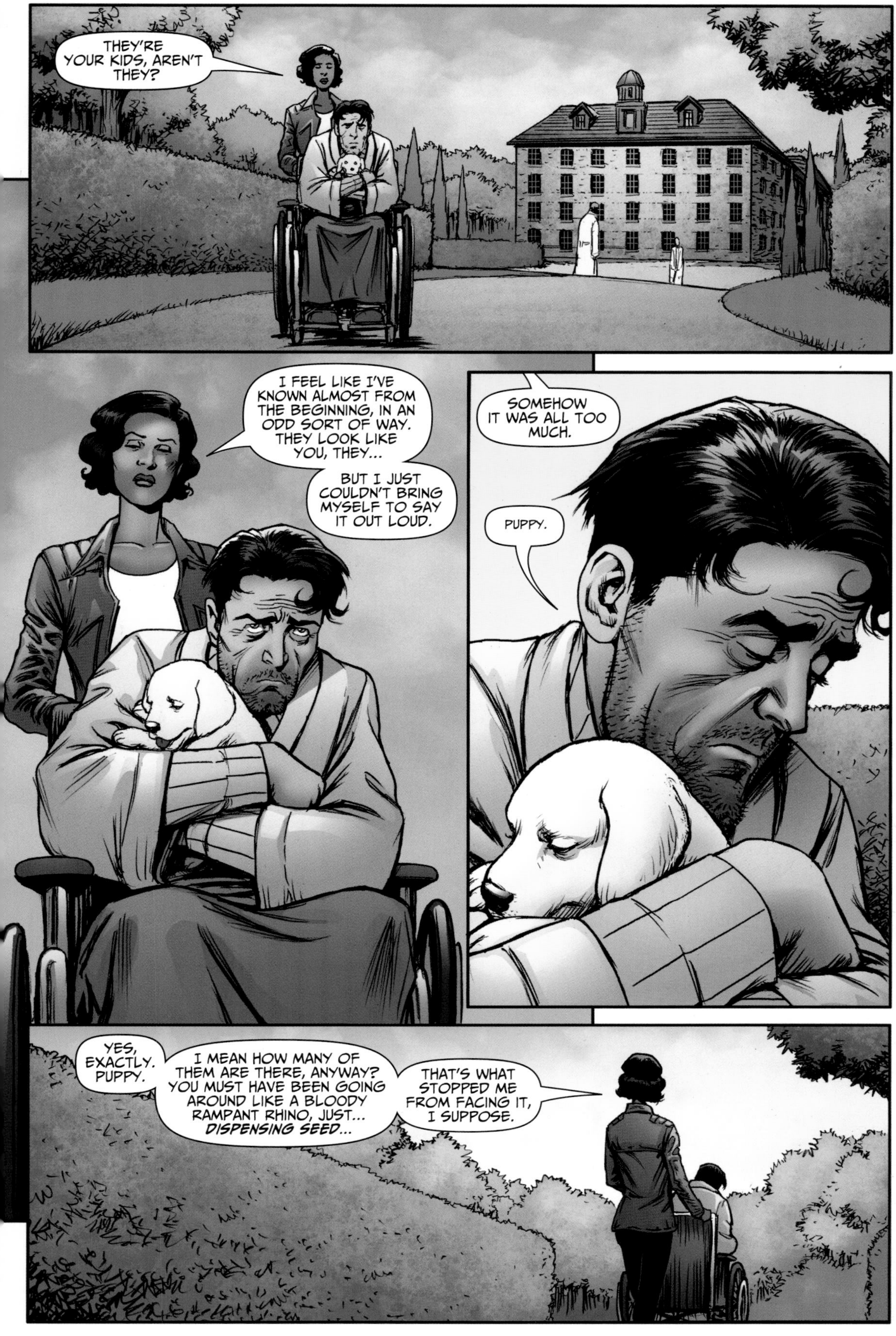
THEY'RE YOUR KIDS, AREN'T THEY?
I FEEL LIKE I'VE KNOWN ALMOST FROM THE BEGINNING, IN AN ODD SORT OF WAY. THEY LOOK LIKE YOU, THEY...
BUT I JUST COULDN'T BRING MYSELF TO SAY IT OUT LOUD.
SOMEHOW IT WAS ALL TOO MUCH.
PUPPY.
YES, EXACTLY. PUPPY.
I MEAN HOW MANY OF THEM ARE THERE, ANYWAY? YOU MUST HAVE BEEN GOING AROUND LIKE A BLOODY RAMPANT RHINO, JUST... *DISPENSING SEED*...
THAT'S WHAT STOPPED ME FROM FACING IT, I SUPPOSE.

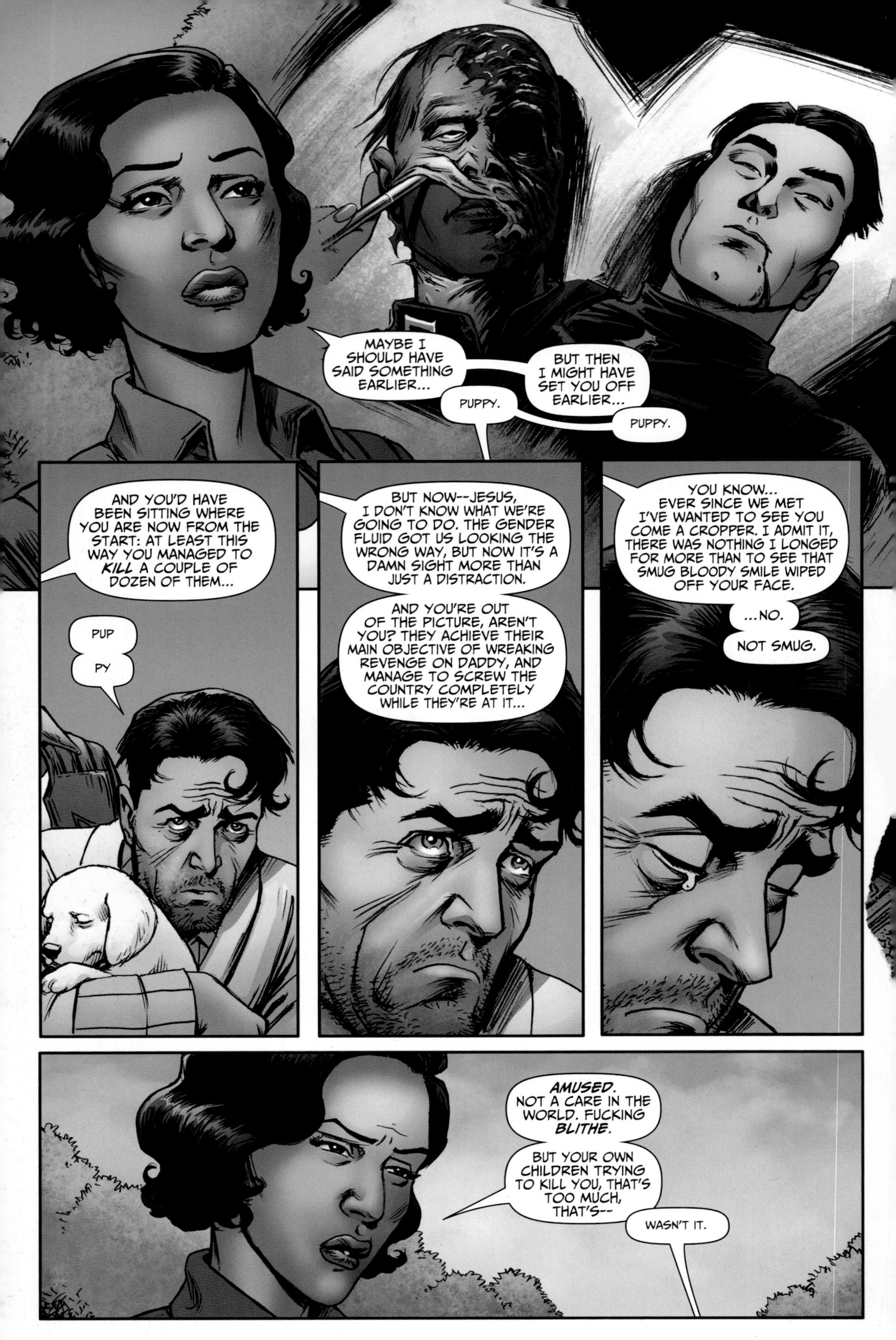
MAYBE I SHOULD HAVE SAID SOMETHING EARLIER...
BUT THEN I MIGHT HAVE SET YOU OFF EARLIER...
PUPPY.
PUPPY.
AND YOU'D HAVE BEEN SITTING WHERE YOU ARE NOW FROM THE START: AT LEAST THIS WAY YOU MANAGED TO *KILL* A COUPLE OF DOZEN OF THEM...
PUP
PY
BUT NOW--JESUS, I DON'T KNOW WHAT WE'RE GOING TO DO. THE GENDER FLUID GOT US LOOKING THE WRONG WAY, BUT NOW IT'S A DAMN SIGHT MORE THAN JUST A DISTRACTION.
AND YOU'RE OUT OF THE PICTURE, AREN'T YOU? THEY ACHIEVE THEIR MAIN OBJECTIVE OF WREAKING REVENGE ON DADDY, AND MANAGE TO SCREW THE COUNTRY COMPLETELY WHILE THEY'RE AT IT...
YOU KNOW... EVER SINCE WE MET I'VE WANTED TO SEE YOU COME A CROPPER. I ADMIT IT, THERE WAS NOTHING I LONGED FOR MORE THAN TO SEE THAT SMUG BLOODY SMILE WIPED OFF YOUR FACE.
...NO.
NOT SMUG.
AMUSED. NOT A CARE IN THE WORLD. FUCKING *BLITHE*.
BUT YOUR OWN CHILDREN TRYING TO KILL YOU, THAT'S TOO MUCH, THAT'S--
WASN'T IT.

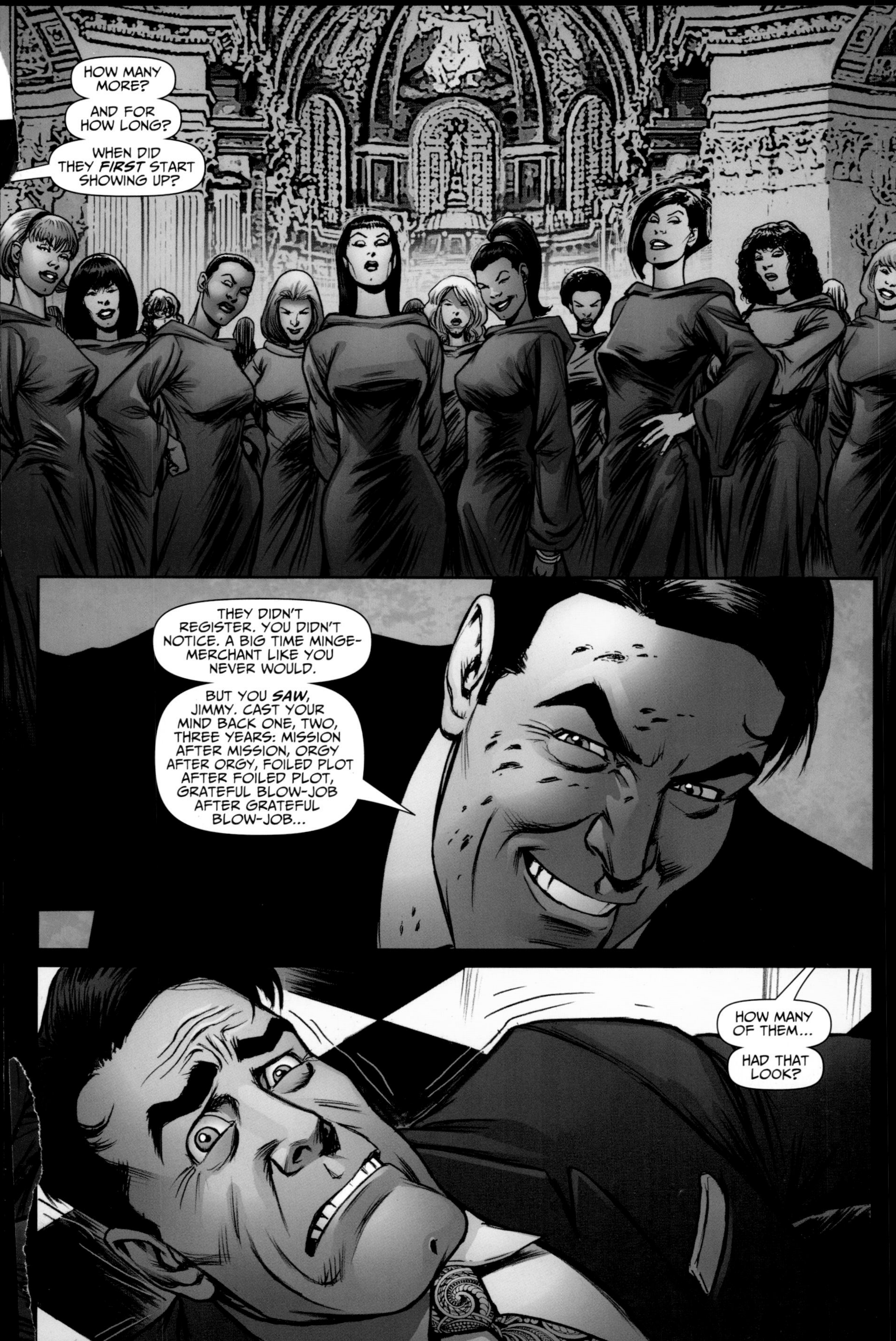
HOW MANY MORE?
AND FOR HOW LONG?
WHEN DID THEY FIRST START SHOWING UP?
THEY DIDN'T REGISTER. YOU DIDN'T NOTICE. A BIG TIME MINGE-MERCHANT LIKE YOU NEVER WOULD.
BUT YOU SAW, JIMMY. CAST YOUR MIND BACK ONE, TWO, THREE YEARS: MISSION AFTER MISSION, ORGY AFTER ORGY, FOILED PLOT AFTER FOILED PLOT, GRATEFUL BLOW-JOB AFTER GRATEFUL BLOW-JOB...
HOW MANY OF THEM...
HAD THAT LOOK?

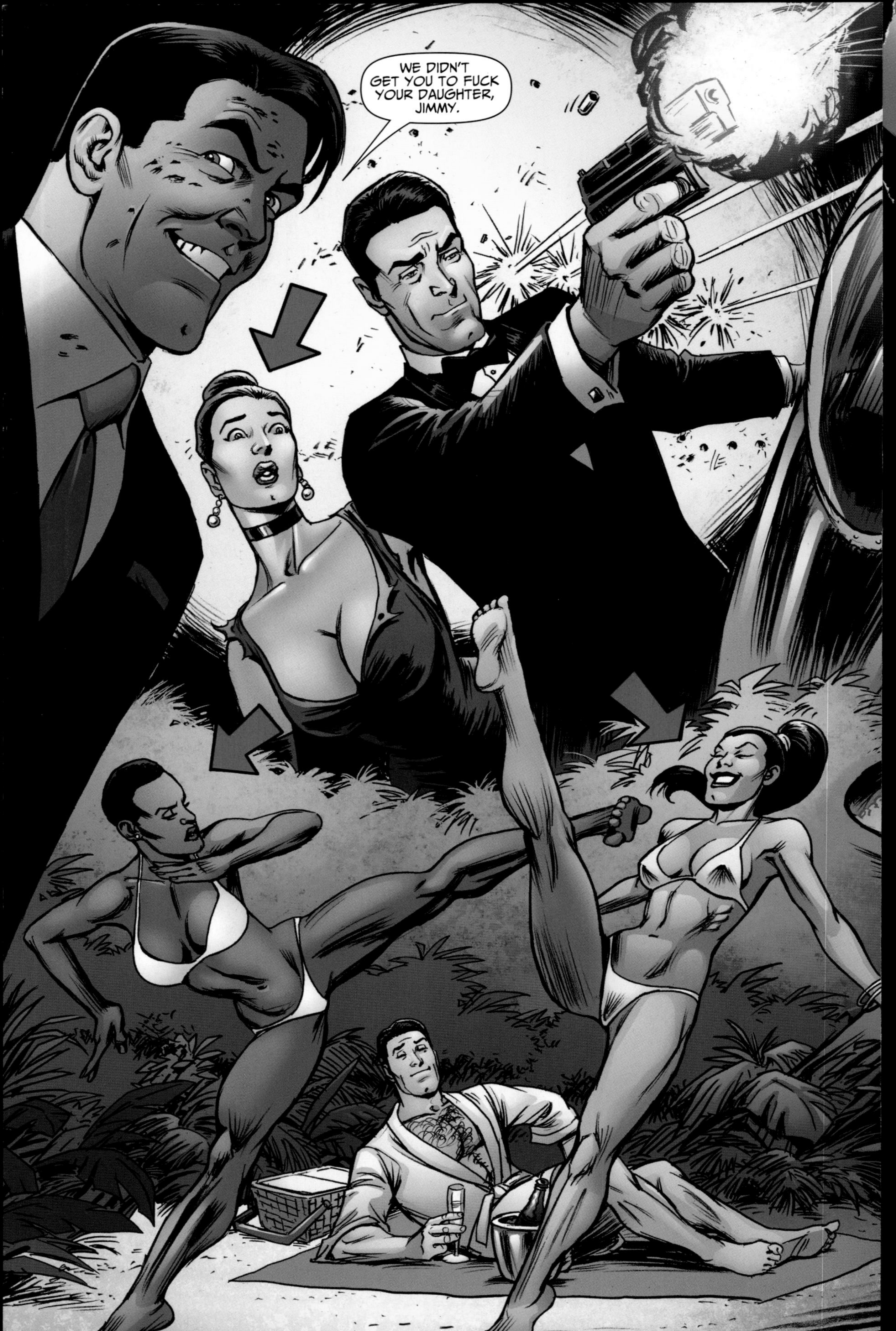
WE DIDN'T GET YOU TO FUCK YOUR DAUGHTER, JIMMY.

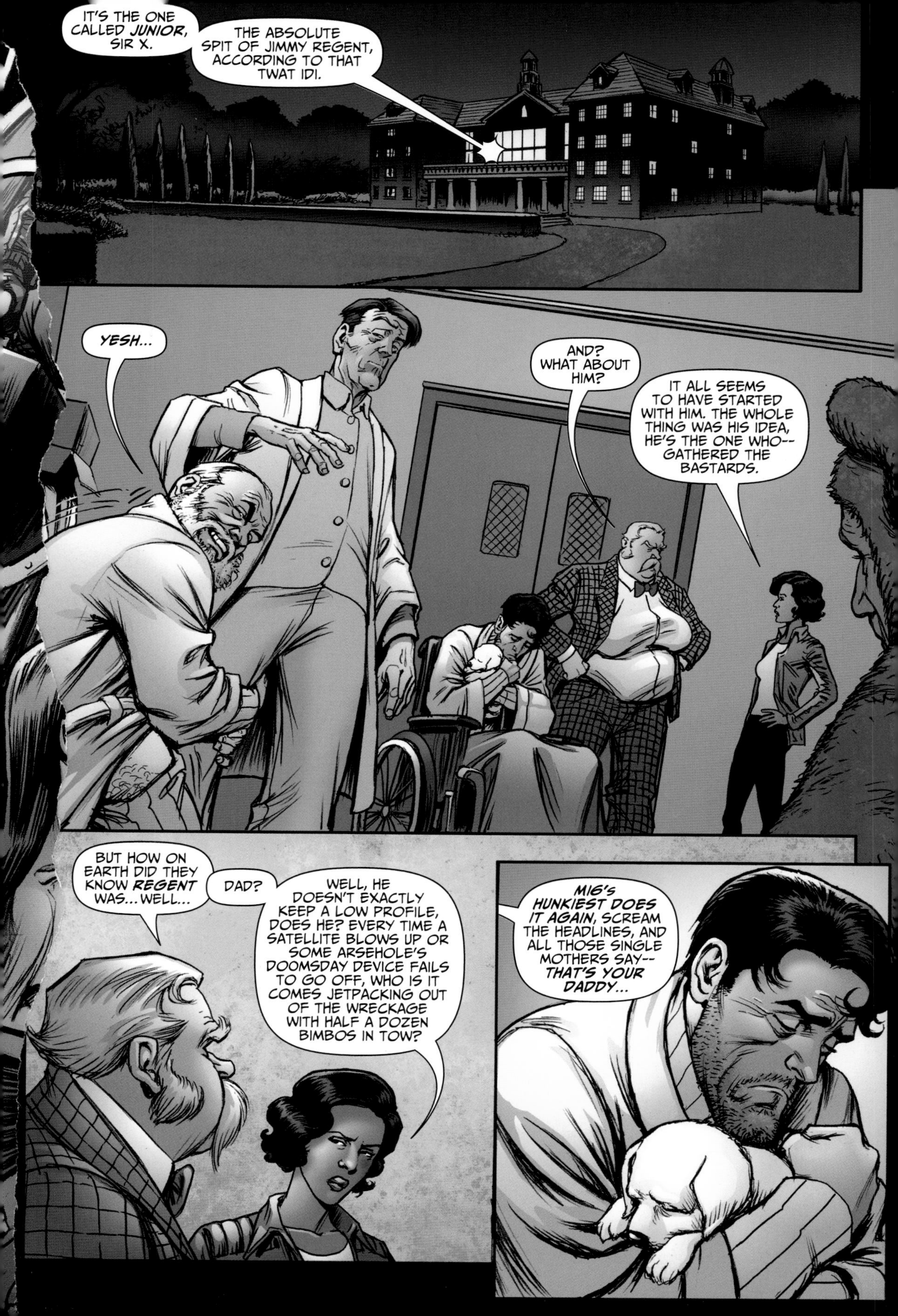
IT'S THE ONE CALLED *JUNIOR*, SIR X.
THE ABSOLUTE SPIT OF JIMMY REGENT, ACCORDING TO THAT TWAT IDI.
YESH...
AND? WHAT ABOUT HIM?
IT ALL SEEMS TO HAVE STARTED WITH HIM. THE WHOLE THING WAS HIS IDEA, HE'S THE ONE WHO-- GATHERED THE BASTARDS.
BUT HOW ON EARTH DID THEY KNOW *REGENT* WAS... WELL...
DAD?
WELL, HE DOESN'T EXACTLY KEEP A LOW PROFILE, DOES HE? EVERY TIME A SATELLITE BLOWS UP OR SOME ARSEHOLE'S DOOMSDAY DEVICE FAILS TO GO OFF, WHO IS IT COMES JETPACKING OUT OF THE WRECKAGE WITH HALF A DOZEN BIMBOS IN TOW?
MI6's HUNKIEST DOES IT AGAIN, SCREAM THE HEADLINES, AND ALL THOSE SINGLE MOTHERS SAY-- *THAT'S YOUR DADDY...*

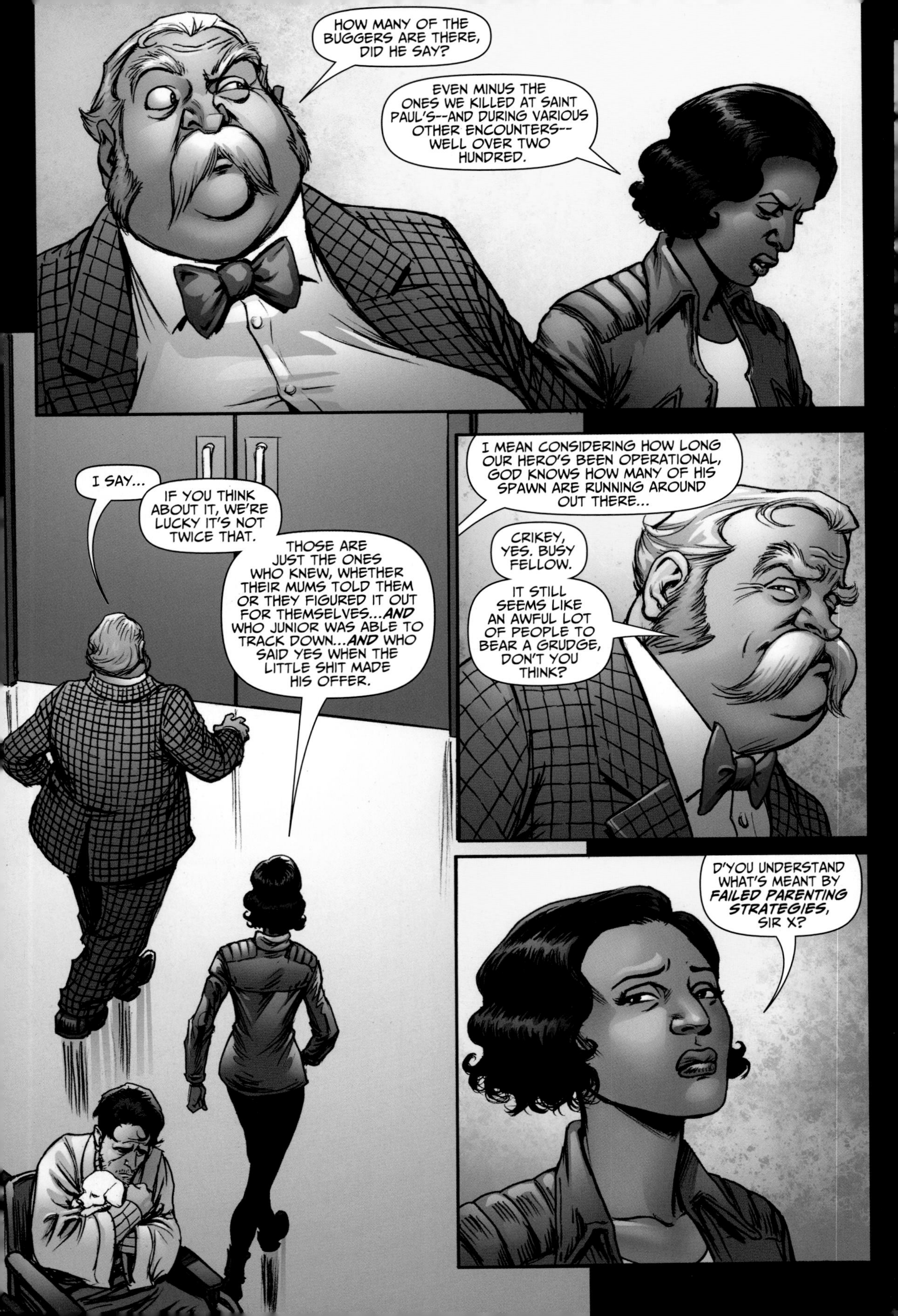
HOW MANY OF THE BUGGERS ARE THERE, DID HE SAY?
EVEN MINUS THE ONES WE KILLED AT SAINT PAUL'S--AND DURING VARIOUS OTHER ENCOUNTERS--WELL OVER TWO HUNDRED.
I SAY...
IF YOU THINK ABOUT IT, WE'RE LUCKY IT'S NOT TWICE THAT.
THOSE ARE JUST THE ONES WHO KNEW, WHETHER THEIR MUMS TOLD THEM OR THEY FIGURED IT OUT FOR THEMSELVES...*AND* WHO JUNIOR WAS ABLE TO TRACK DOWN...*AND* WHO SAID YES WHEN THE LITTLE SHIT MADE HIS OFFER.
I MEAN CONSIDERING HOW LONG OUR HERO'S BEEN OPERATIONAL, GOD KNOWS HOW MANY OF HIS SPAWN ARE RUNNING AROUND OUT THERE...
CRIKEY, YES. BUSY FELLOW.
IT STILL SEEMS LIKE AN AWFUL LOT OF PEOPLE TO BEAR A GRUDGE, DON'T YOU THINK?
D'YOU UNDERSTAND WHAT'S MEANT BY ***FAILED PARENTING STRATEGIES***, SIR X?

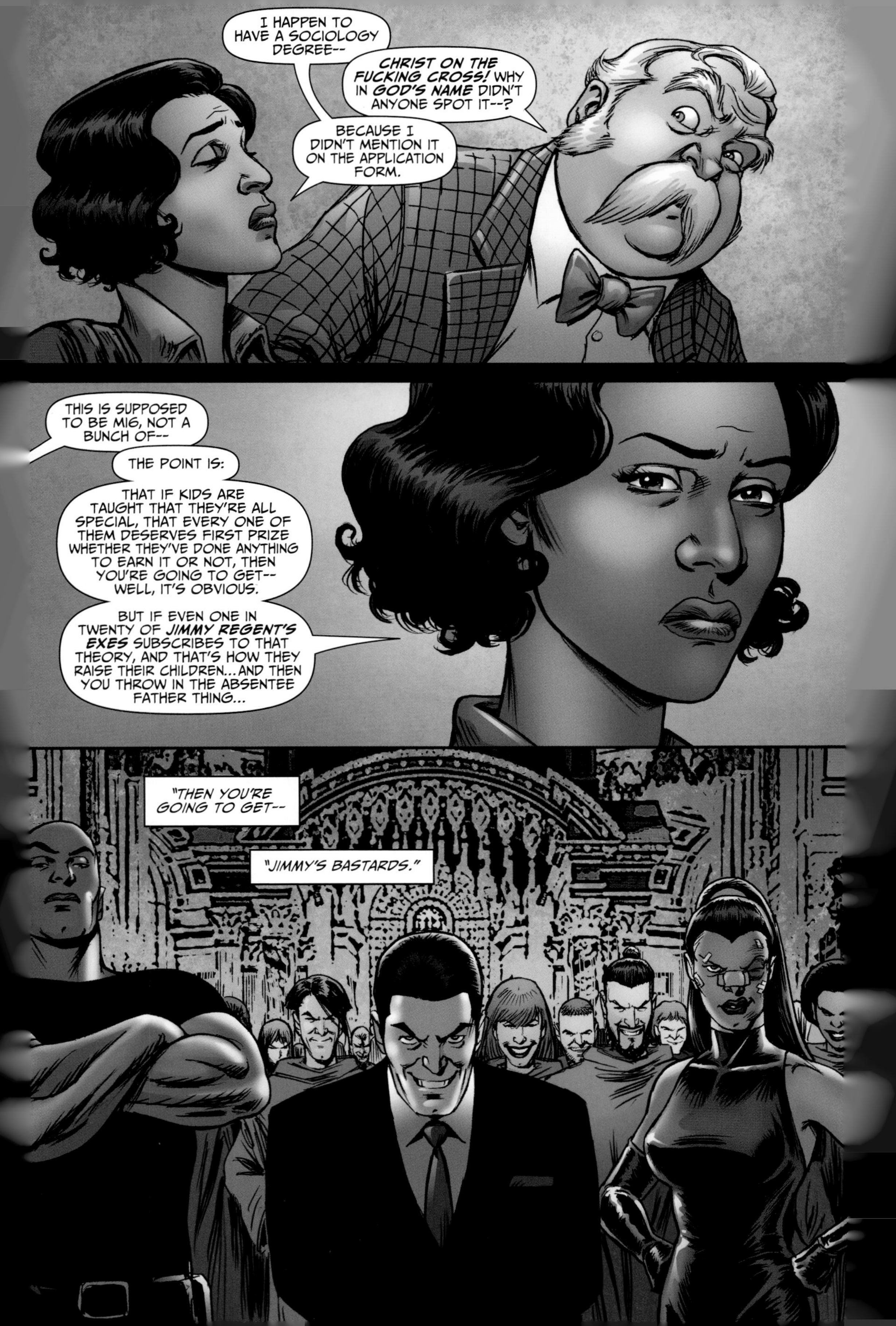
I HAPPEN TO HAVE A SOCIOLOGY DEGREE--
CHRIST ON THE FUCKING CROSS! WHY IN GOD'S NAME DIDN'T ANYONE SPOT IT--?
BECAUSE I DIDN'T MENTION IT ON THE APPLICATION FORM.
THIS IS SUPPOSED TO BE MI6, NOT A BUNCH OF--
THE POINT IS:
THAT IF KIDS ARE TAUGHT THAT THEY'RE ALL SPECIAL, THAT EVERY ONE OF THEM DESERVES FIRST PRIZE WHETHER THEY'VE DONE ANYTHING TO EARN IT OR NOT, THEN YOU'RE GOING TO GET-- WELL, IT'S OBVIOUS.
BUT IF EVEN ONE IN TWENTY OF JIMMY REGENT'S EXES SUBSCRIBES TO THAT THEORY, AND THAT'S HOW THEY RAISE THEIR CHILDREN...AND THEN YOU THROW IN THE ABSENTEE FATHER THING...
"THEN YOU'RE GOING TO GET--
"JIMMY'S BASTARDS."

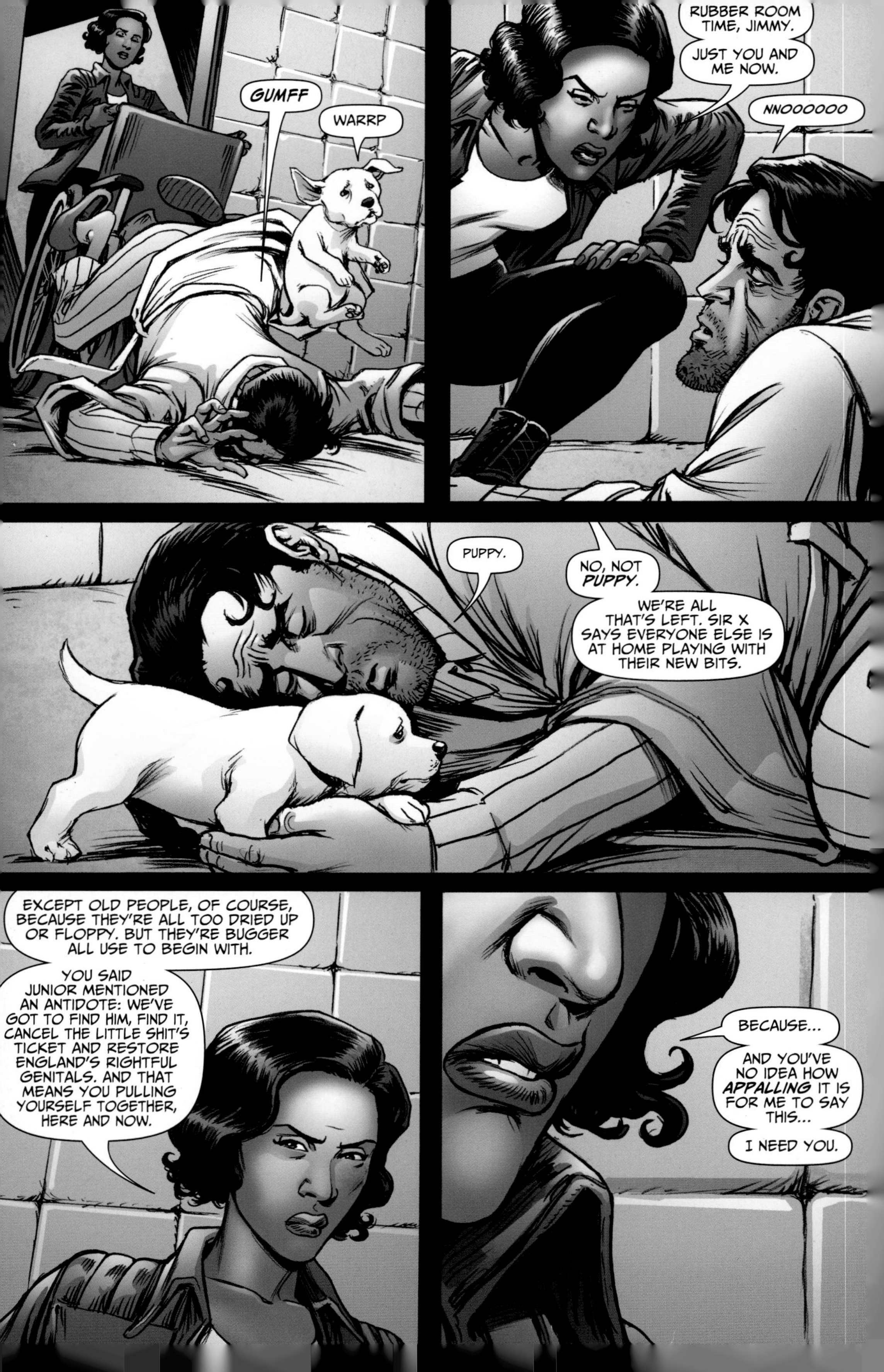
GUMFF
WARRP
RUBBER ROOM TIME, JIMMY.
JUST YOU AND ME NOW.
NNOOOOOO
PUPPY.
NO, NOT *PUPPY*.
WE'RE ALL THAT'S LEFT. SIR X SAYS EVERYONE ELSE IS AT HOME PLAYING WITH THEIR NEW BITS.
EXCEPT OLD PEOPLE, OF COURSE, BECAUSE THEY'RE ALL TOO DRIED UP OR FLOPPY. BUT THEY'RE BUGGER ALL USE TO BEGIN WITH.
YOU SAID JUNIOR MENTIONED AN ANTIDOTE: WE'VE GOT TO FIND HIM, FIND IT, CANCEL THE LITTLE SHIT'S TICKET AND RESTORE ENGLAND'S RIGHTFUL GENITALS. AND THAT MEANS YOU PULLING YOURSELF TOGETHER, HERE AND NOW.
BECAUSE...
AND YOU'VE NO IDEA HOW *APPALLING* IT IS FOR ME TO SAY THIS...
I NEED YOU.

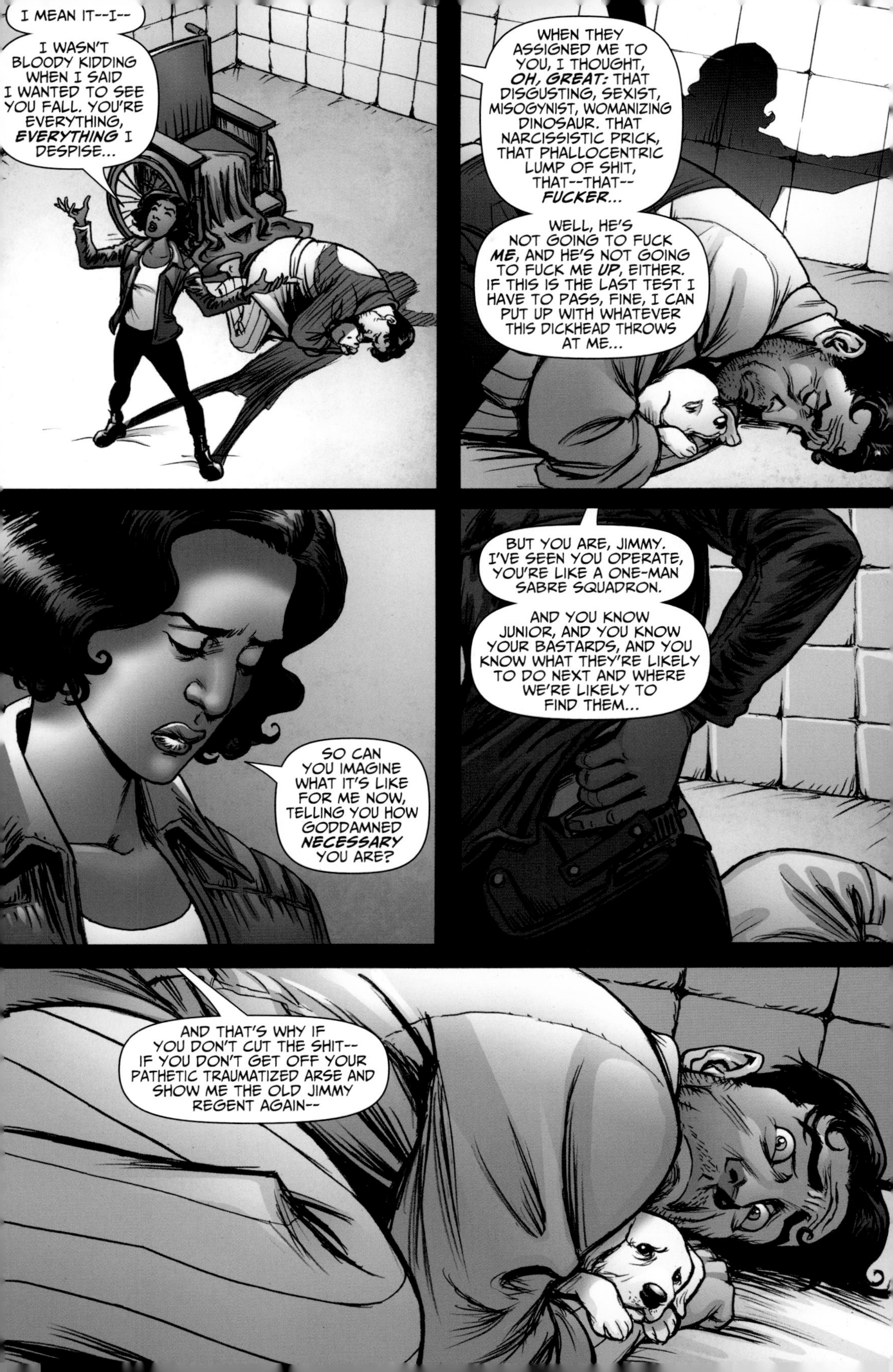

I MEAN IT--I--
I WASN'T BLOODY KIDDING WHEN I SAID I WANTED TO SEE YOU FALL. YOU'RE EVERYTHING, **EVERYTHING** I DESPISE...
WHEN THEY ASSIGNED ME TO YOU, I THOUGHT, ***OH, GREAT:*** THAT DISGUSTING, SEXIST, MISOGYNIST, WOMANIZING DINOSAUR. THAT NARCISSISTIC PRICK, THAT PHALLOCENTRIC LUMP OF SHIT, THAT--THAT-- ***FUCKER***...
WELL, HE'S NOT GOING TO FUCK ***ME***, AND HE'S NOT GOING TO FUCK ME ***UP***, EITHER. IF THIS IS THE LAST TEST I HAVE TO PASS, FINE, I CAN PUT UP WITH WHATEVER THIS DICKHEAD THROWS AT ME...
SO CAN YOU IMAGINE WHAT IT'S LIKE FOR ME NOW, TELLING YOU HOW GODDAMNED ***NECESSARY*** YOU ARE?
BUT YOU ARE, JIMMY. I'VE SEEN YOU OPERATE, YOU'RE LIKE A ONE-MAN SABRE SQUADRON.
AND YOU KNOW JUNIOR, AND YOU KNOW YOUR BASTARDS, AND YOU KNOW WHAT THEY'RE LIKELY TO DO NEXT AND WHERE WE'RE LIKELY TO FIND THEM...
AND THAT'S WHY IF YOU DON'T CUT THE SHIT-- IF YOU DON'T GET OFF YOUR PATHETIC TRAUMATIZED ARSE AND SHOW ME THE OLD JIMMY REGENT AGAIN--

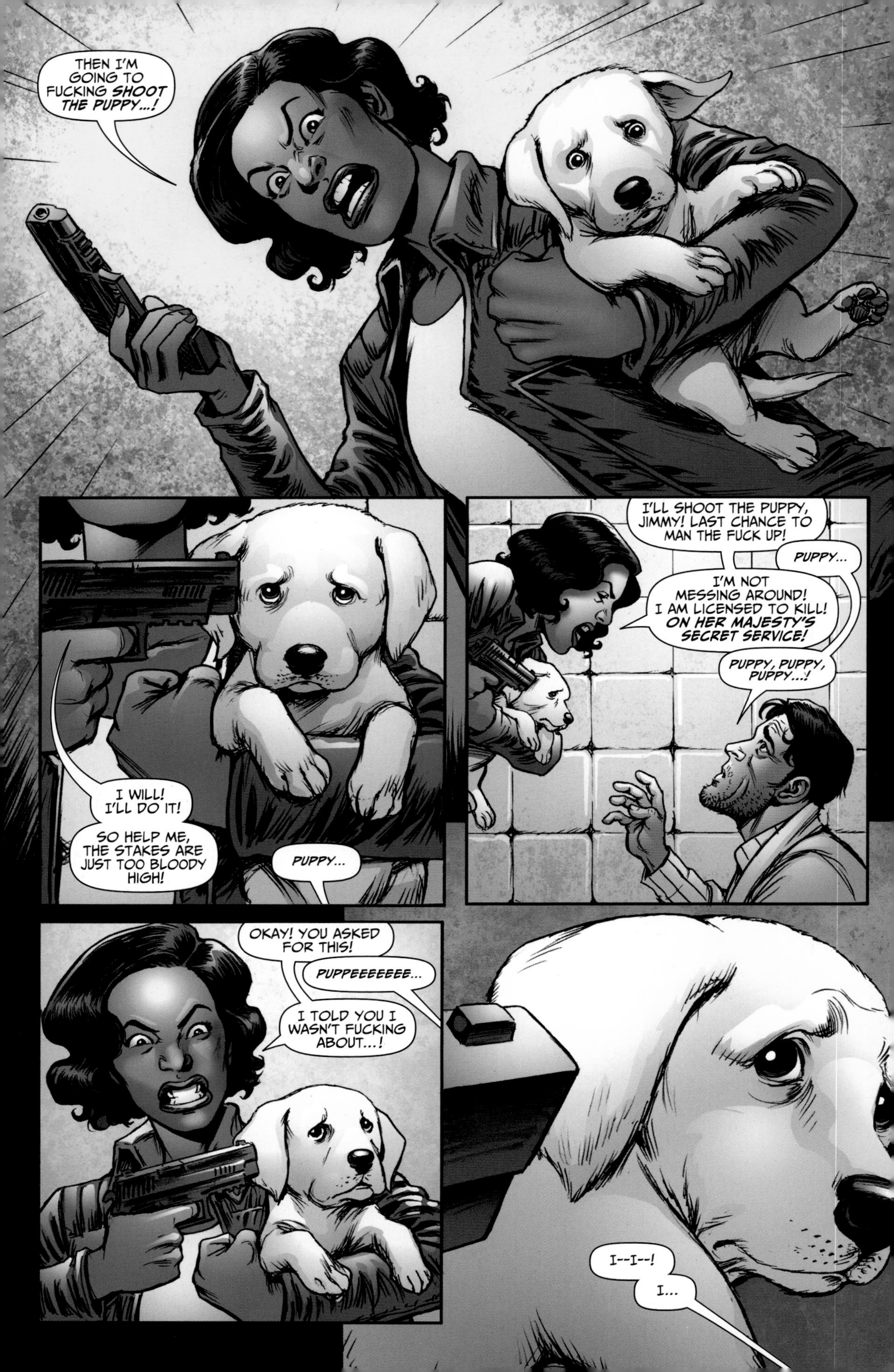
THEN I'M GOING TO FUCKING *SHOOT THE PUPPY...!*
I WILL! I'LL DO IT!
SO HELP ME, THE STAKES ARE JUST TOO BLOODY HIGH!
PUPPY...
I'LL SHOOT THE PUPPY, JIMMY! LAST CHANCE TO MAN THE FUCK UP!
PUPPY...
I'M NOT MESSING AROUND! I AM LICENSED TO KILL! ***ON HER MAJESTY'S SECRET SERVICE!***
PUPPY, PUPPY, PUPPY...!
OKAY! YOU ASKED FOR THIS!
PUPPEEEEEEE...
I TOLD YOU I WASN'T FUCKING ABOUT...!
I--I--!
I...

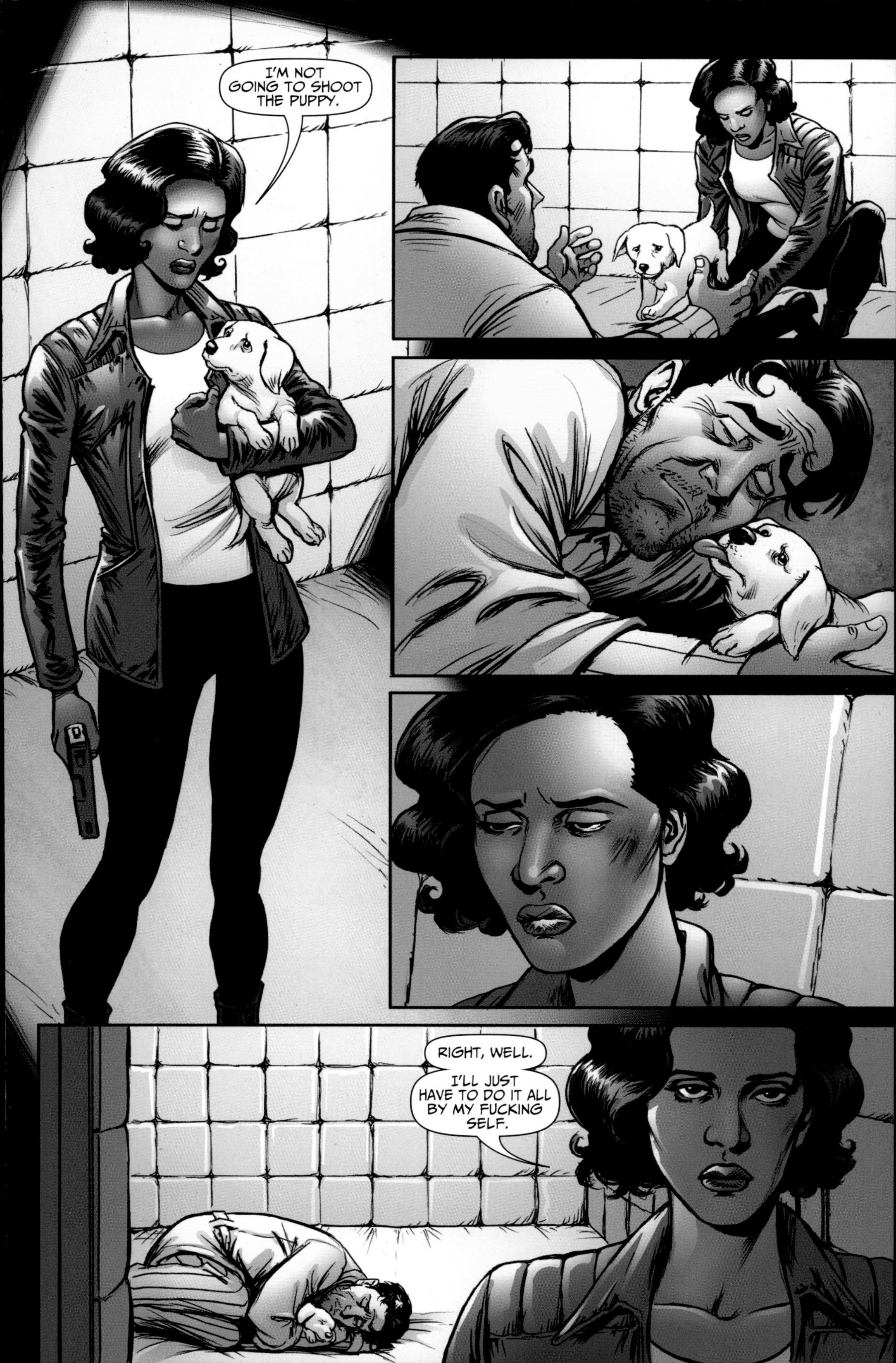
I'M NOT GOING TO SHOOT THE PUPPY.
RIGHT, WELL.
I'LL JUST HAVE TO DO IT ALL BY MY FUCKING SELF.

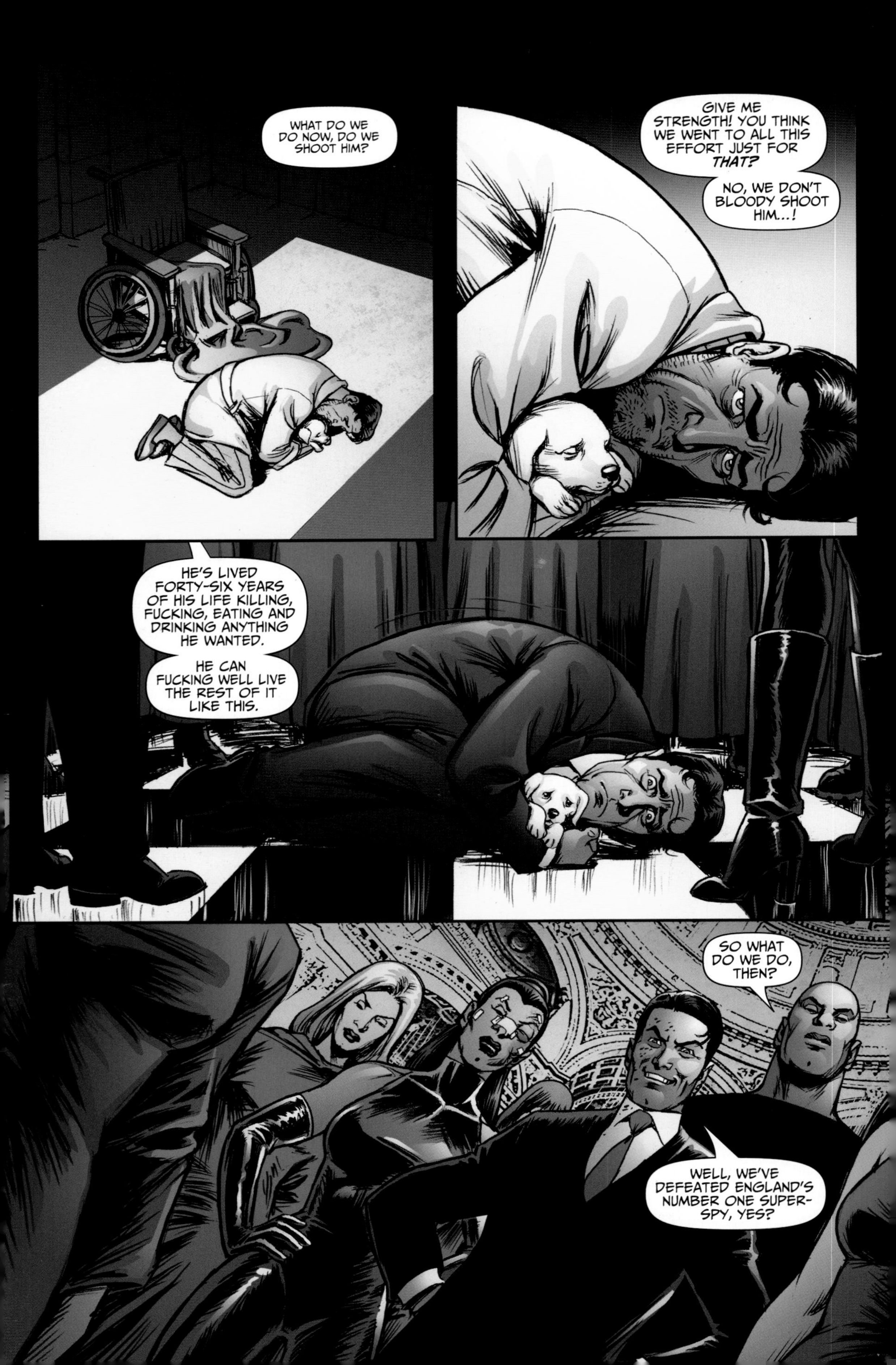
WHAT DO WE DO NOW, DO WE SHOOT HIM?
GIVE ME STRENGTH! YOU THINK WE WENT TO ALL THIS EFFORT JUST FOR *THAT?*
NO, WE DON'T BLOODY SHOOT HIM...!
HE'S LIVED FORTY-SIX YEARS OF HIS LIFE KILLING, FUCKING, EATING AND DRINKING ANYTHING HE WANTED.
HE CAN FUCKING WELL LIVE THE REST OF IT LIKE THIS.
SO WHAT DO WE DO, THEN?
WELL, WE'VE DEFEATED ENGLAND'S NUMBER ONE SUPER-SPY, YES?

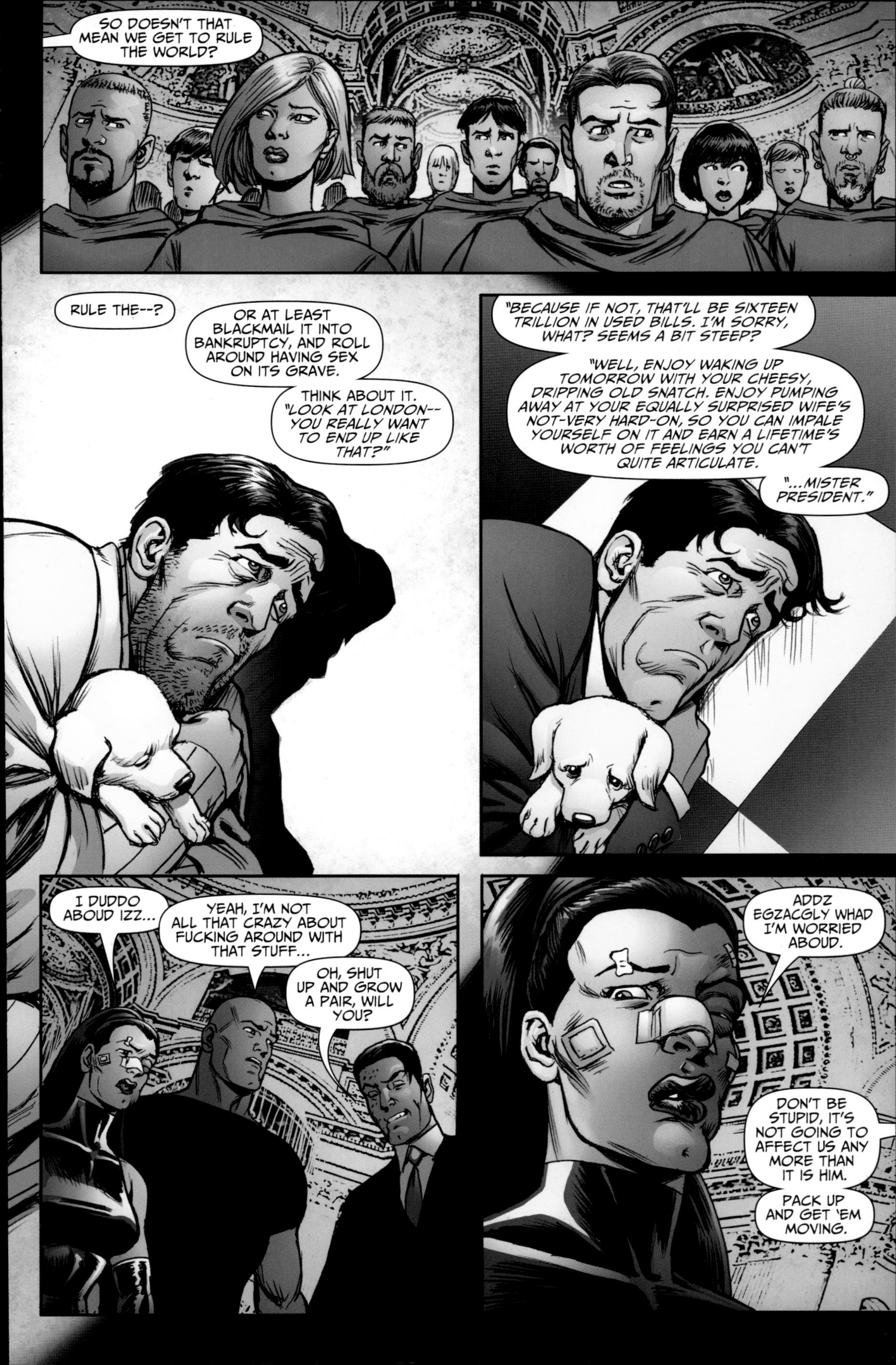
SO DOESN'T THAT MEAN WE GET TO RULE THE WORLD?
RULE THE--?
OR AT LEAST BLACKMAIL IT INTO BANKRUPTCY, AND ROLL AROUND HAVING SEX ON ITS GRAVE.
THINK ABOUT IT. "LOOK AT LONDON-- YOU REALLY WANT TO END UP LIKE THAT?"
"BECAUSE IF NOT, THAT'LL BE SIXTEEN TRILLION IN USED BILLS. I'M SORRY, WHAT? SEEMS A BIT STEEP?
"WELL, ENJOY WAKING UP TOMORROW WITH YOUR CHEESY, DRIPPING OLD SNATCH. ENJOY PUMPING AWAY AT YOUR EQUALLY SURPRISED WIFE'S NOT-VERY HARD-ON, SO YOU CAN IMPALE YOURSELF ON IT AND EARN A LIFETIME'S WORTH OF FEELINGS YOU CAN'T QUITE ARTICULATE.
"...MISTER PRESIDENT."
I DUDDO ABOUD IZZ...
YEAH, I'M NOT ALL THAT CRAZY ABOUT FUCKING AROUND WITH THAT STUFF...
OH, SHUT UP AND GROW A PAIR, WILL YOU?
ADDZ EGZACGLY WHAD I'M WORRIED ABOUD.
DON'T BE STUPID, IT'S NOT GOING TO AFFECT US ANY MORE THAN IT IS HIM.
PACK UP AND GET 'EM MOVING.

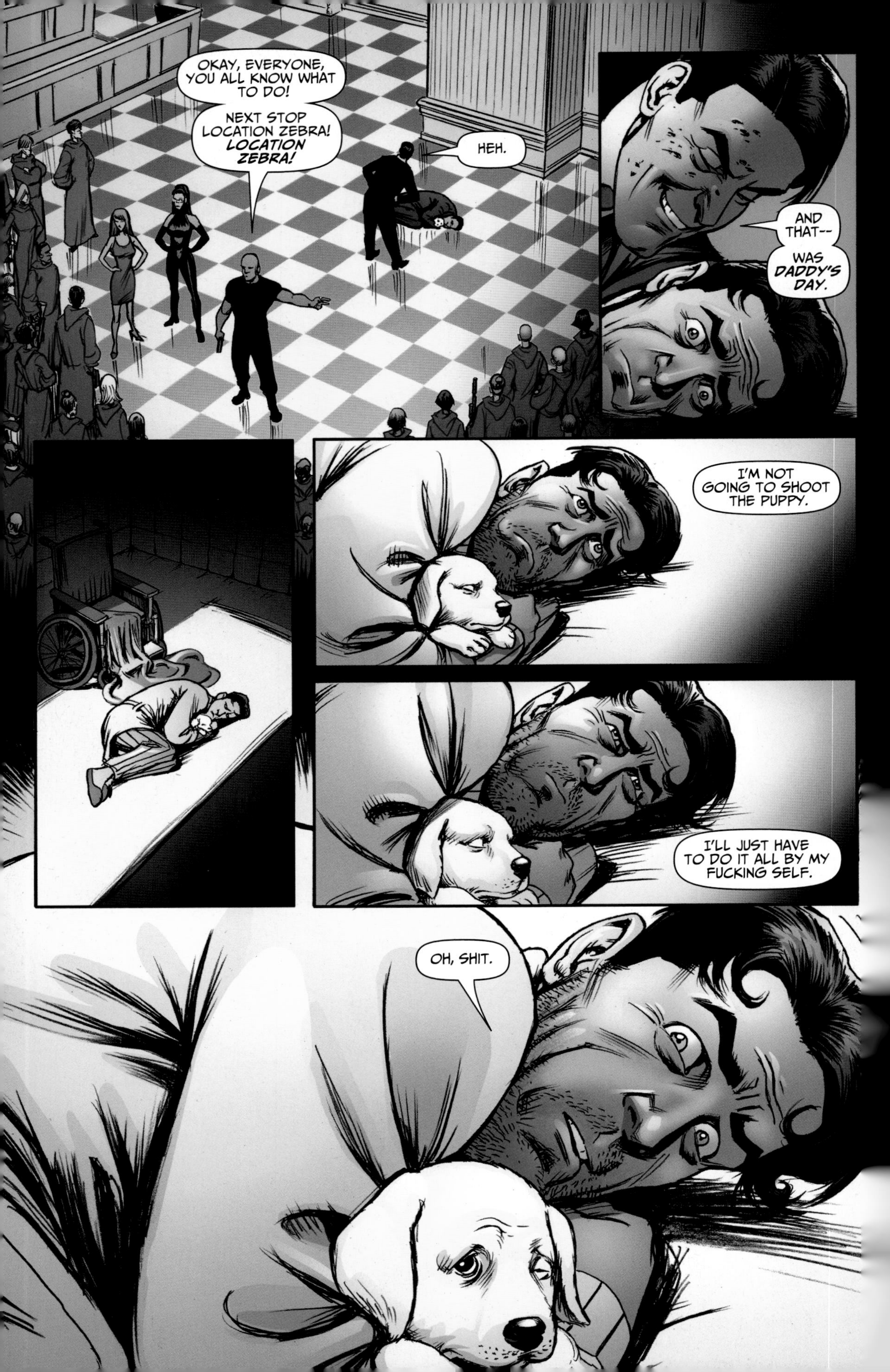
OKAY, EVERYONE, YOU ALL KNOW WHAT TO DO!
NEXT STOP LOCATION ZEBRA! LOCATION ZEBRA!
HEH.
AND THAT--
WAS DADDY'S DAY.
I'M NOT GOING TO SHOOT THE PUPPY.
I'LL JUST HAVE TO DO IT ALL BY MY FUCKING SELF.
OH, SHIT.

7

I NEVER GET TIRED OF THAT SOUND

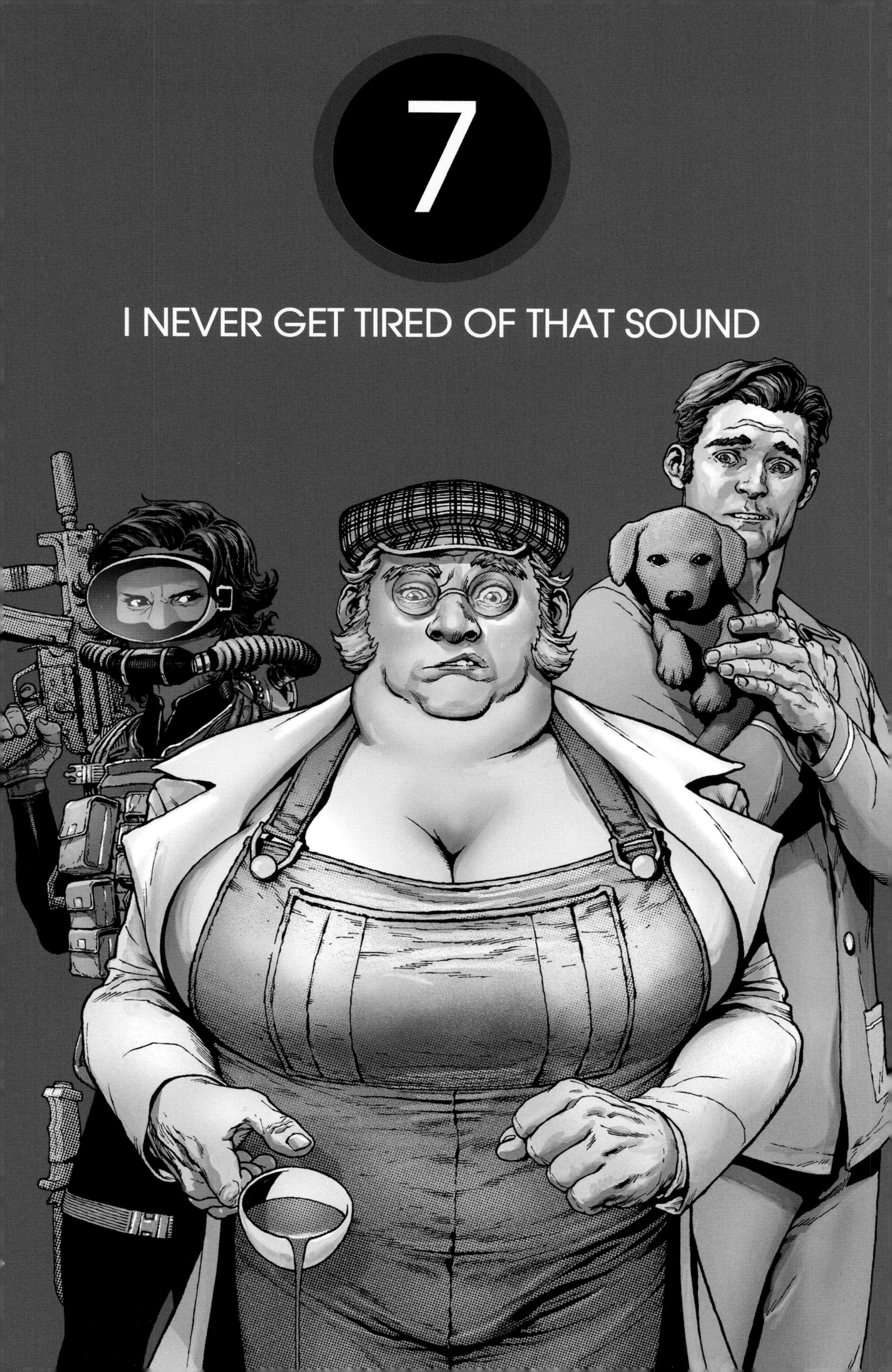

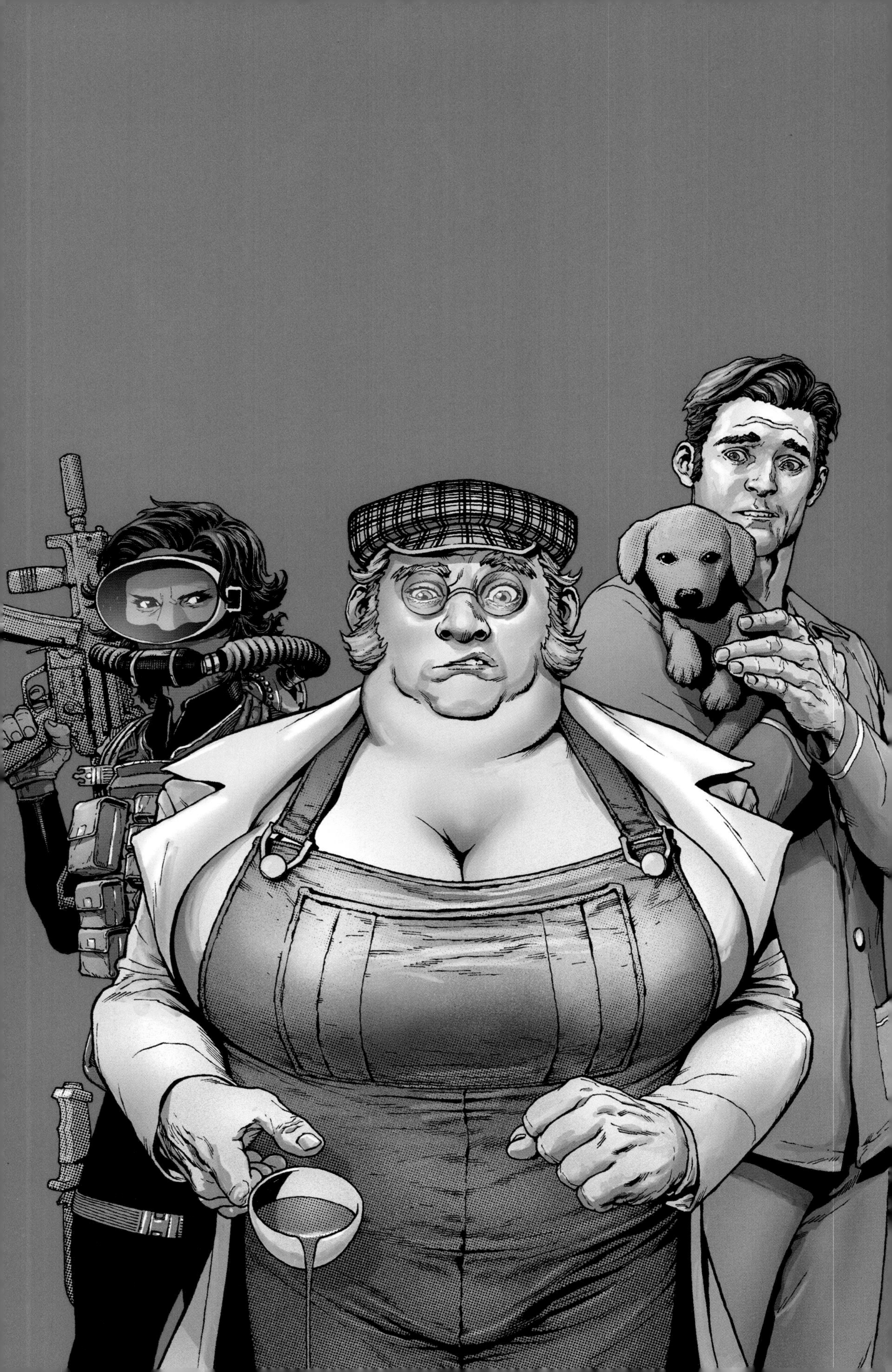

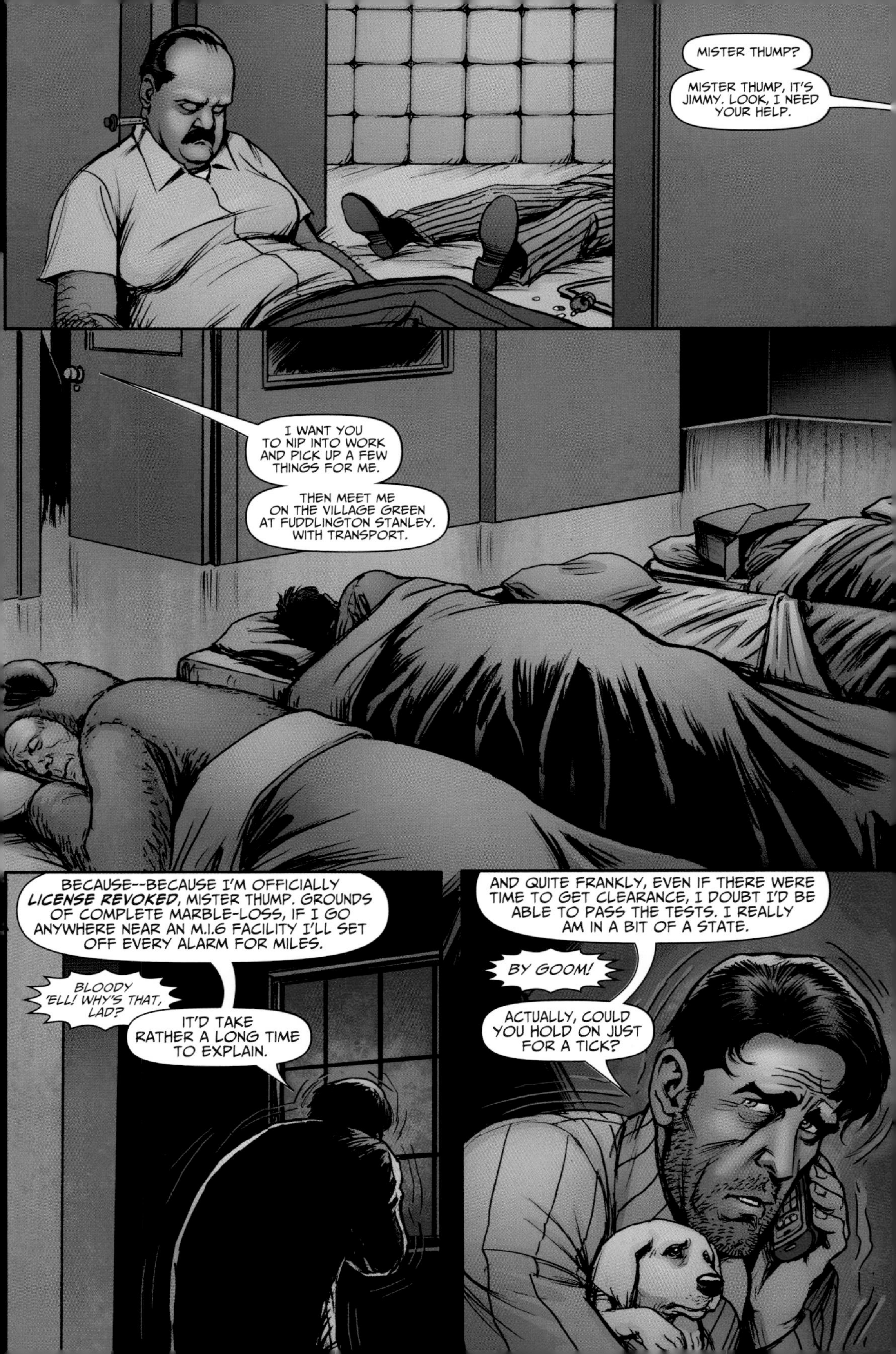
MISTER THUMP?
MISTER THUMP, IT'S JIMMY. LOOK, I NEED YOUR HELP.
I WANT YOU TO NIP INTO WORK AND PICK UP A FEW THINGS FOR ME.
THEN MEET ME ON THE VILLAGE GREEN AT FUDDLINGTON STANLEY. WITH TRANSPORT.
BLOODY 'ELL! WHY'S THAT, LAD?
BECAUSE--BECAUSE I'M OFFICIALLY LICENSE REVOKED, MISTER THUMP. GROUNDS OF COMPLETE MARBLE-LOSS, IF I GO ANYWHERE NEAR AN M.I.6 FACILITY I'LL SET OFF EVERY ALARM FOR MILES.
IT'D TAKE RATHER A LONG TIME TO EXPLAIN.
AND QUITE FRANKLY, EVEN IF THERE WERE TIME TO GET CLEARANCE, I DOUBT I'D BE ABLE TO PASS THE TESTS. I REALLY AM IN A BIT OF A STATE.
BY GOOM!
ACTUALLY, COULD YOU HOLD ON JUST FOR A TICK?

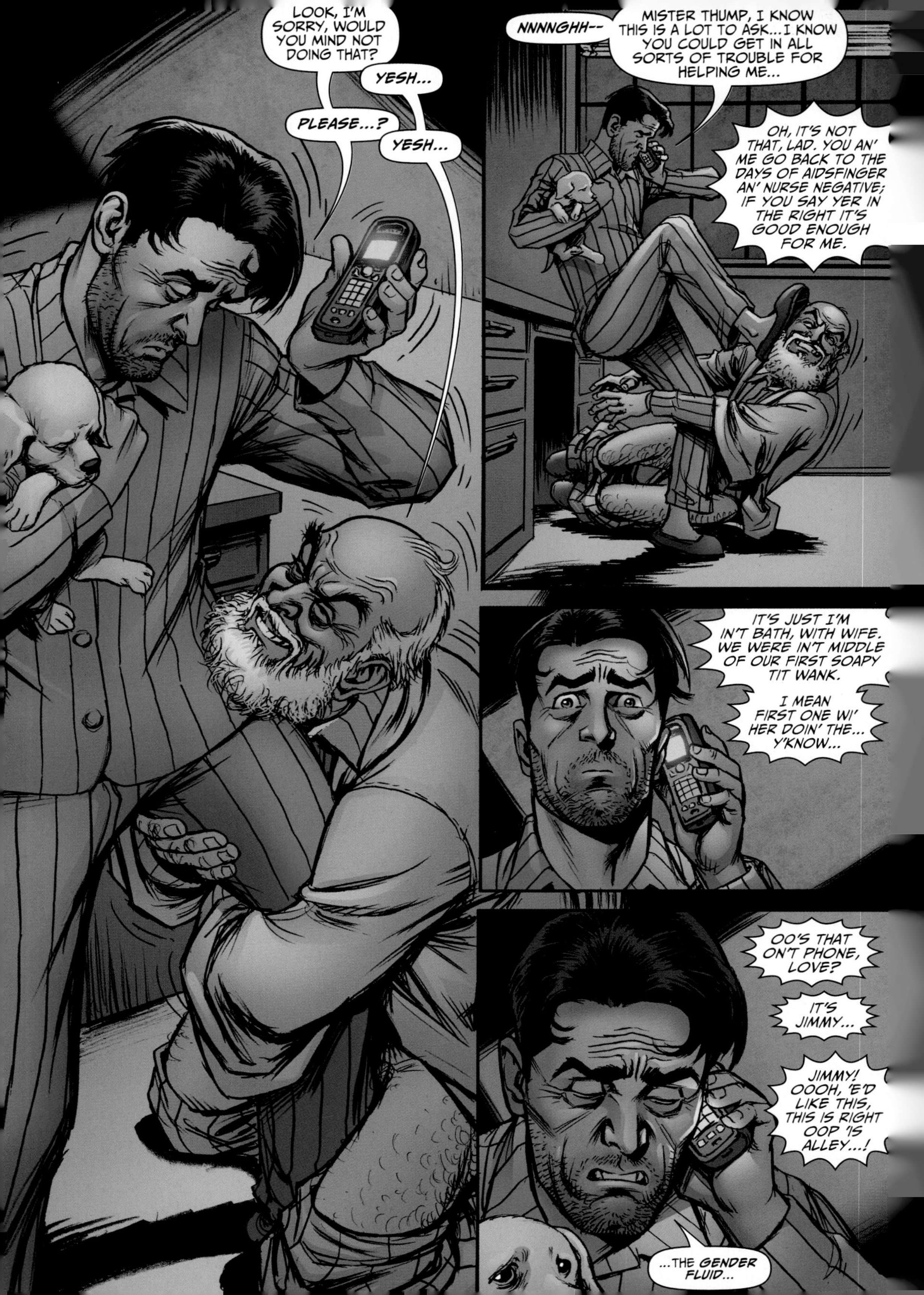
LOOK, I'M SORRY, WOULD YOU MIND NOT DOING THAT?
YESH...
PLEASE...?
YESH...
NNNNGHH--
MISTER THUMP, I KNOW THIS IS A LOT TO ASK...I KNOW YOU COULD GET IN ALL SORTS OF TROUBLE FOR HELPING ME...
OH, IT'S NOT THAT, LAD. YOU AN' ME GO BACK TO THE DAYS OF AIDSFINGER AN' NURSE NEGATIVE; IF YOU SAY YER IN THE RIGHT IT'S GOOD ENOUGH FOR ME.
IT'S JUST I'M IN'T BATH, WITH WIFE. WE WERE IN'T MIDDLE OF OUR FIRST SOAPY TIT WANK.
I MEAN FIRST ONE WI' HER DOIN' THE... Y'KNOW...
OO'S THAT ON'T PHONE, LOVE?
IT'S JIMMY...
JIMMY! OOOH, 'E'D LIKE THIS, THIS IS RIGHT OOP 'IS ALLEY...!
...THE GENDER FLUID...

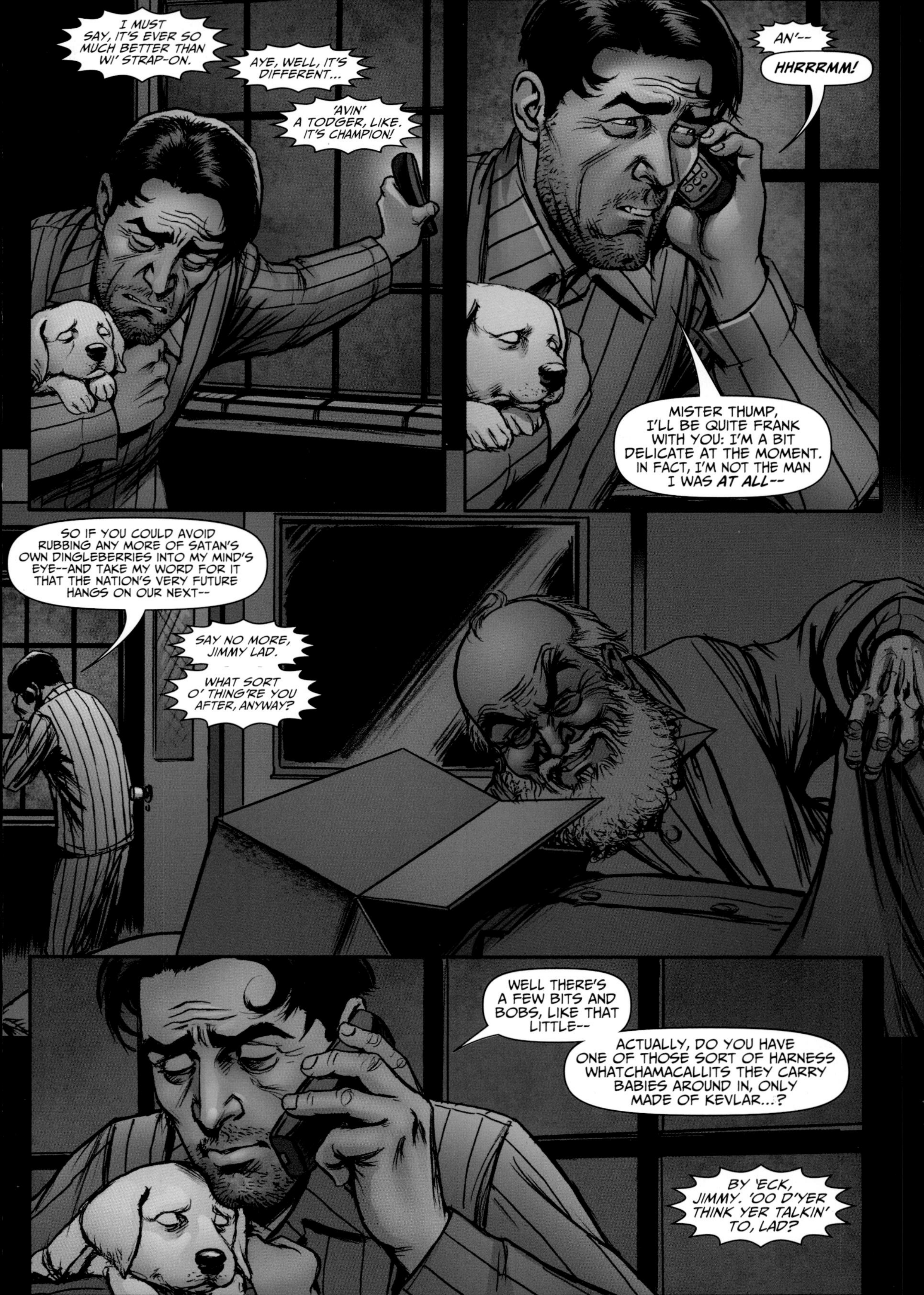
I MUST SAY, IT'S EVER SO MUCH BETTER THAN WI' STRAP-ON.
AYE, WELL, IT'S DIFFERENT...
'AVIN' A TODGER, LIKE. IT'S CHAMPION!
AN'--
HHRRRMM!
MISTER THUMP, I'LL BE QUITE FRANK WITH YOU: I'M A BIT DELICATE AT THE MOMENT. IN FACT, I'M NOT THE MAN I WAS AT ALL--
SO IF YOU COULD AVOID RUBBING ANY MORE OF SATAN'S OWN DINGLEBERRIES INTO MY MIND'S EYE--AND TAKE MY WORD FOR IT THAT THE NATION'S VERY FUTURE HANGS ON OUR NEXT--
SAY NO MORE, JIMMY LAD.
WHAT SORT O' THING'RE YOU AFTER, ANYWAY?
WELL THERE'S A FEW BITS AND BOBS, LIKE THAT LITTLE--
ACTUALLY, DO YOU HAVE ONE OF THOSE SORT OF HARNESS WHATCHAMACALLITS THEY CARRY BABIES AROUND IN, ONLY MADE OF KEVLAR...?
BY 'ECK, JIMMY. 'OO D'YER THINK YER TALKIN' TO, LAD?

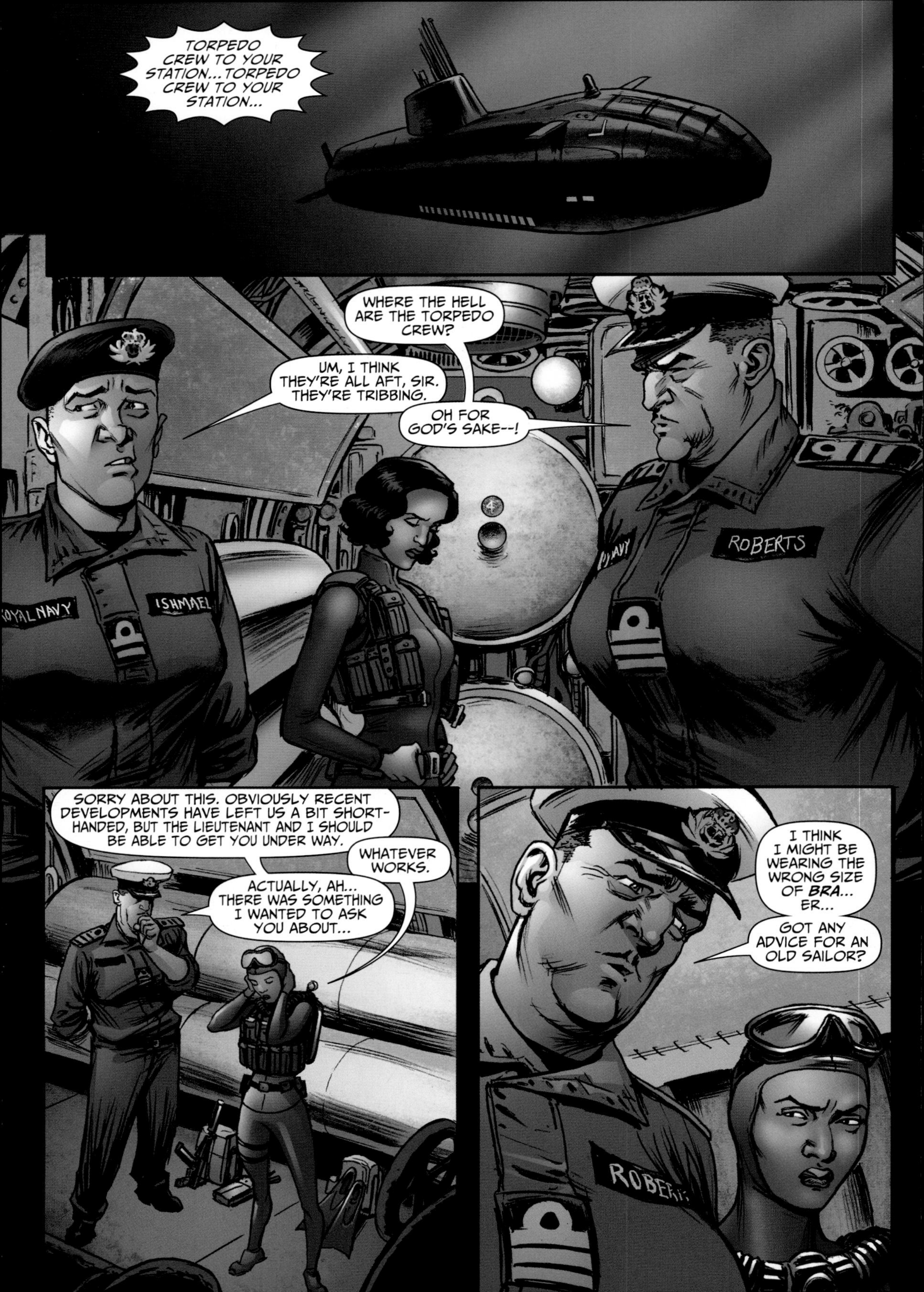
TORPEDO CREW TO YOUR STATION...TORPEDO CREW TO YOUR STATION...
WHERE THE HELL ARE THE TORPEDO CREW?
UM, I THINK THEY'RE ALL AFT, SIR. THEY'RE TRIBBING.
OH FOR GOD'S SAKE--!
ROYAL NAVY
ISHMAEL
ROBERTS
SORRY ABOUT THIS. OBVIOUSLY RECENT DEVELOPMENTS HAVE LEFT US A BIT SHORT-HANDED, BUT THE LIEUTENANT AND I SHOULD BE ABLE TO GET YOU UNDER WAY.
WHATEVER WORKS.
ACTUALLY, AH... THERE WAS SOMETHING I WANTED TO ASK YOU ABOUT...
I THINK I MIGHT BE WEARING THE WRONG SIZE OF **BRA**... ER...
GOT ANY ADVICE FOR AN OLD SAILOR?
ROBERTS

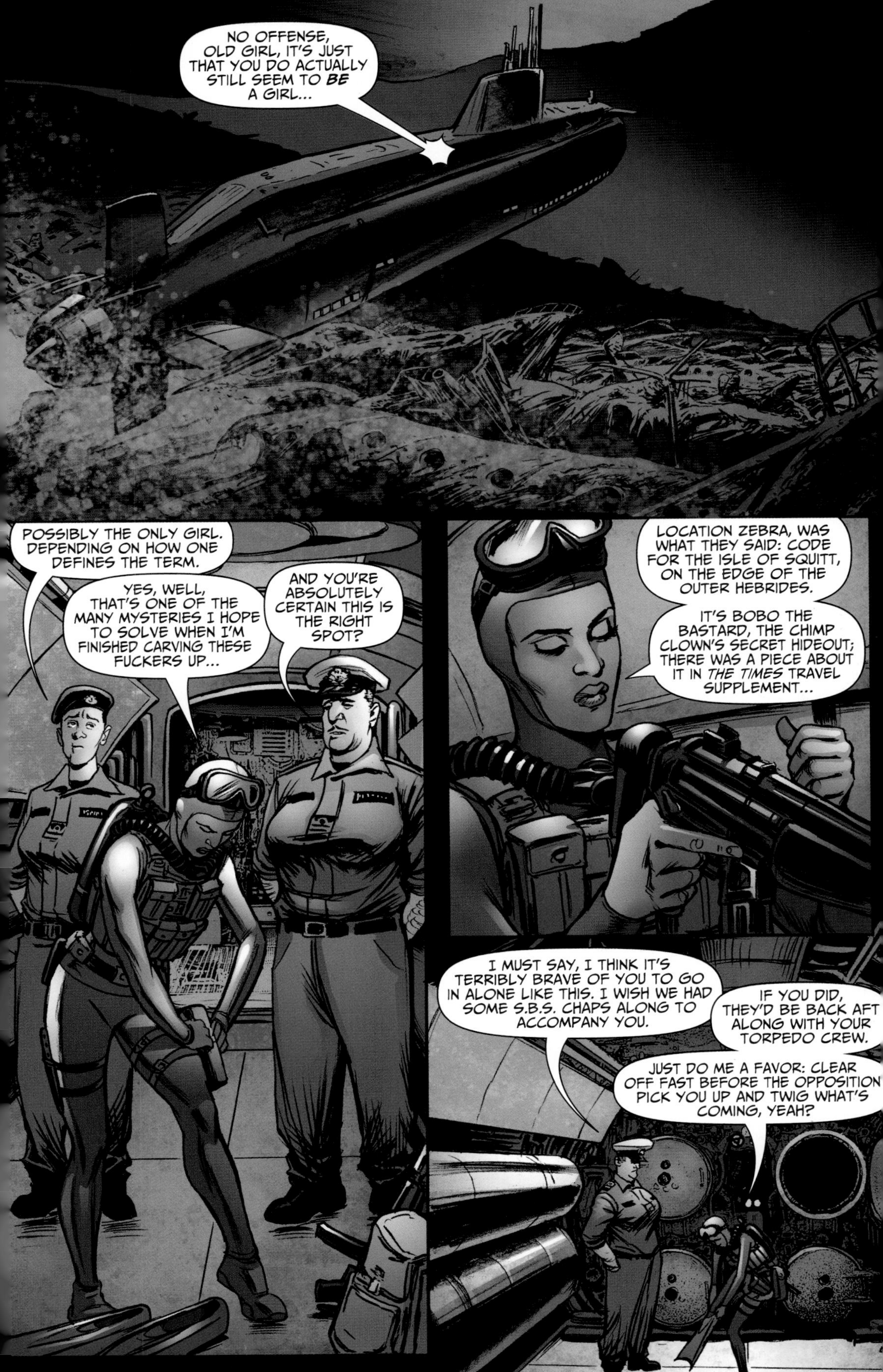
NO OFFENSE, OLD GIRL, IT'S JUST THAT YOU DO ACTUALLY STILL SEEM TO *BE* A GIRL...
POSSIBLY THE ONLY GIRL. DEPENDING ON HOW ONE DEFINES THE TERM.
YES, WELL, THAT'S ONE OF THE MANY MYSTERIES I HOPE TO SOLVE WHEN I'M FINISHED CARVING THESE FUCKERS UP...
AND YOU'RE ABSOLUTELY CERTAIN THIS IS THE RIGHT SPOT?
LOCATION ZEBRA, WAS WHAT THEY SAID: CODE FOR THE ISLE OF SQUITT, ON THE EDGE OF THE OUTER HEBRIDES.
IT'S BOBO THE BASTARD, THE CHIMP CLOWN'S SECRET HIDEOUT; THERE WAS A PIECE ABOUT IT IN *THE TIMES* TRAVEL SUPPLEMENT...
I MUST SAY, I THINK IT'S TERRIBLY BRAVE OF YOU TO GO IN ALONE LIKE THIS. I WISH WE HAD SOME S.B.S. CHAPS ALONG TO ACCOMPANY YOU.
IF YOU DID, THEY'D BE BACK AFT ALONG WITH YOUR TORPEDO CREW.
JUST DO ME A FAVOR: CLEAR OFF FAST BEFORE THE OPPOSITION PICK YOU UP AND TWIG WHAT'S COMING, YEAH?

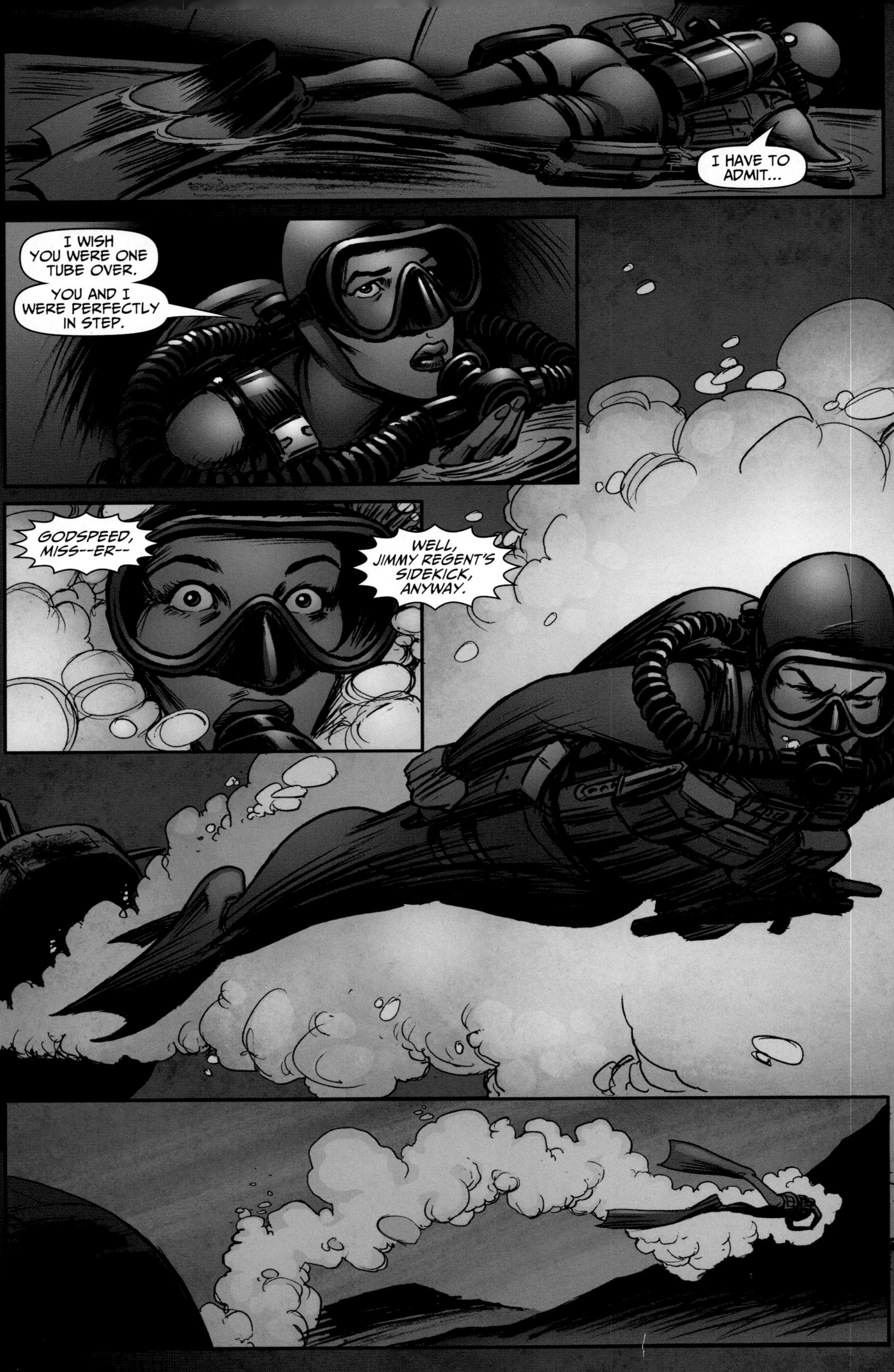
I HAVE TO ADMIT...
I WISH YOU WERE ONE TUBE OVER.
YOU AND I WERE PERFECTLY IN STEP.
GODSPEED, MISS--ER--
WELL, JIMMY REGENT'S SIDEKICK, ANYWAY.

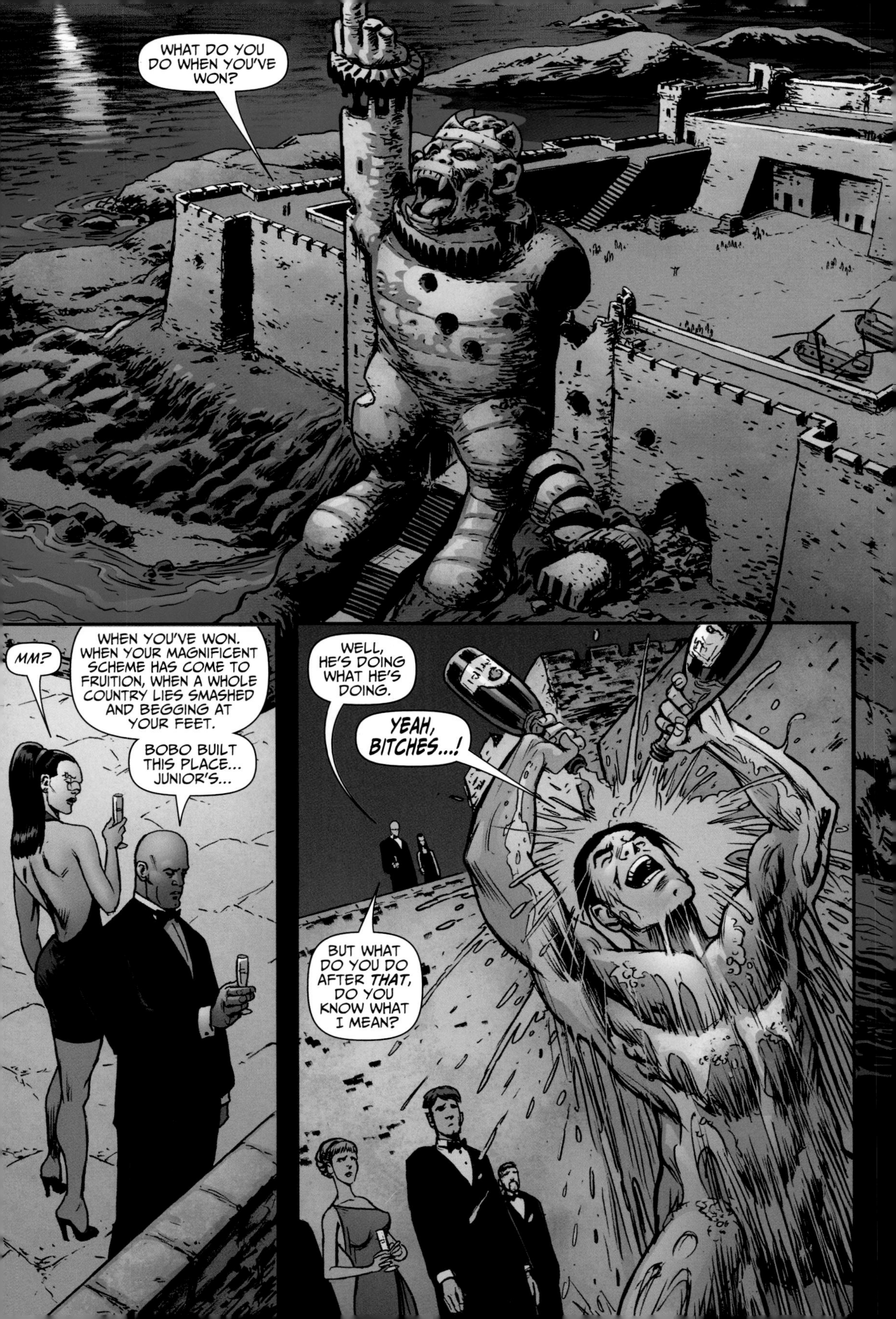
WHAT DO YOU DO WHEN YOU'VE WON?
MM?
WHEN YOU'VE WON. WHEN YOUR MAGNIFICENT SCHEME HAS COME TO FRUITION, WHEN A WHOLE COUNTRY LIES SMASHED AND BEGGING AT YOUR FEET.
BOBO BUILT THIS PLACE... JUNIOR'S...
WELL, HE'S DOING WHAT HE'S DOING.
YEAH, BITCHES...!
BUT WHAT DO YOU DO AFTER *THAT*, DO YOU KNOW WHAT I MEAN?

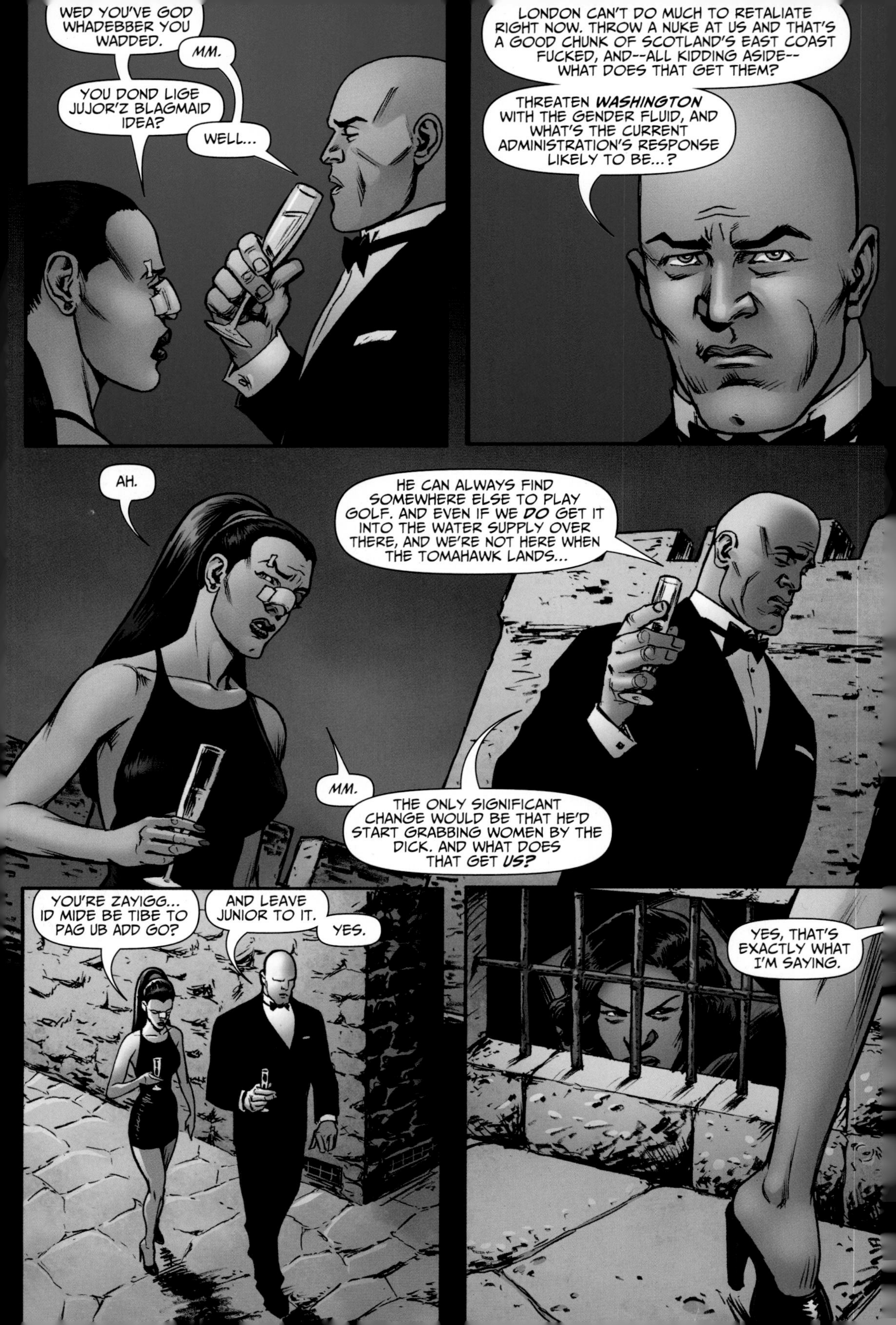
WED YOU'VE GOD WHADEBBER YOU WADDED.
MM.
YOU DOND LIGE JUJOR'Z BLAGMAID IDEA?
WELL...
LONDON CAN'T DO MUCH TO RETALIATE RIGHT NOW. THROW A NUKE AT US AND THAT'S A GOOD CHUNK OF SCOTLAND'S EAST COAST FUCKED, AND--ALL KIDDING ASIDE-- WHAT DOES THAT GET THEM?
THREATEN *WASHINGTON* WITH THE GENDER FLUID, AND WHAT'S THE CURRENT ADMINISTRATION'S RESPONSE LIKELY TO BE...?
AH.
HE CAN ALWAYS FIND SOMEWHERE ELSE TO PLAY GOLF. AND EVEN IF WE *DO* GET IT INTO THE WATER SUPPLY OVER THERE, AND WE'RE NOT HERE WHEN THE TOMAHAWK LANDS...
MM.
THE ONLY SIGNIFICANT CHANGE WOULD BE THAT HE'D START GRABBING WOMEN BY THE DICK. AND WHAT DOES THAT GET *US?*
YOU'RE ZAYIGG... ID MIDE BE TIBE TO PAG UB ADD GO?
AND LEAVE JUNIOR TO IT.
YES.
YES, THAT'S EXACTLY WHAT I'M SAYING.

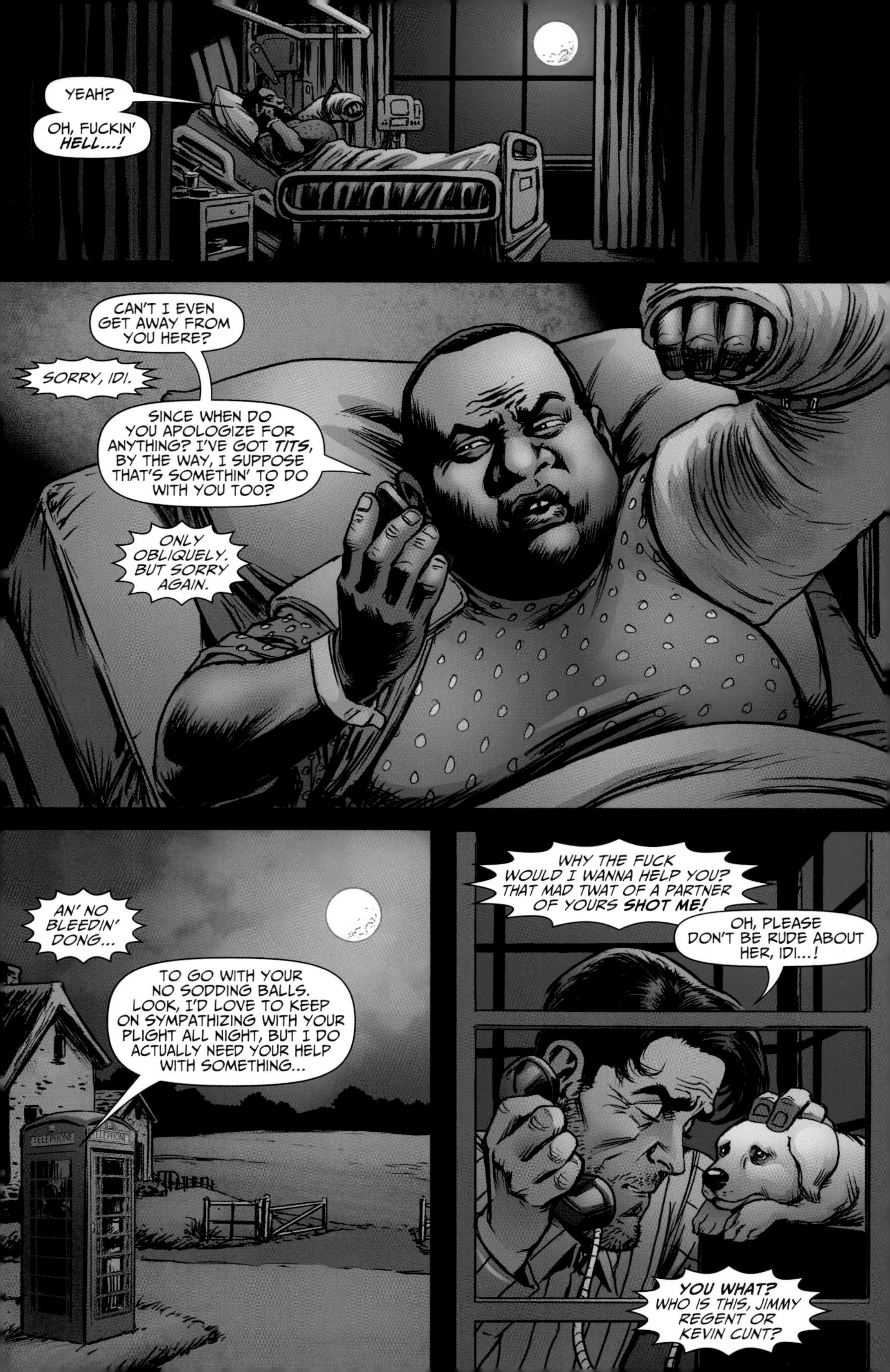
YEAH?
OH, FUCKIN' HELL...!
CAN'T I EVEN GET AWAY FROM YOU HERE?
SORRY, IDI.
SINCE WHEN DO YOU APOLOGIZE FOR ANYTHING? I'VE GOT TITS, BY THE WAY, I SUPPOSE THAT'S SOMETHIN' TO DO WITH YOU TOO?
ONLY OBLIQUELY. BUT SORRY AGAIN.
AN' NO BLEEDIN' DONG...
TO GO WITH YOUR NO SODDING BALLS. LOOK, I'D LOVE TO KEEP ON SYMPATHIZING WITH YOUR PLIGHT ALL NIGHT, BUT I DO ACTUALLY NEED YOUR HELP WITH SOMETHING...
TELEPHONE
TELEPHONE
WHY THE FUCK WOULD I WANNA HELP YOU? THAT MAD TWAT OF A PARTNER OF YOURS SHOT ME!
OH, PLEASE DON'T BE RUDE ABOUT HER, IDI...!
YOU WHAT? WHO IS THIS, JIMMY REGENT OR KEVIN CUNT?

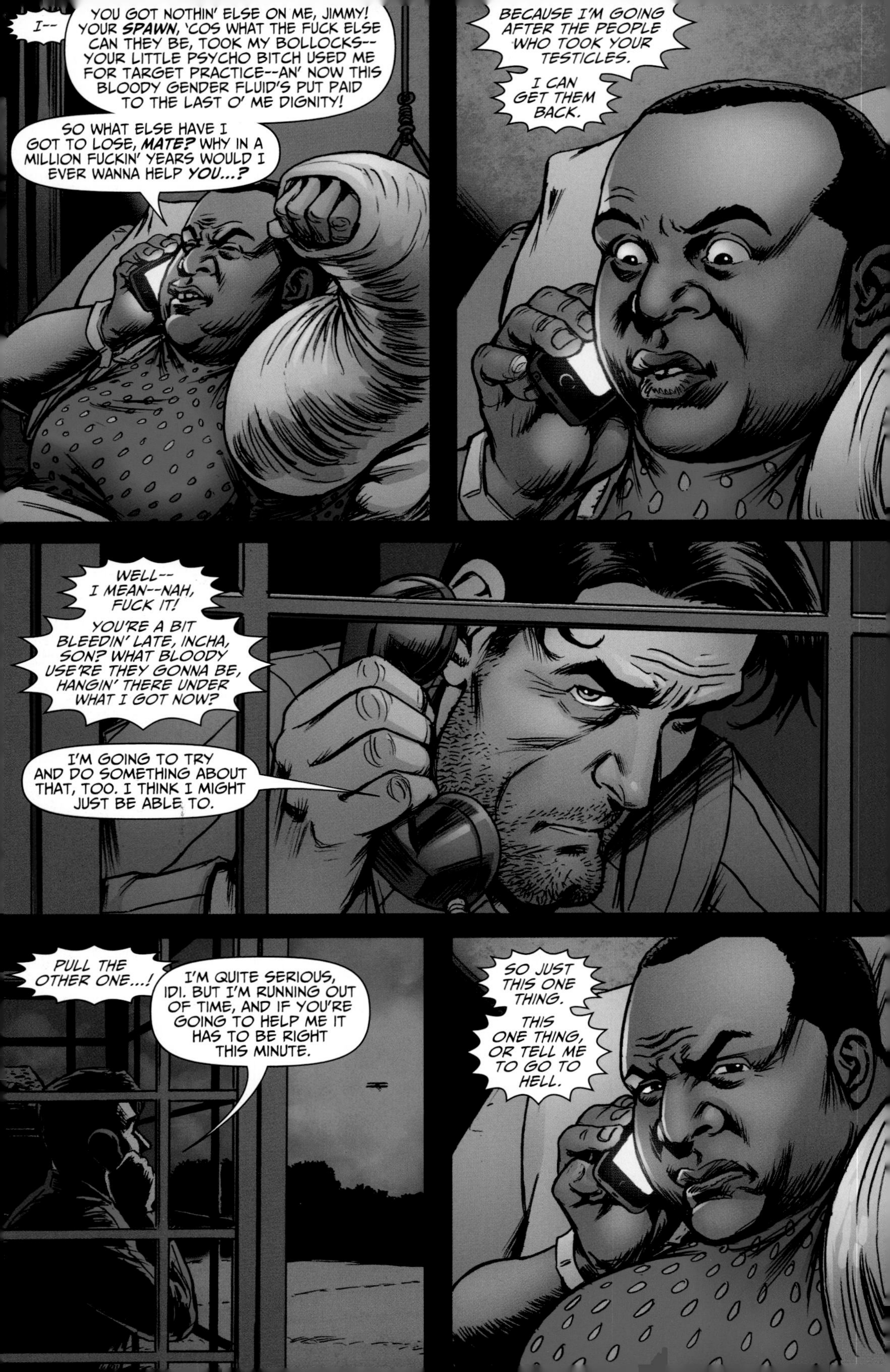
I--
YOU GOT NOTHIN' ELSE ON ME, JIMMY! YOUR SPAWN, 'COS WHAT THE FUCK ELSE CAN THEY BE, TOOK MY BOLLOCKS--YOUR LITTLE PSYCHO BITCH USED ME FOR TARGET PRACTICE--AN' NOW THIS BLOODY GENDER FLUID'S PUT PAID TO THE LAST O' ME DIGNITY!
SO WHAT ELSE HAVE I GOT TO LOSE, MATE? WHY IN A MILLION FUCKIN' YEARS WOULD I EVER WANNA HELP YOU...?
BECAUSE I'M GOING AFTER THE PEOPLE WHO TOOK YOUR TESTICLES.
I CAN GET THEM BACK.
WELL-- I MEAN--NAH, FUCK IT!
YOU'RE A BIT BLEEDIN' LATE, INCHA, SON? WHAT BLOODY USE'RE THEY GONNA BE, HANGIN' THERE UNDER WHAT I GOT NOW?
I'M GOING TO TRY AND DO SOMETHING ABOUT THAT, TOO. I THINK I MIGHT JUST BE ABLE TO.
PULL THE OTHER ONE...!
I'M QUITE SERIOUS, IDI. BUT I'M RUNNING OUT OF TIME, AND IF YOU'RE GOING TO HELP ME IT HAS TO BE RIGHT THIS MINUTE.
SO JUST THIS ONE THING.
THIS ONE THING, OR TELL ME TO GO TO HELL.

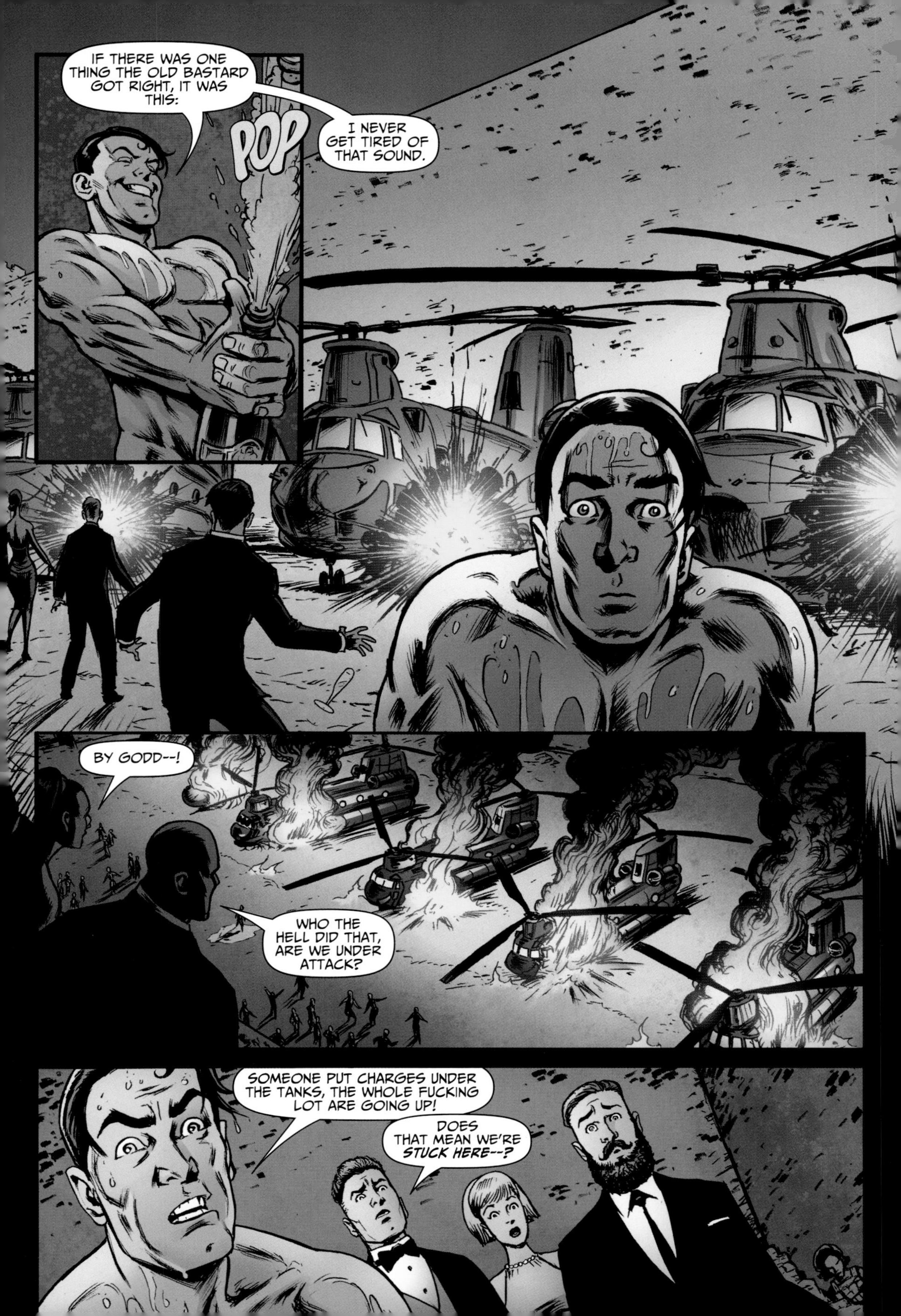
IF THERE WAS ONE THING THE OLD BASTARD GOT RIGHT, IT WAS THIS:
POP
I NEVER GET TIRED OF THAT SOUND.
BY GODD--!
WHO THE HELL DID THAT, ARE WE UNDER ATTACK?
SOMEONE PUT CHARGES UNDER THE TANKS, THE WHOLE FUCKING LOT ARE GOING UP!
DOES THAT MEAN WE'RE *STUCK HERE*--?

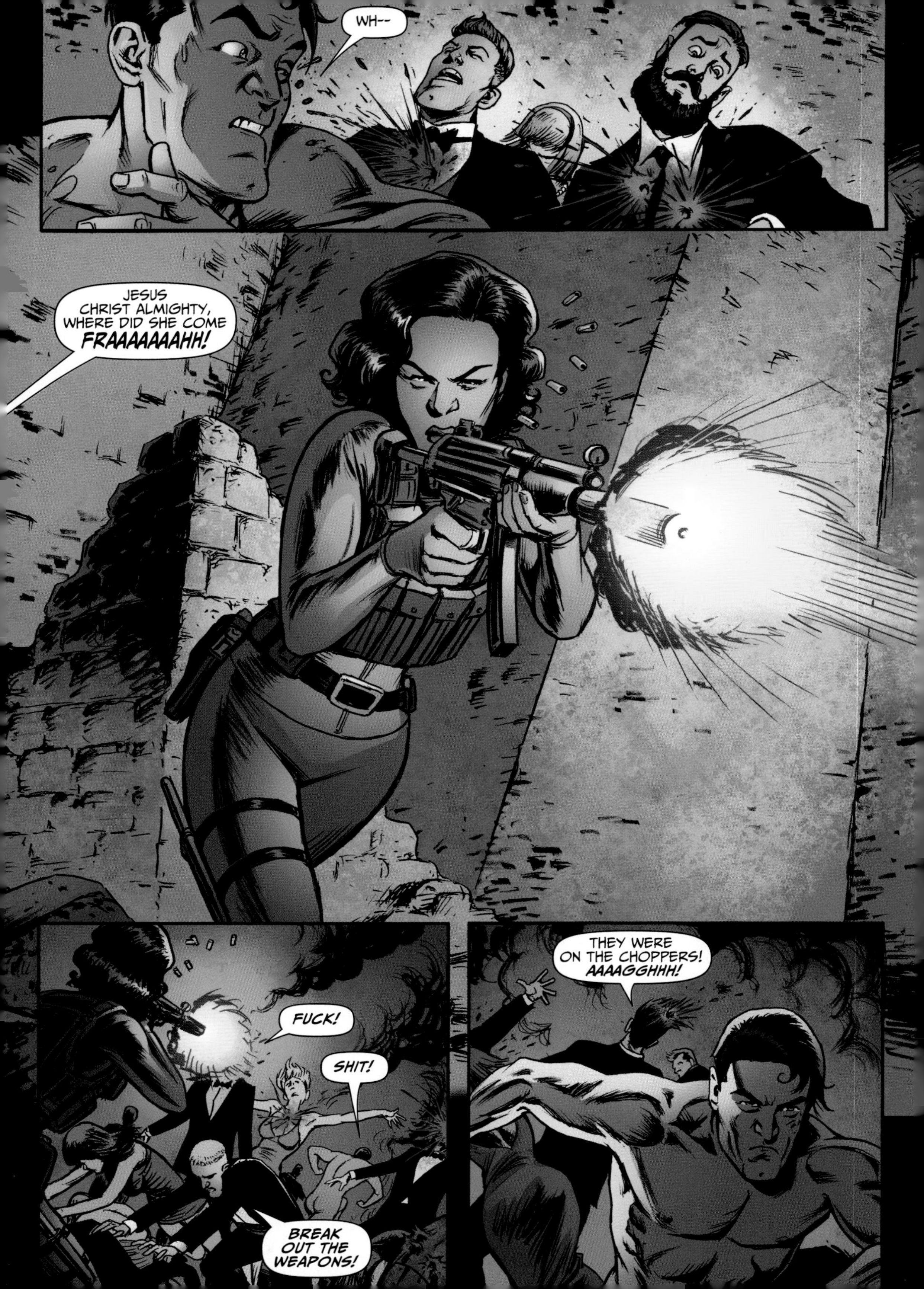
WH--
JESUS CHRIST ALMIGHTY, WHERE DID SHE COME FRAAAAAAAHH!
FUCK!
SHIT!
BREAK OUT THE WEAPONS!
THEY WERE ON THE CHOPPERS! AAAAGGHHH!

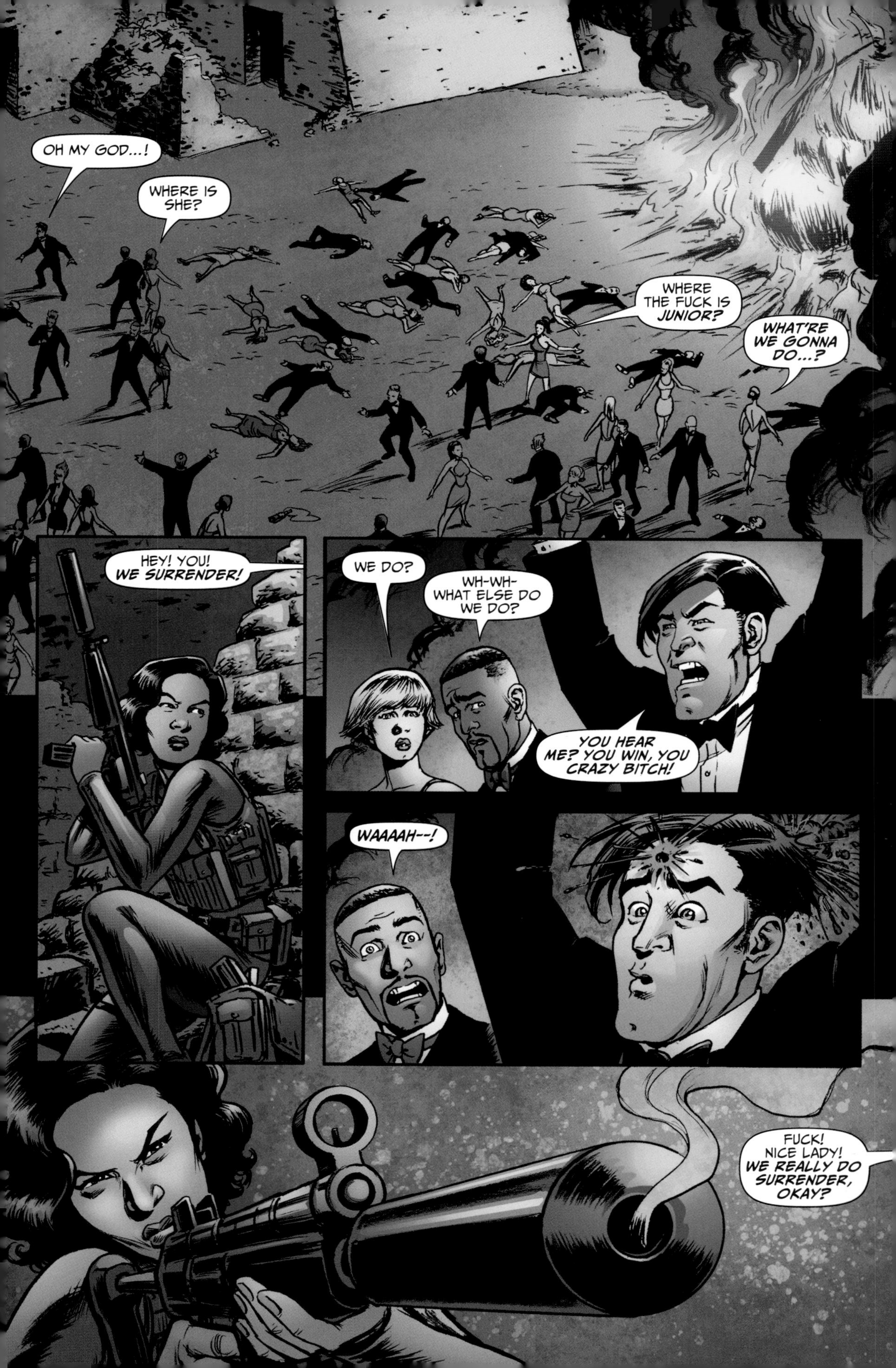
OH MY GOD...!
WHERE IS SHE?
WHERE THE FUCK IS JUNIOR?
WHAT'RE WE GONNA DO...?
HEY! YOU! WE SURRENDER!
WE DO?
WH-WH- WHAT ELSE DO WE DO?
YOU HEAR ME? YOU WIN, YOU CRAZY BITCH!
WAAAAH--!
FUCK! NICE LADY! WE REALLY DO SURRENDER, OKAY?

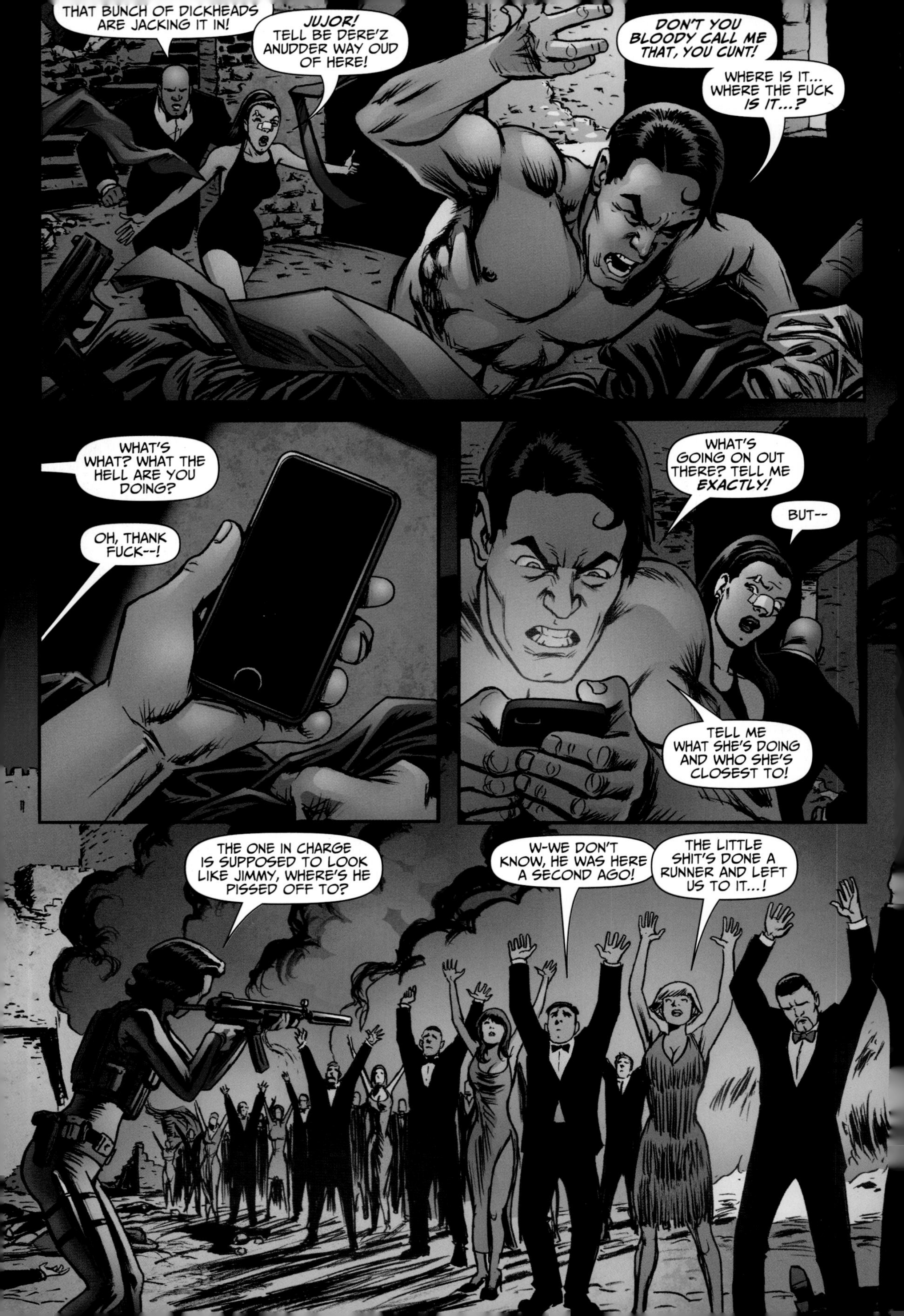
THAT BUNCH OF DICKHEADS ARE JACKING IT IN!
JUJOR! TELL BE DERE'Z ANUDDER WAY OUD OF HERE!
DON'T YOU BLOODY CALL ME THAT, YOU CUNT!
WHERE IS IT... WHERE THE FUCK IS IT...?
WHAT'S WHAT? WHAT THE HELL ARE YOU DOING?
OH, THANK FUCK--!
WHAT'S GOING ON OUT THERE? TELL ME EXACTLY!
BUT--
TELL ME WHAT SHE'S DOING AND WHO SHE'S CLOSEST TO!
THE ONE IN CHARGE IS SUPPOSED TO LOOK LIKE JIMMY, WHERE'S HE PISSED OFF TO?
W-WE DON'T KNOW, HE WAS HERE A SECOND AGO!
THE LITTLE SHIT'S DONE A RUNNER AND LEFT US TO IT...!

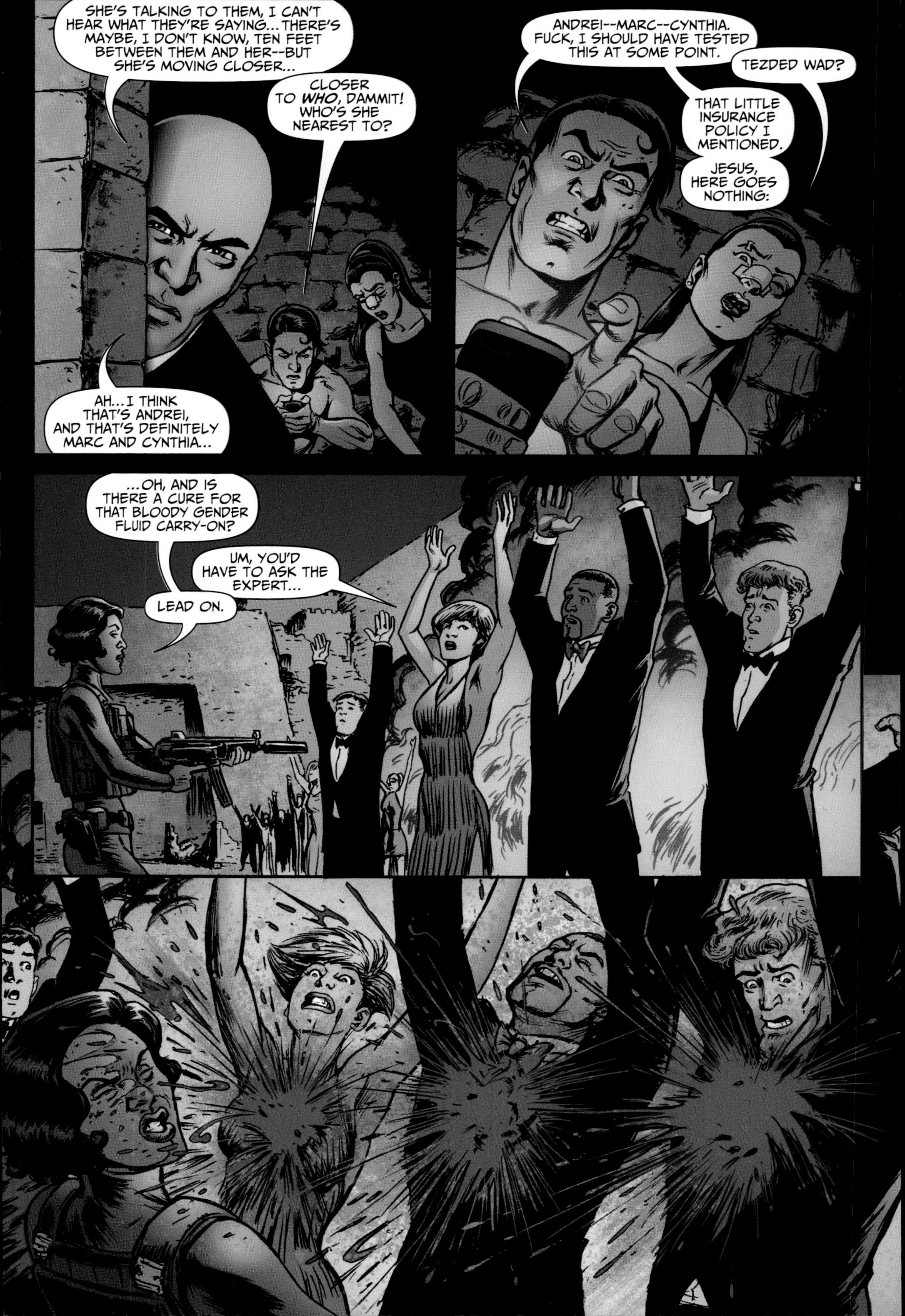
SHE'S TALKING TO THEM, I CAN'T HEAR WHAT THEY'RE SAYING... THERE'S MAYBE, I DON'T KNOW, TEN FEET BETWEEN THEM AND HER--BUT SHE'S MOVING CLOSER...
CLOSER TO **WHO**, DAMMIT! WHO'S SHE NEAREST TO?
AH... I THINK THAT'S ANDREI, AND THAT'S DEFINITELY MARC AND CYNTHIA...
ANDREI--MARC--CYNTHIA. FUCK, I SHOULD HAVE TESTED THIS AT SOME POINT.
TEZDED WAD?
THAT LITTLE INSURANCE POLICY I MENTIONED.
JESUS, HERE GOES NOTHING:
...OH, AND IS THERE A CURE FOR THAT BLOODY GENDER FLUID CARRY-ON?
UM, YOU'D HAVE TO ASK THE EXPERT...
LEAD ON.

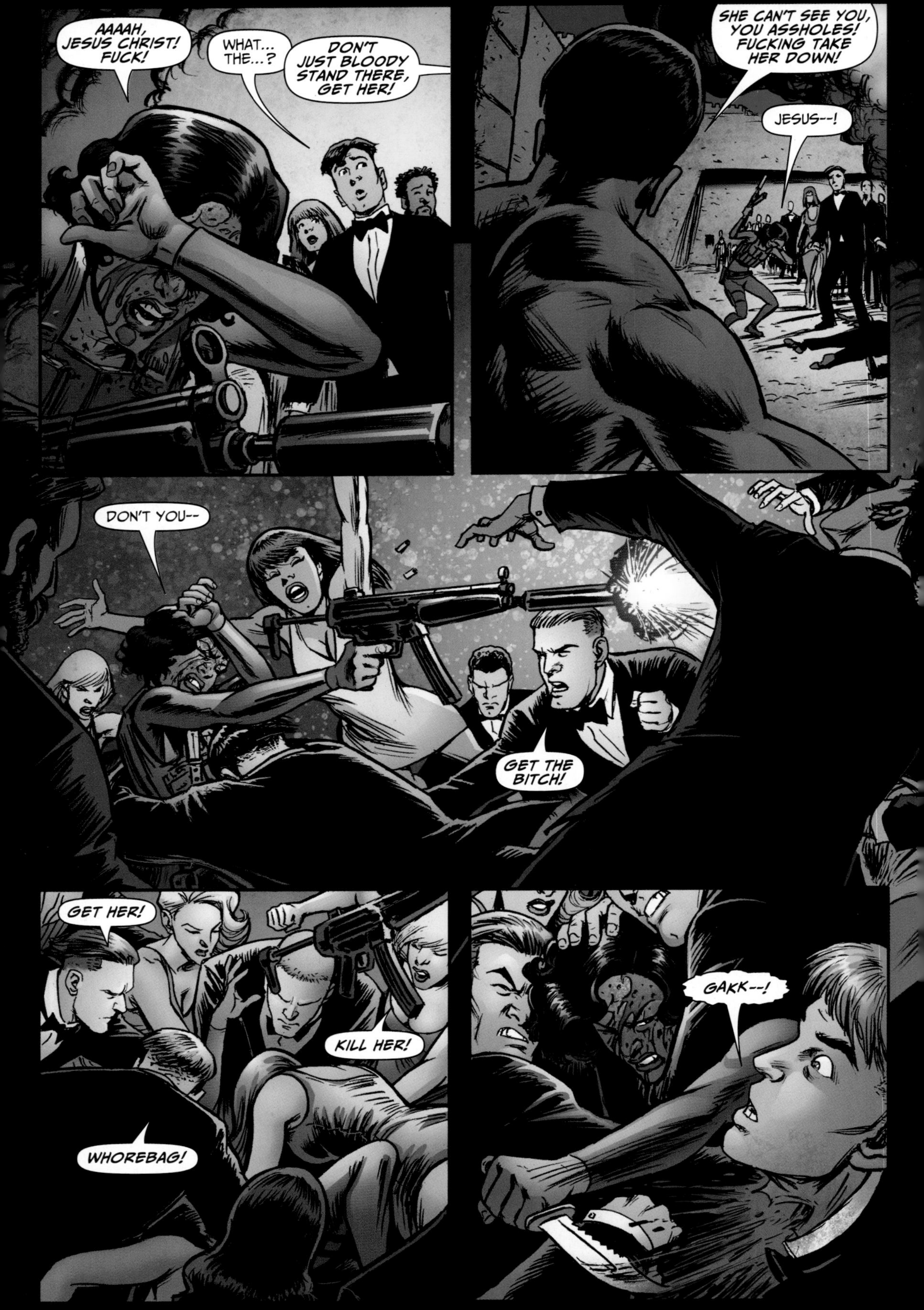
AAAAH, JESUS CHRIST! FUCK!
WHAT... THE...?
DON'T JUST BLOODY STAND THERE, GET HER!
SHE CAN'T SEE YOU, YOU ASSHOLES! FUCKING TAKE HER DOWN!
JESUS--!
DON'T YOU--
GET THE BITCH!
GET HER!
KILL HER!
WHOREBAG!
GAKK--!

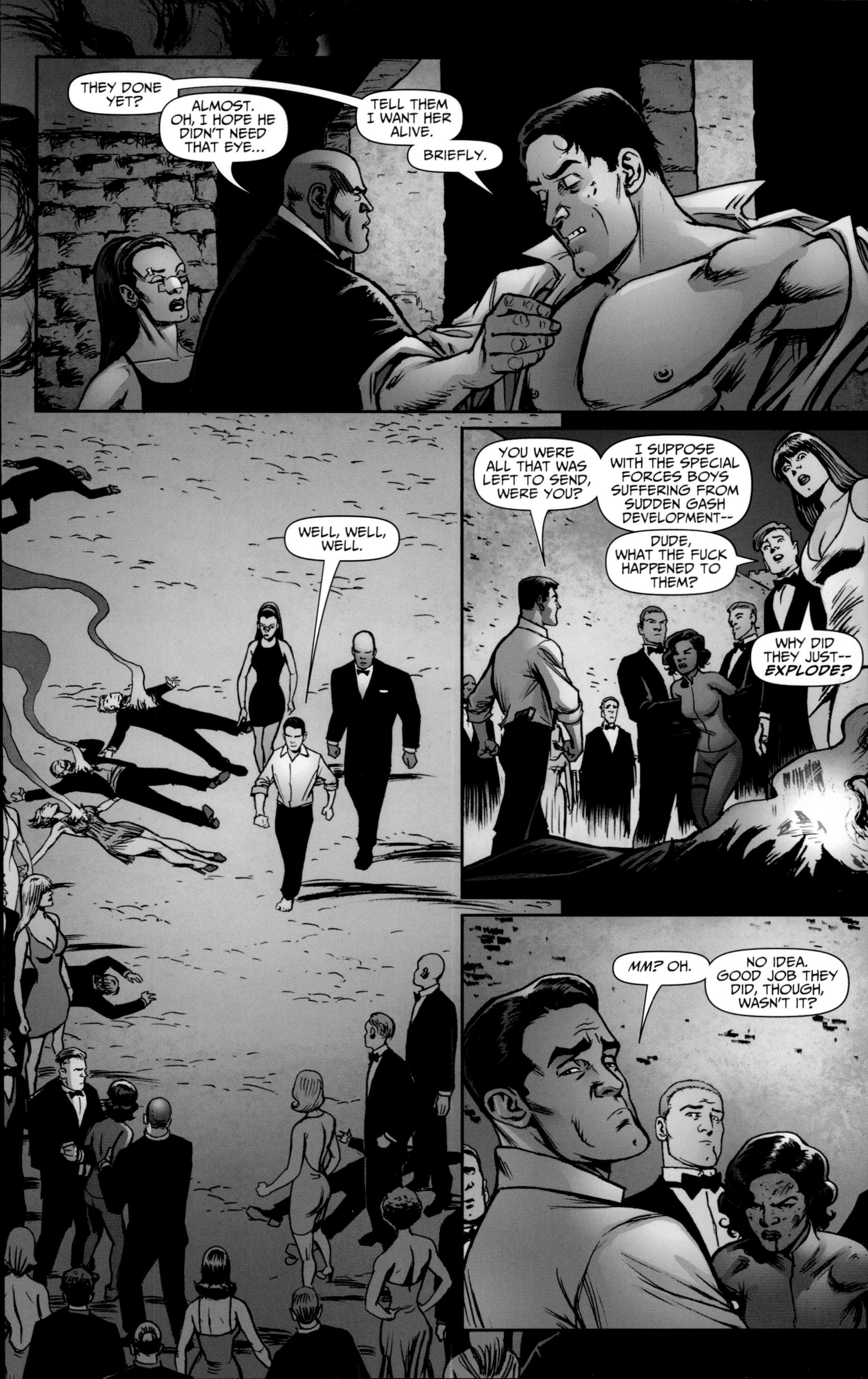
THEY DONE YET?
ALMOST. OH, I HOPE HE DIDN'T NEED THAT EYE...
TELL THEM I WANT HER ALIVE.
BRIEFLY.
WELL, WELL, WELL.
YOU WERE ALL THAT WAS LEFT TO SEND, WERE YOU?
I SUPPOSE WITH THE SPECIAL FORCES BOYS SUFFERING FROM SUDDEN GASH DEVELOPMENT--
DUDE, WHAT THE FUCK HAPPENED TO THEM?
WHY DID THEY JUST-- *EXPLODE?*
MM? OH.
NO IDEA. GOOD JOB THEY DID, THOUGH, WASN'T IT?

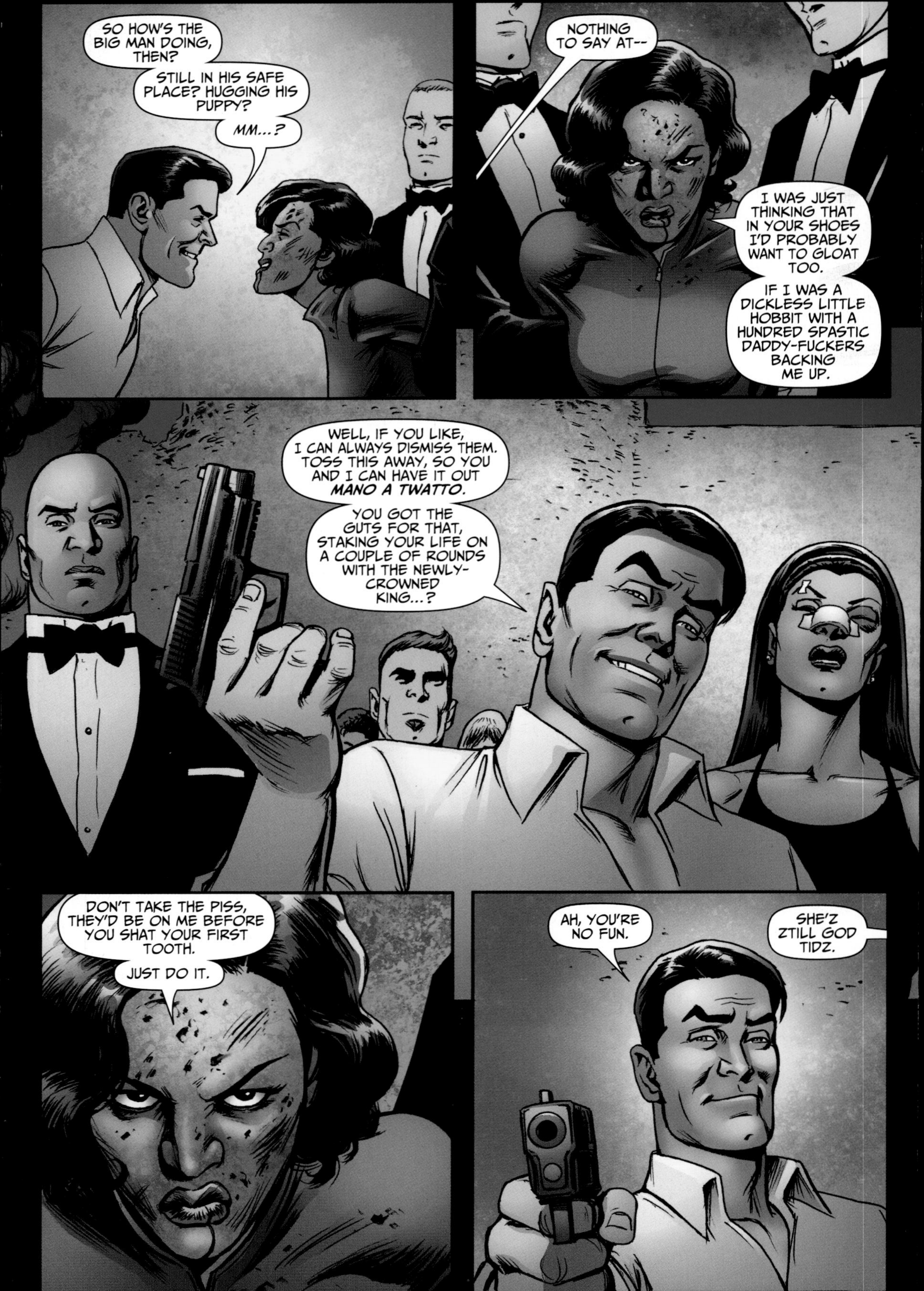

SO HOW'S THE BIG MAN DOING, THEN?
STILL IN HIS SAFE PLACE? HUGGING HIS PUPPY?
MM...?
NOTHING TO SAY AT--
I WAS JUST THINKING THAT IN YOUR SHOES I'D PROBABLY WANT TO GLOAT TOO.
IF I WAS A DICKLESS LITTLE HOBBIT WITH A HUNDRED SPASTIC DADDY-FUCKERS BACKING ME UP.
WELL, IF YOU LIKE, I CAN ALWAYS DISMISS THEM. TOSS THIS AWAY, SO YOU AND I CAN HAVE IT OUT *MANO A TWATTO.*
YOU GOT THE GUTS FOR THAT, STAKING YOUR LIFE ON A COUPLE OF ROUNDS WITH THE NEWLY-CROWNED KING...?
DON'T TAKE THE PISS, THEY'D BE ON ME BEFORE YOU SHAT YOUR FIRST TOOTH.
JUST DO IT.
AH, YOU'RE NO FUN.
SHE'Z ZTILL GOD TIDZ.

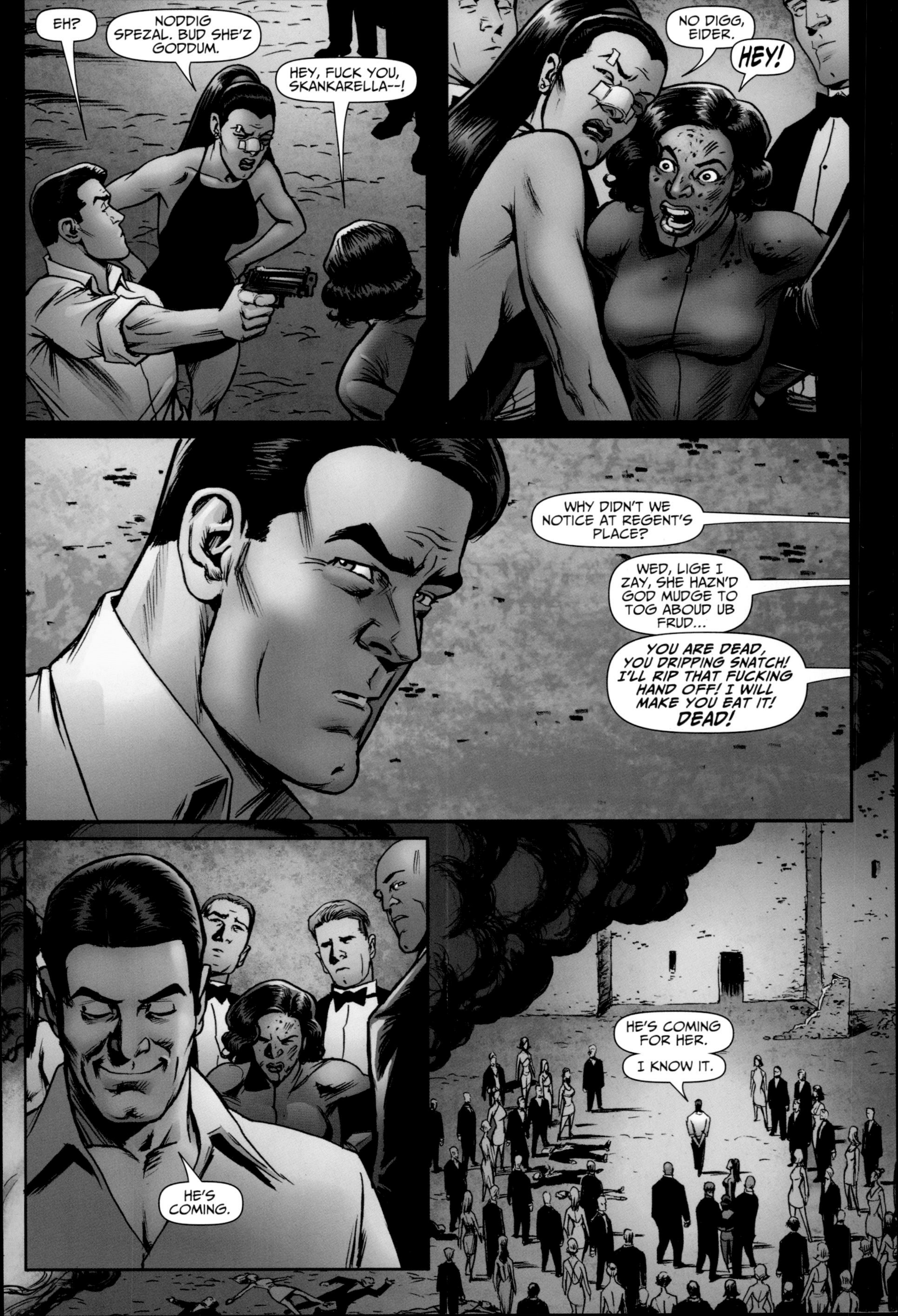
EH?
NODDIG SPEZAL. BUD SHE'Z GODDUM.
HEY, FUCK YOU, SKANKARELLA--!
NO DIGG, EIDER.
HEY!
WHY DIDN'T WE NOTICE AT REGENT'S PLACE?
WED, LIGE I ZAY, SHE HAZN'D GOD MUDGE TO TOG ABOUD UB FRUD...
YOU ARE DEAD, YOU DRIPPING SNATCH! I'LL RIP THAT FUCKING HAND OFF! I WILL MAKE YOU EAT IT! DEAD!
HE'S COMING.
HE'S COMING FOR HER.
I KNOW IT.

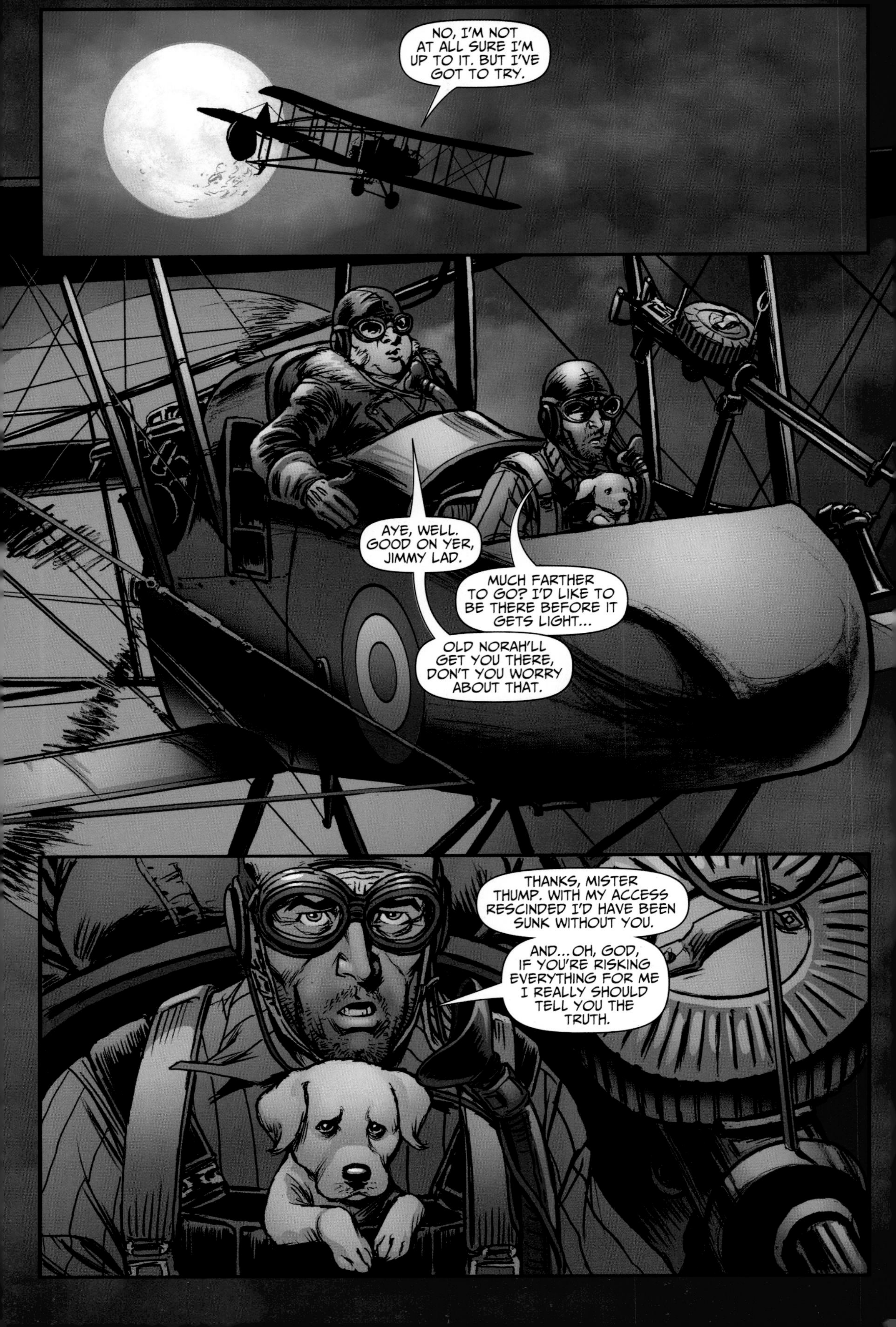
NO, I'M NOT AT ALL SURE I'M UP TO IT. BUT I'VE GOT TO TRY.
AYE, WELL. GOOD ON YER, JIMMY LAD.
MUCH FARTHER TO GO? I'D LIKE TO BE THERE BEFORE IT GETS LIGHT...
OLD NORAH'LL GET YOU THERE, DON'T YOU WORRY ABOUT THAT.
THANKS, MISTER THUMP. WITH MY ACCESS RESCINDED I'D HAVE BEEN SUNK WITHOUT YOU.
AND...OH, GOD, IF YOU'RE RISKING EVERYTHING FOR ME I REALLY SHOULD TELL YOU THE TRUTH.

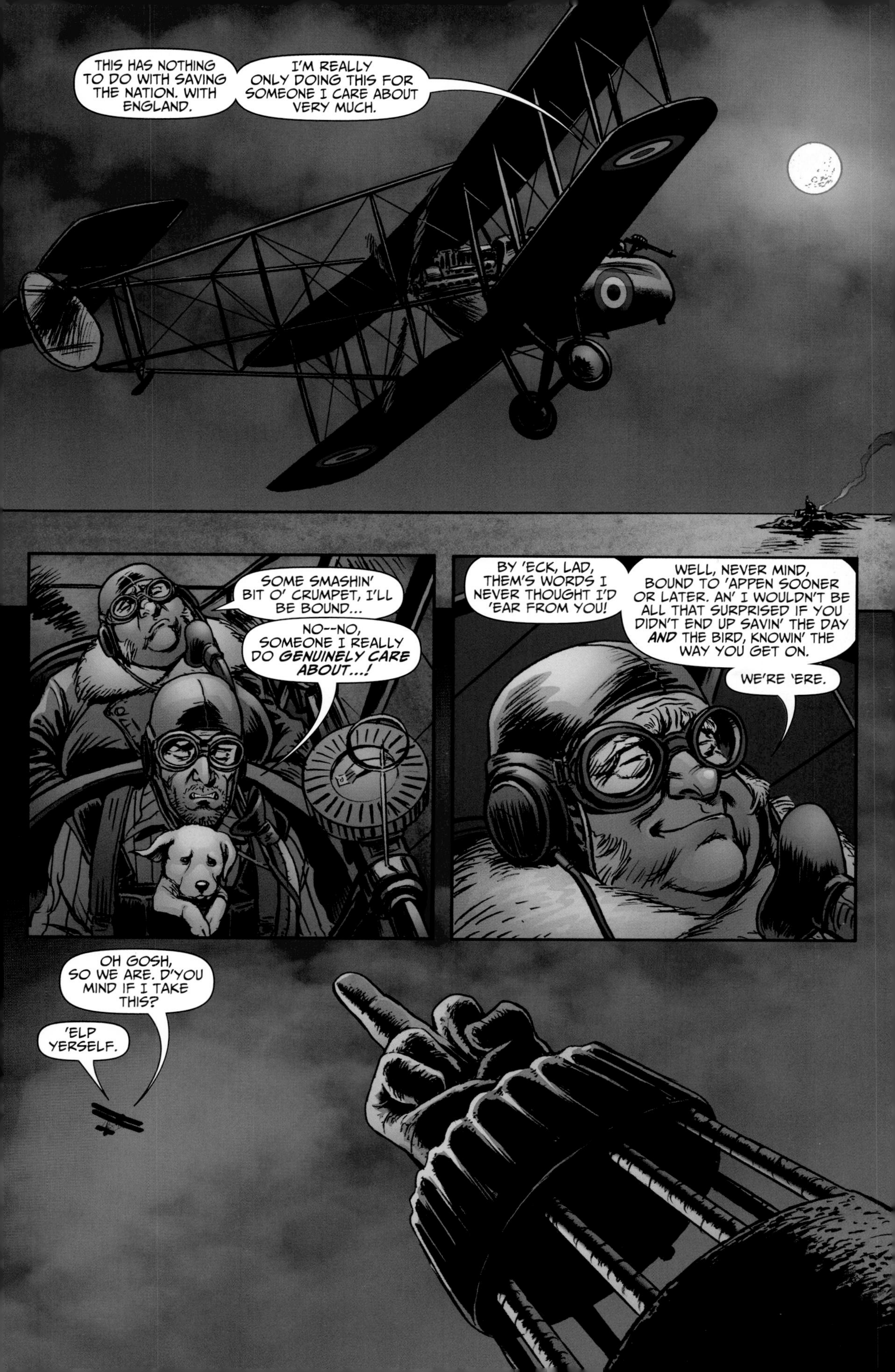
THIS HAS NOTHING TO DO WITH SAVING THE NATION. WITH ENGLAND.
I'M REALLY ONLY DOING THIS FOR SOMEONE I CARE ABOUT VERY MUCH.
SOME SMASHIN' BIT O' CRUMPET, I'LL BE BOUND...
NO--NO, SOMEONE I REALLY DO **GENUINELY CARE ABOUT**...!
BY 'ECK, LAD, THEM'S WORDS I NEVER THOUGHT I'D 'EAR FROM YOU!
WELL, NEVER MIND, BOUND TO 'APPEN SOONER OR LATER. AN' I WOULDN'T BE ALL THAT SURPRISED IF YOU DIDN'T END UP SAVIN' THE DAY **AND** THE BIRD, KNOWIN' THE WAY YOU GET ON.
WE'RE 'ERE.
OH GOSH, SO WE ARE. D'YOU MIND IF I TAKE THIS?
'ELP YERSELF.

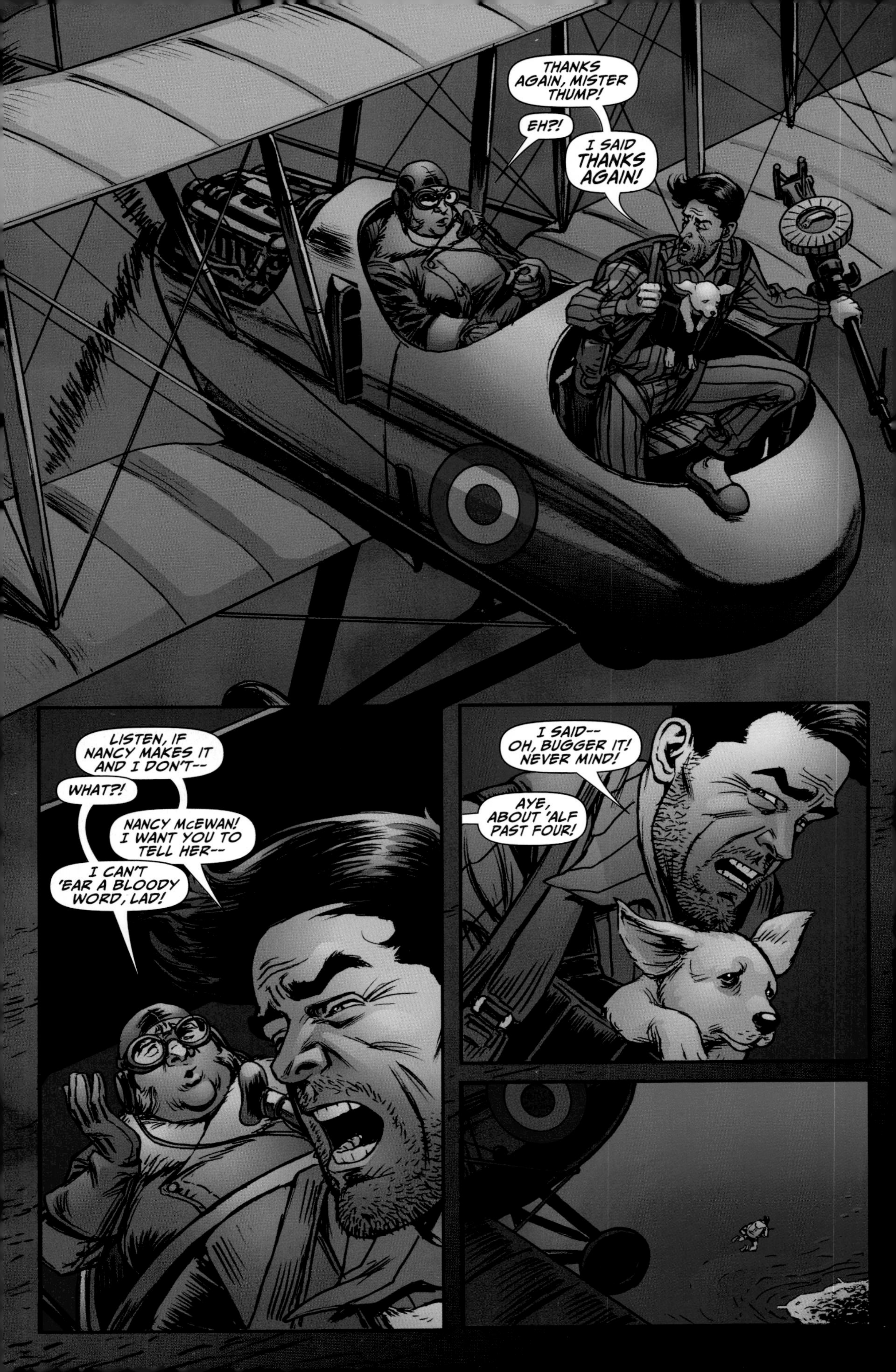
THANKS AGAIN, MISTER THUMP!
EH?!
I SAID THANKS AGAIN!
LISTEN, IF NANCY MAKES IT AND I DON'T--
WHAT?!
NANCY McEWAN! I WANT YOU TO TELL HER--
I CAN'T 'EAR A BLOODY WORD, LAD!
I SAID-- OH, BUGGER IT! NEVER MIND!
AYE, ABOUT 'ALF PAST FOUR!

8

GO FULL VILLAIN

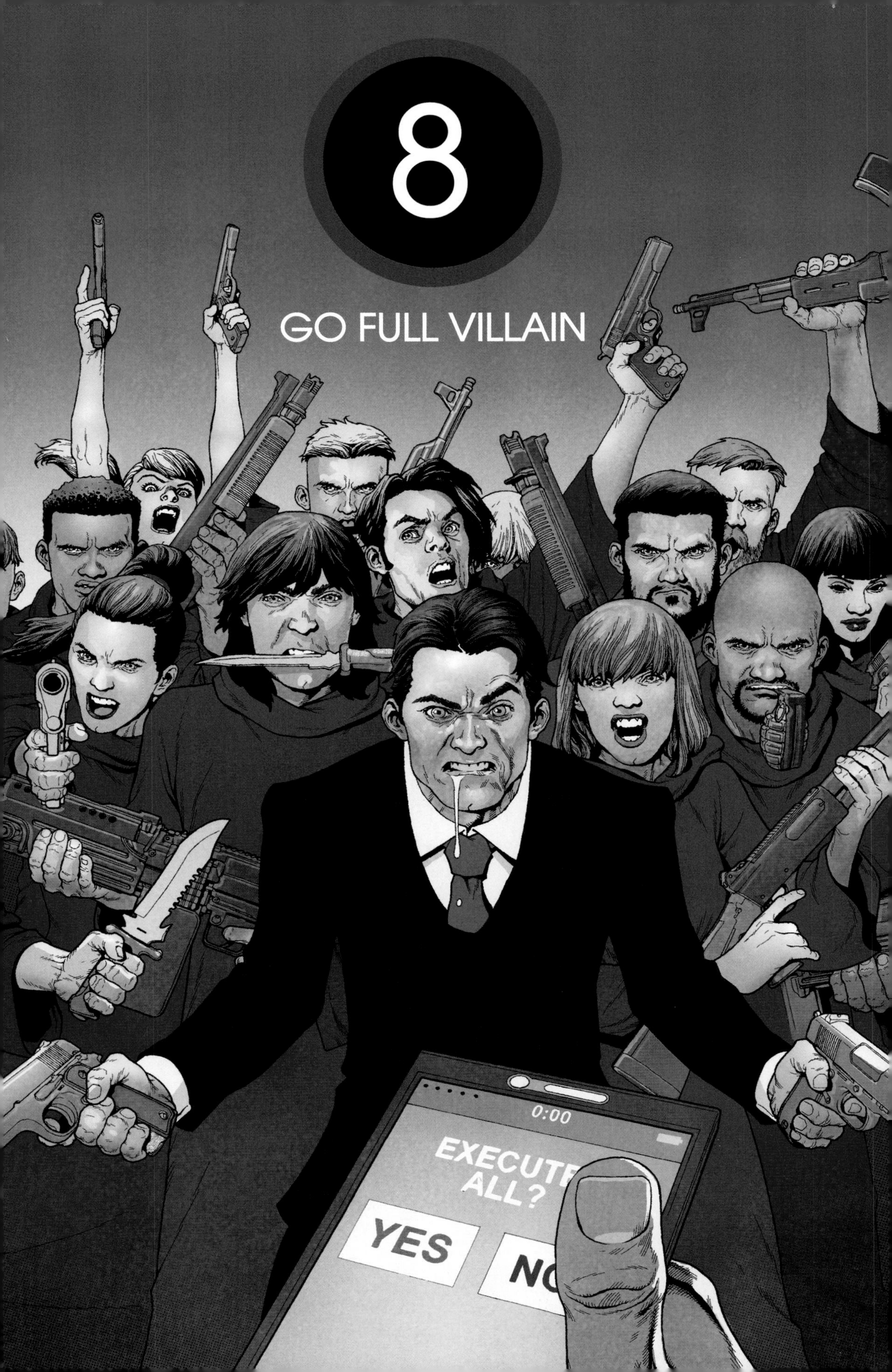
0:00
EXECUT
ALL?
YES
N

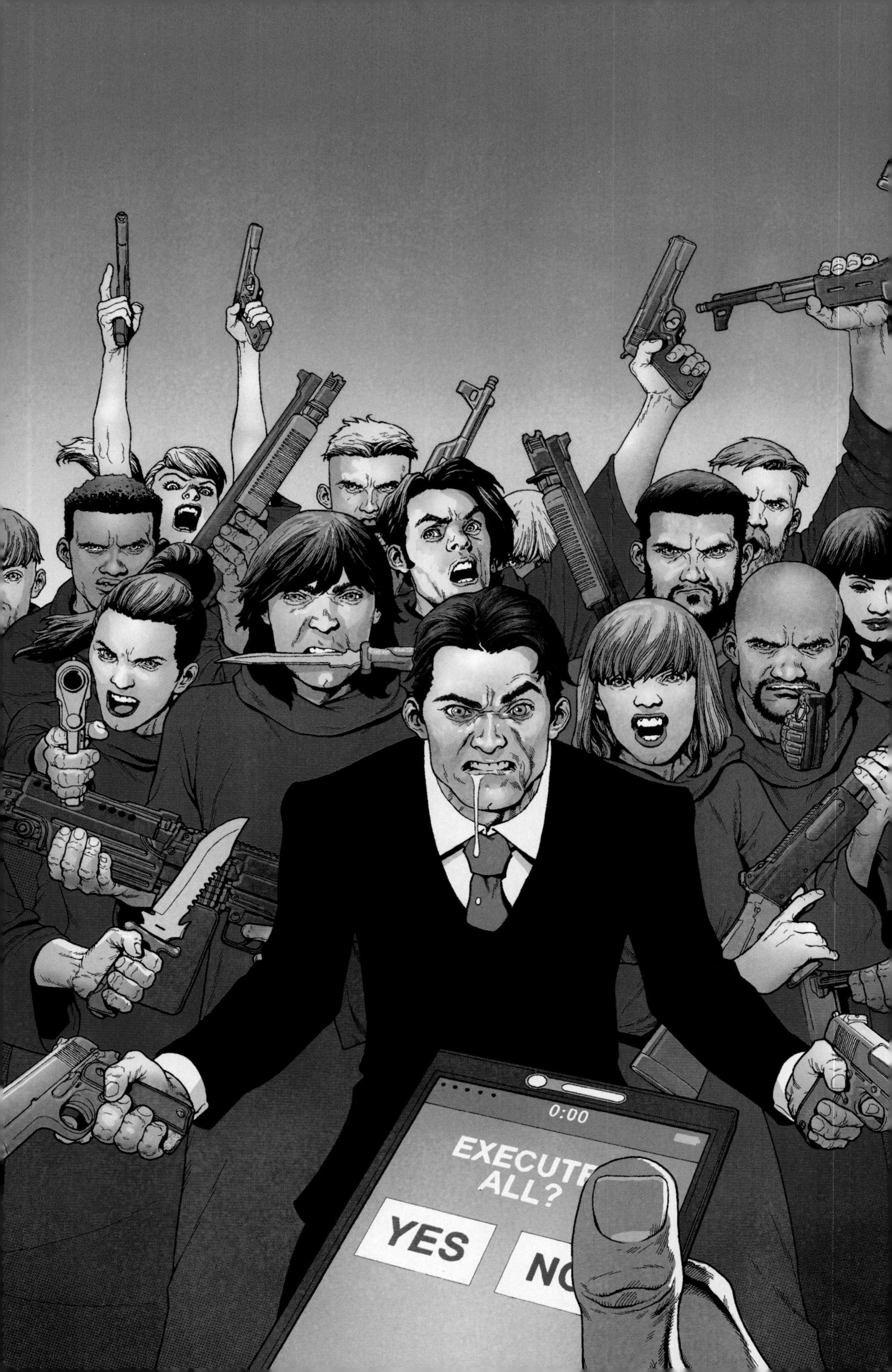
0:00
EXECUTE
ALL?
YES
NO

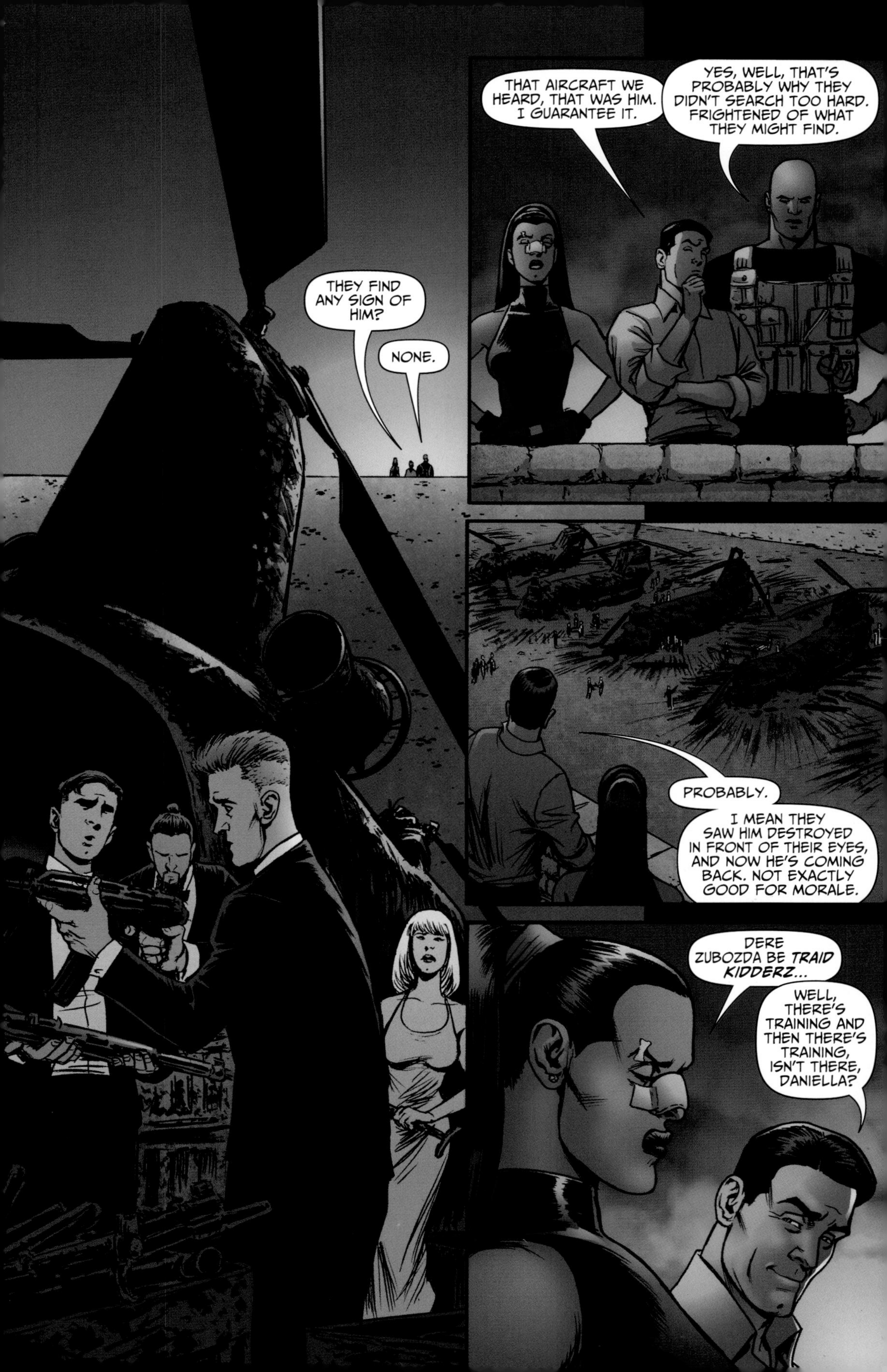
THEY FIND ANY SIGN OF HIM?
NONE.
THAT AIRCRAFT WE HEARD, THAT WAS HIM. I GUARANTEE IT.
YES, WELL, THAT'S PROBABLY WHY THEY DIDN'T SEARCH TOO HARD. FRIGHTENED OF WHAT THEY MIGHT FIND.
PROBABLY.
I MEAN THEY SAW HIM DESTROYED IN FRONT OF THEIR EYES, AND NOW HE'S COMING BACK. NOT EXACTLY GOOD FOR MORALE.
DERE ZUBOZDA BE *TRAID KIDDERZ*...
WELL, THERE'S TRAINING AND THEN THERE'S TRAINING, ISN'T THERE, DANIELLA?

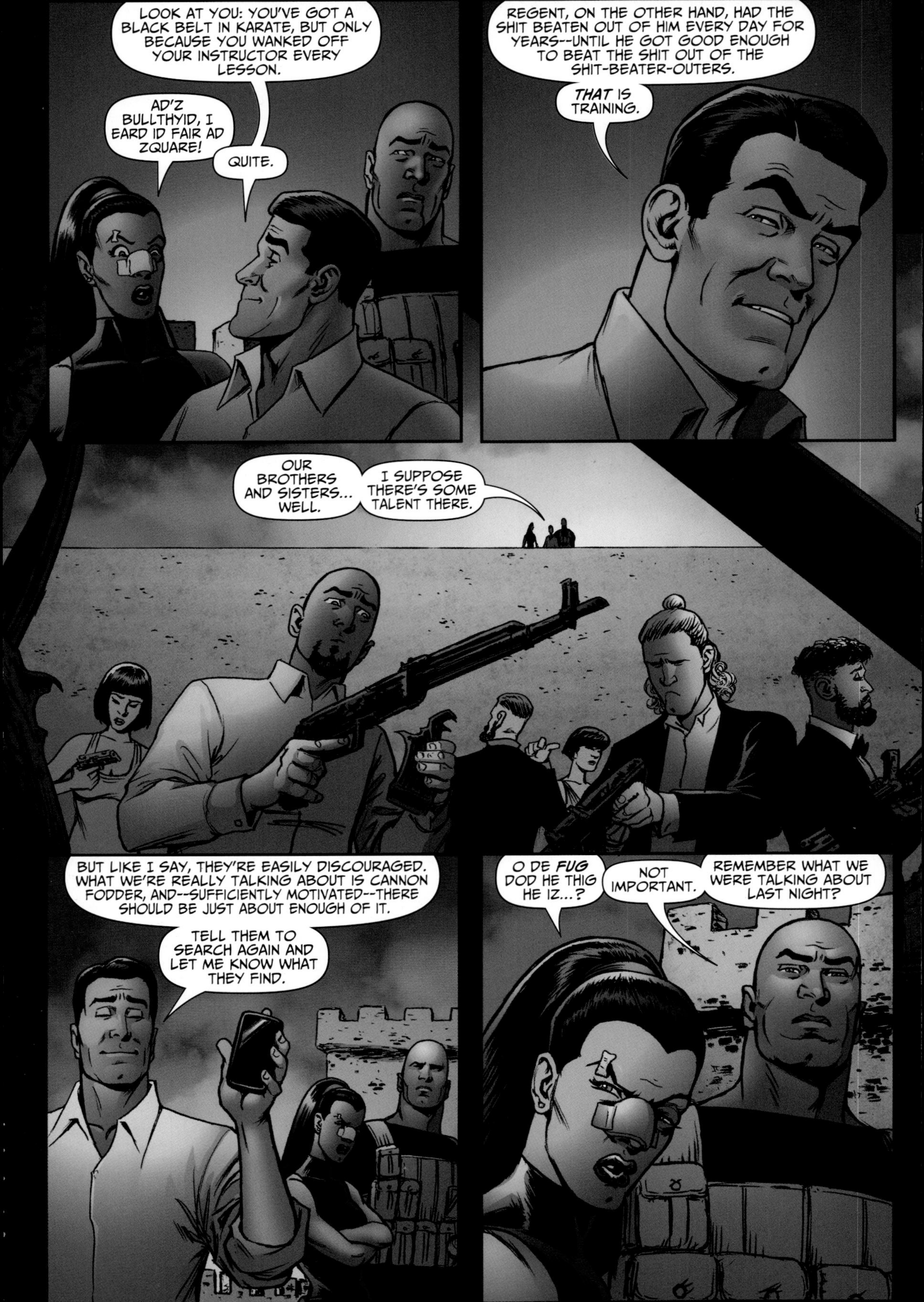
LOOK AT YOU: YOU'VE GOT A BLACK BELT IN KARATE, BUT ONLY BECAUSE YOU WANKED OFF YOUR INSTRUCTOR EVERY LESSON.
AD'Z BULLTHYID, I EARD ID FAIR AD ZQUARE!
QUITE.
REGENT, ON THE OTHER HAND, HAD THE SHIT BEATEN OUT OF HIM EVERY DAY FOR YEARS--UNTIL HE GOT GOOD ENOUGH TO BEAT THE SHIT OUT OF THE SHIT-BEATER-OUTERS.
THAT IS TRAINING.
OUR BROTHERS AND SISTERS... WELL.
I SUPPOSE THERE'S SOME TALENT THERE.
BUT LIKE I SAY, THEY'RE EASILY DISCOURAGED. WHAT WE'RE REALLY TALKING ABOUT IS CANNON FODDER, AND--SUFFICIENTLY MOTIVATED--THERE SHOULD BE JUST ABOUT ENOUGH OF IT.
TELL THEM TO SEARCH AGAIN AND LET ME KNOW WHAT THEY FIND.
O DE *FUG* DOD HE THIG HE IZ...?
NOT IMPORTANT.
REMEMBER WHAT WE WERE TALKING ABOUT LAST NIGHT?

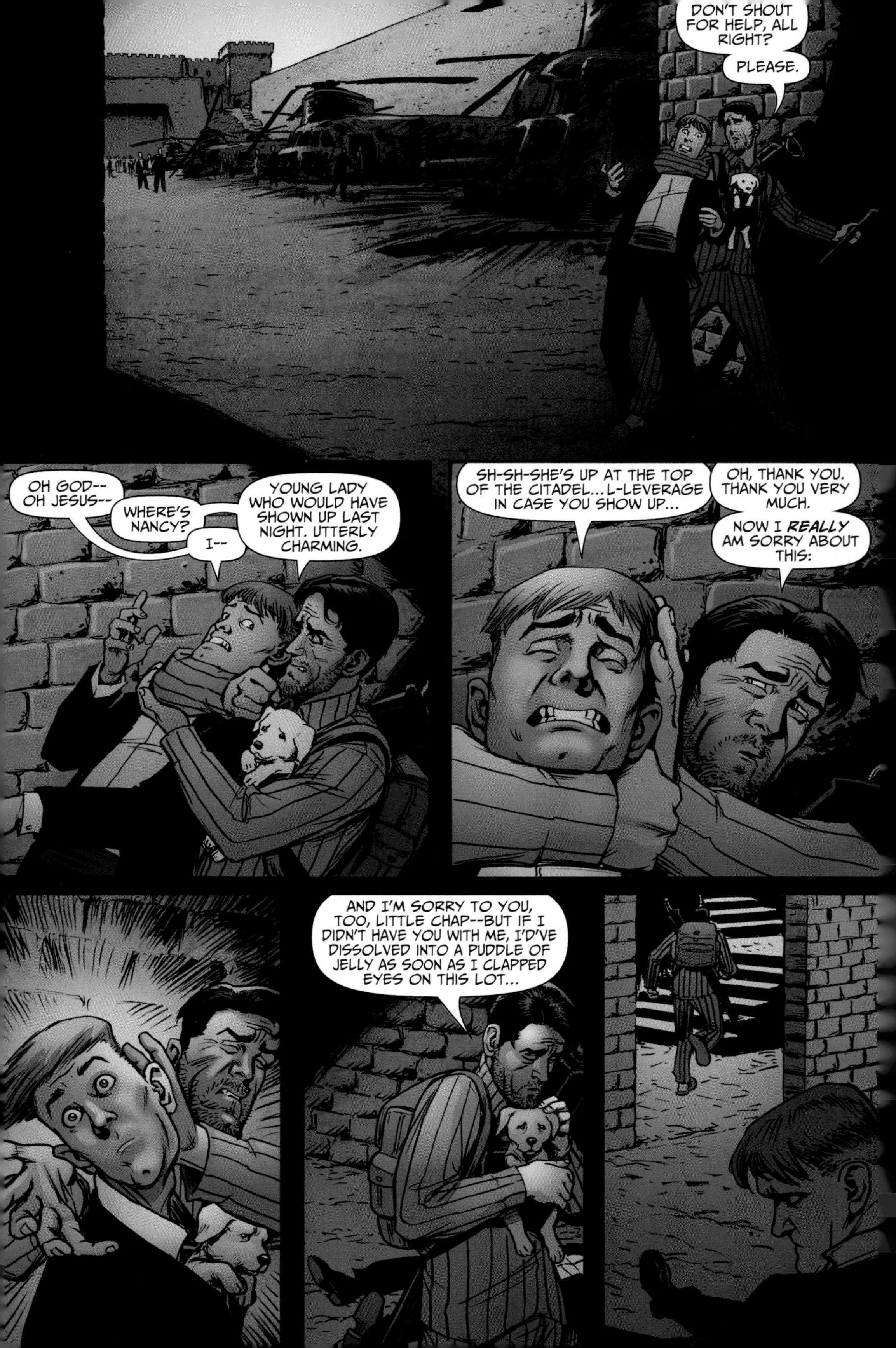
DON'T SHOUT FOR HELP, ALL RIGHT?
PLEASE.
OH GOD-- OH JESUS--
WHERE'S NANCY?
I--
YOUNG LADY WHO WOULD HAVE SHOWN UP LAST NIGHT. UTTERLY CHARMING.
SH-SH-SHE'S UP AT THE TOP OF THE CITADEL...L-LEVERAGE IN CASE YOU SHOW UP...
OH, THANK YOU. THANK YOU VERY MUCH.
NOW I *REALLY* AM SORRY ABOUT THIS:
AND I'M SORRY TO YOU, TOO, LITTLE CHAP--BUT IF I DIDN'T HAVE YOU WITH ME, I'D'VE DISSOLVED INTO A PUDDLE OF JELLY AS SOON AS I CLAPPED EYES ON THIS LOT...

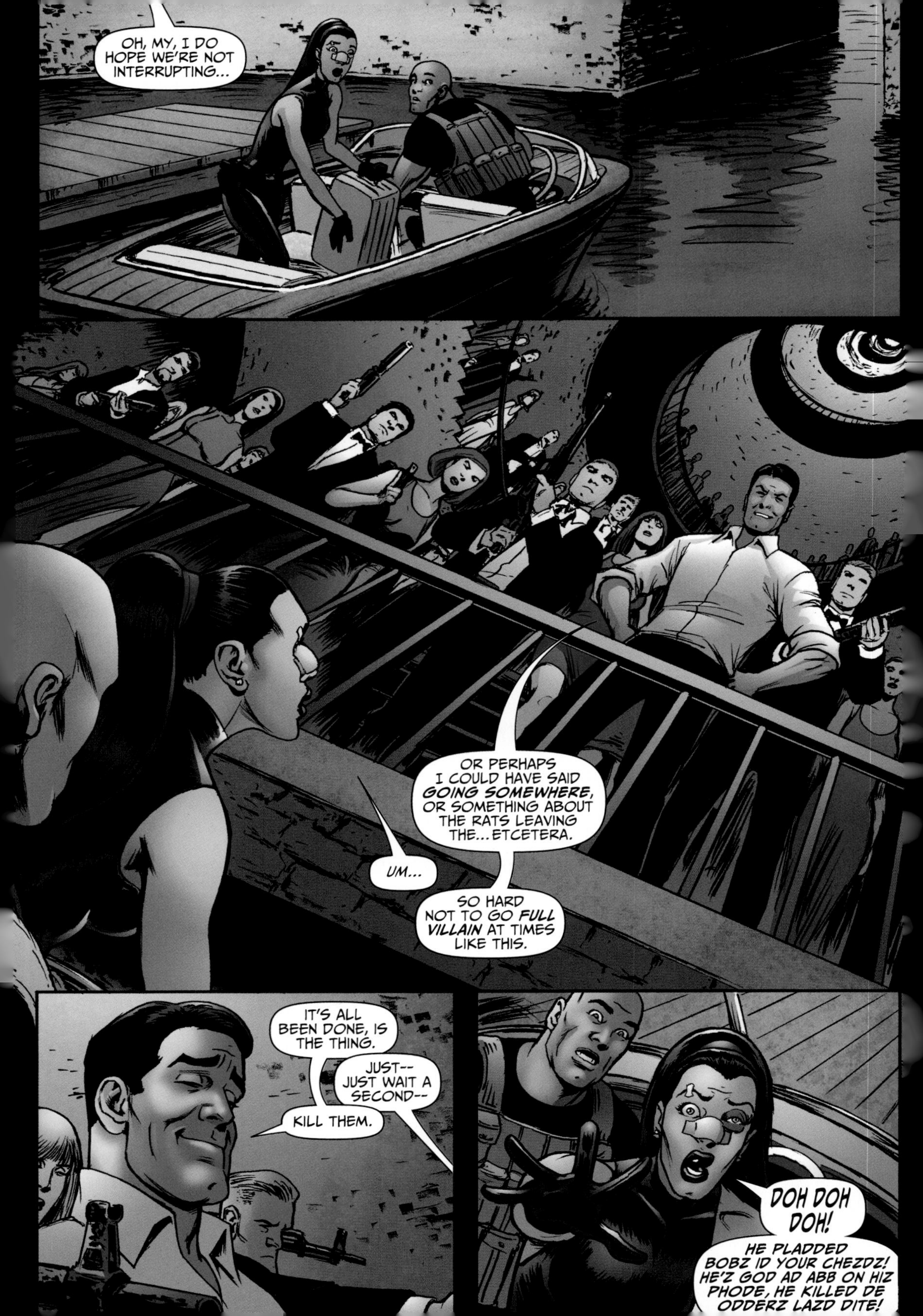
OH, MY, I DO HOPE WE'RE NOT INTERRUPTING...
OR PERHAPS I COULD HAVE SAID *GOING SOMEWHERE*, OR SOMETHING ABOUT THE RATS LEAVING THE... ETCETERA.
UM...
SO HARD NOT TO GO *FULL VILLAIN* AT TIMES LIKE THIS.
IT'S ALL BEEN DONE, IS THE THING.
JUST-- JUST WAIT A SECOND--
KILL THEM.
DOH DOH DOH!
HE PLADDED BOBZ ID YOUR CHEZDZ! HE'Z GOD AD ABB ON HIZ PHODE, HE KILLED DE ODDERZ LAZD DITE!

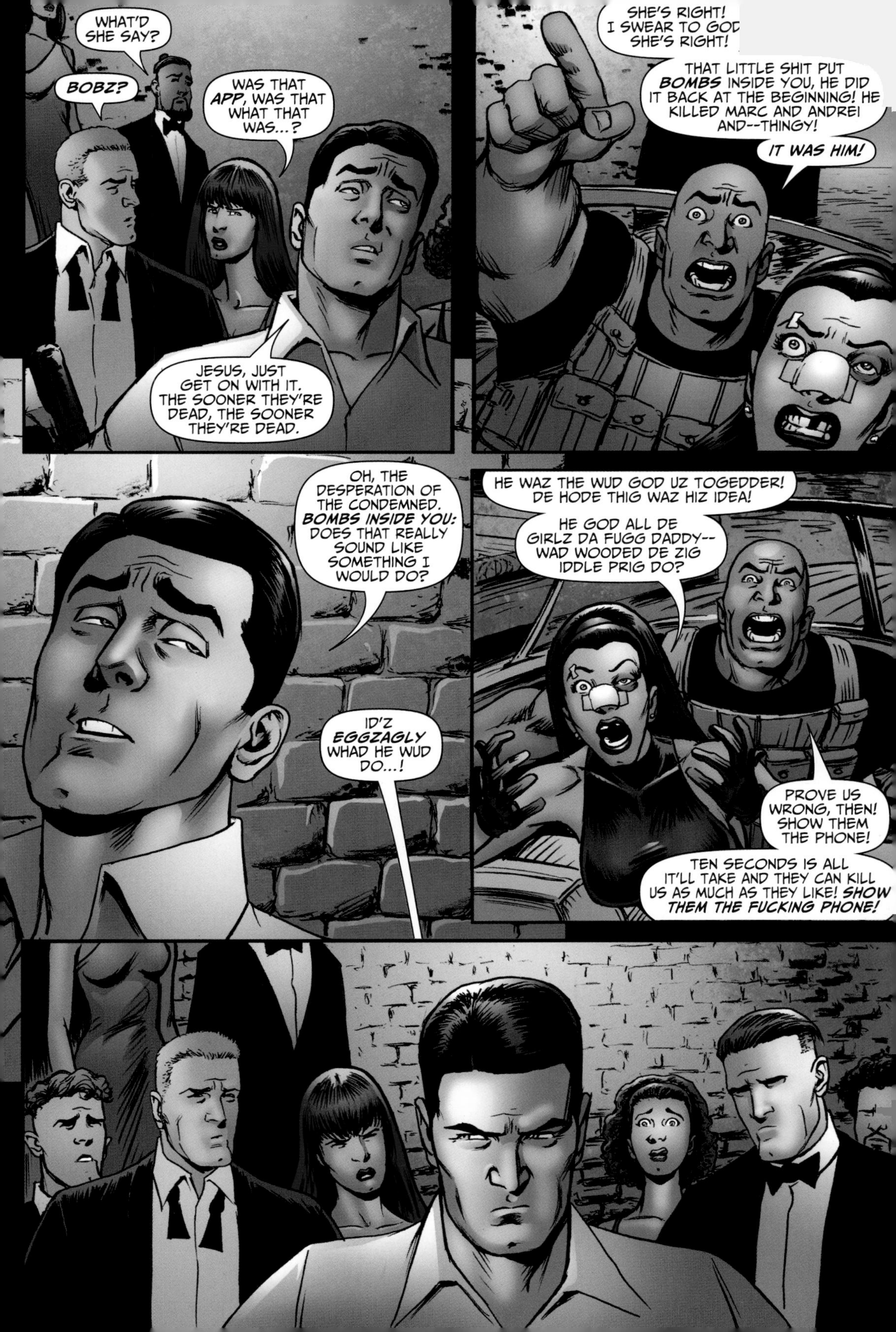
WHAT'D SHE SAY?
BOBZ?
WAS THAT APP, WAS THAT WHAT THAT WAS...?
JESUS, JUST GET ON WITH IT. THE SOONER THEY'RE DEAD, THE SOONER THEY'RE DEAD.
SHE'S RIGHT! I SWEAR TO GOD SHE'S RIGHT!
THAT LITTLE SHIT PUT BOMBS INSIDE YOU, HE DID IT BACK AT THE BEGINNING! HE KILLED MARC AND ANDREI AND--THINGY!
IT WAS HIM!
OH, THE DESPERATION OF THE CONDEMNED. BOMBS INSIDE YOU: DOES THAT REALLY SOUND LIKE SOMETHING I WOULD DO?
ID'Z EGGZAGLY WHAD HE WUD DO...!
HE WAZ THE WUD GOD UZ TOGEDDER! DE HODE THIG WAZ HIZ IDEA!
HE GOD ALL DE GIRLZ DA FUGG DADDY-- WAD WOODED DE ZIG IDDLE PRIG DO?
PROVE US WRONG, THEN! SHOW THEM THE PHONE!
TEN SECONDS IS ALL IT'LL TAKE AND THEY CAN KILL US AS MUCH AS THEY LIKE! SHOW THEM THE FUCKING PHONE!

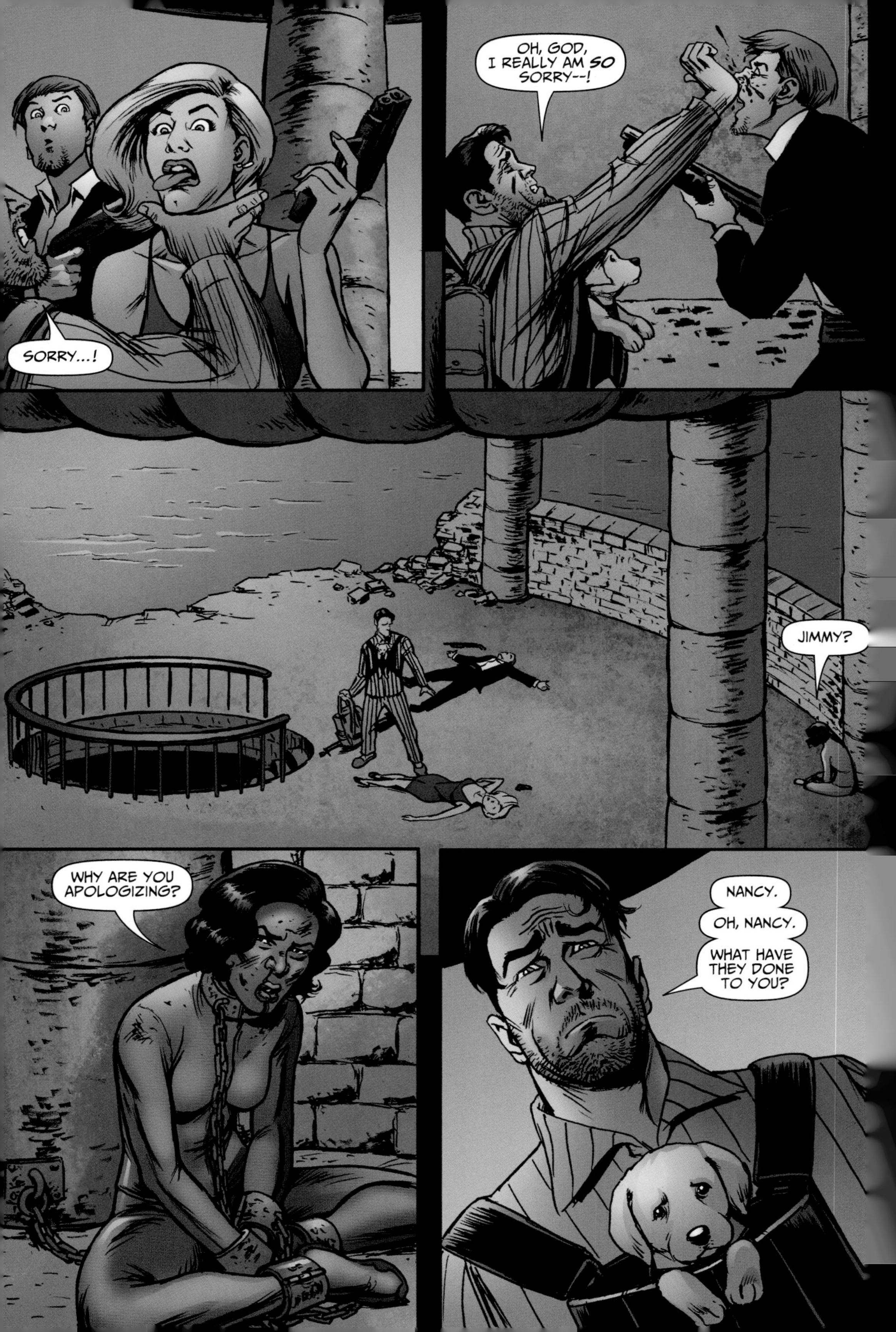
SORRY...!
OH, GOD, I REALLY AM SO SORRY--!
JIMMY?
WHY ARE YOU APOLOGIZING?
NANCY.
OH, NANCY.
WHAT HAVE THEY DONE TO YOU?

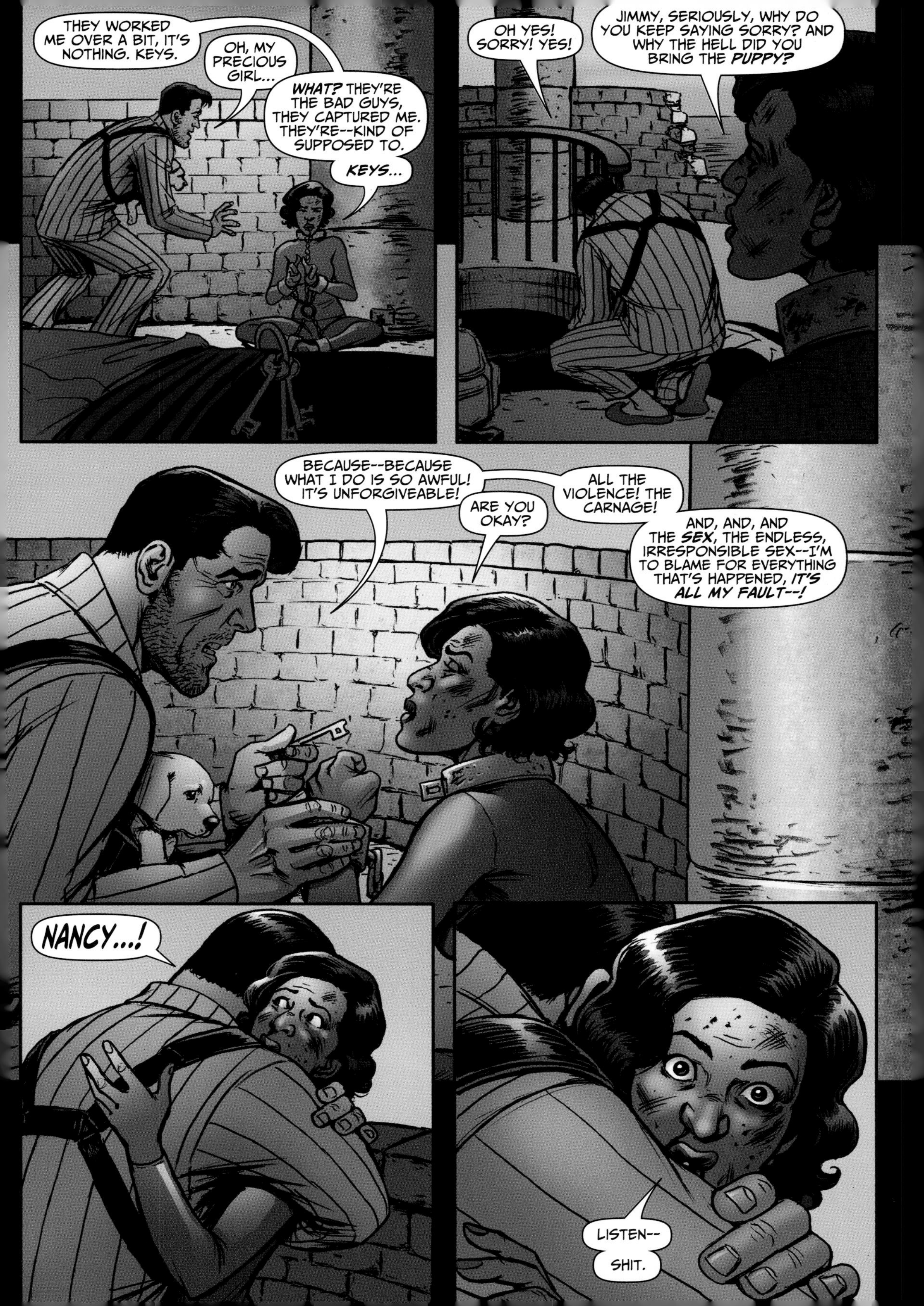
THEY WORKED ME OVER A BIT, IT'S NOTHING. KEYS.
OH, MY PRECIOUS GIRL...
WHAT? THEY'RE THE BAD GUYS, THEY CAPTURED ME. THEY'RE--KIND OF SUPPOSED TO.
KEYS...
OH YES! SORRY! YES!
JIMMY, SERIOUSLY, WHY DO YOU KEEP SAYING SORRY? AND WHY THE HELL DID YOU BRING THE PUPPY?
BECAUSE--BECAUSE WHAT I DO IS SO AWFUL! IT'S UNFORGIVEABLE!
ARE YOU OKAY?
ALL THE VIOLENCE! THE CARNAGE!
AND, AND, AND THE SEX, THE ENDLESS, IRRESPONSIBLE SEX--I'M TO BLAME FOR EVERYTHING THAT'S HAPPENED, IT'S ALL MY FAULT--!
NANCY...!
LISTEN--
SHIT.

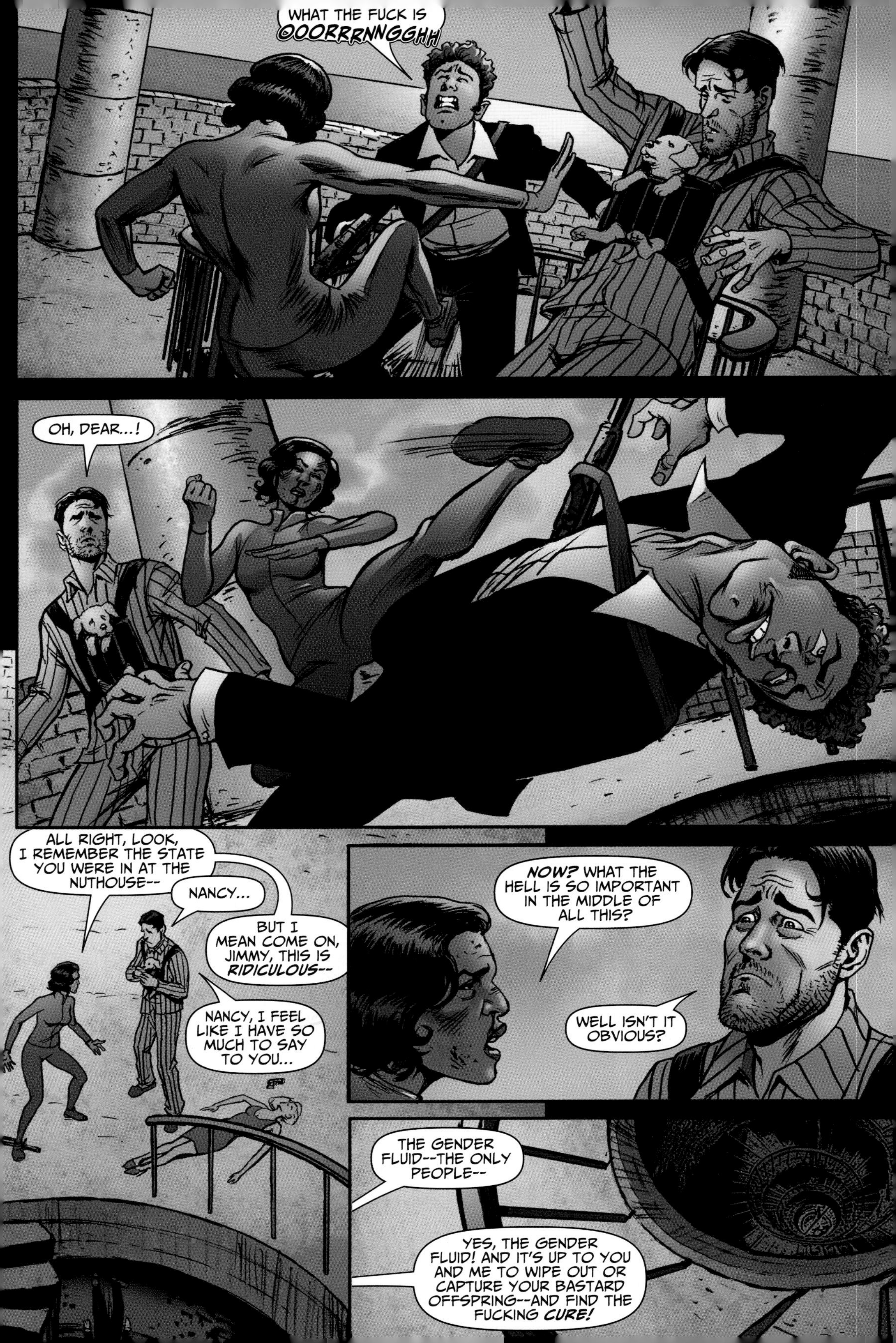
WHAT THE FUCK IS OOORRRNNGGHH
OH, DEAR...!
ALL RIGHT, LOOK, I REMEMBER THE STATE YOU WERE IN AT THE NUTHOUSE--
NANCY...
BUT I MEAN COME ON, JIMMY, THIS IS RIDICULOUS--
NANCY, I FEEL LIKE I HAVE SO MUCH TO SAY TO YOU...
NOW? WHAT THE HELL IS SO IMPORTANT IN THE MIDDLE OF ALL THIS?
WELL ISN'T IT OBVIOUS?
THE GENDER FLUID--THE ONLY PEOPLE--
YES, THE GENDER FLUID! AND IT'S UP TO YOU AND ME TO WIPE OUT OR CAPTURE YOUR BASTARD OFFSPRING--AND FIND THE FUCKING CURE!

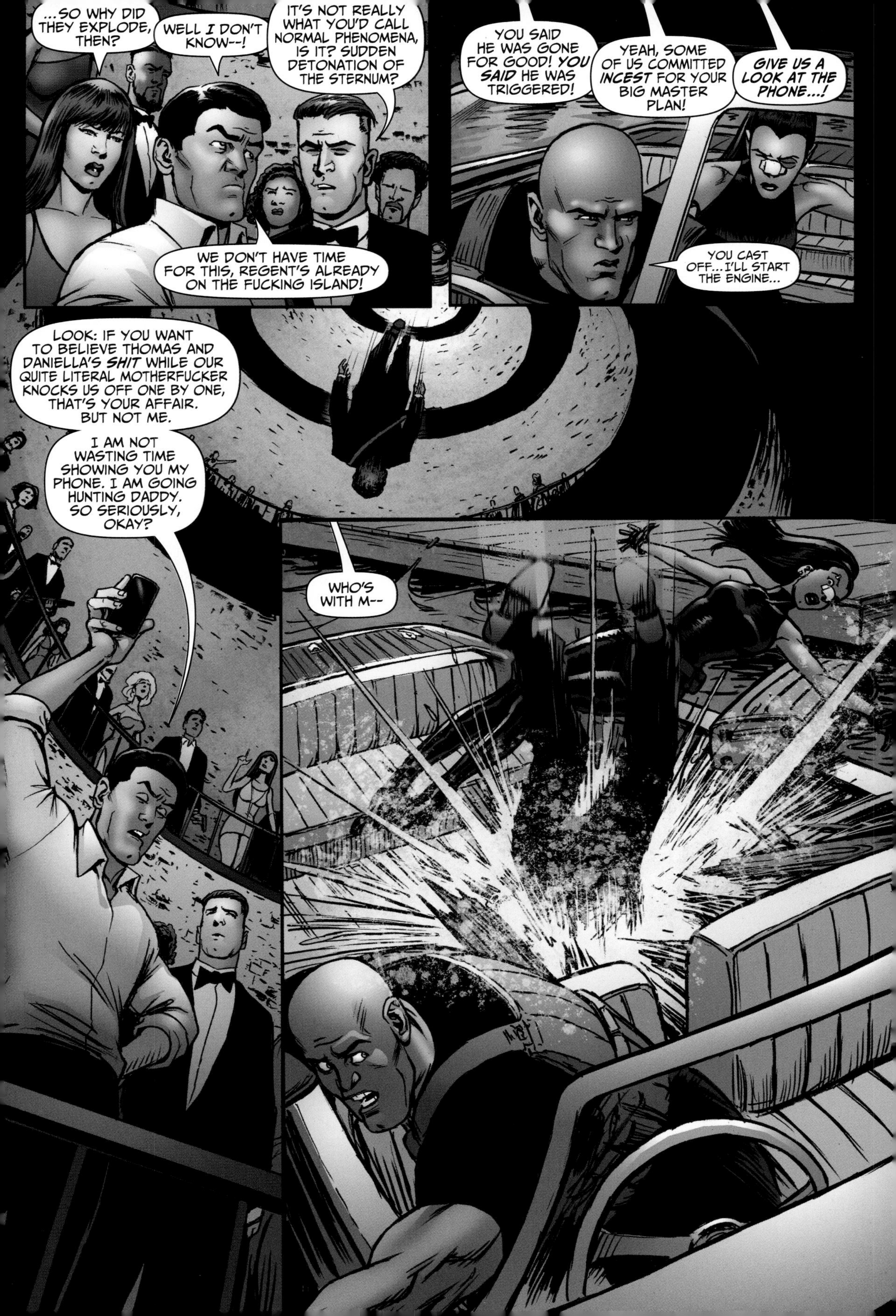
...SO WHY DID THEY EXPLODE, THEN?
WELL I DON'T KNOW--!
IT'S NOT REALLY WHAT YOU'D CALL NORMAL PHENOMENA, IS IT? SUDDEN DETONATION OF THE STERNUM?
WE DON'T HAVE TIME FOR THIS, REGENT'S ALREADY ON THE FUCKING ISLAND!
YOU SAID HE WAS GONE FOR GOOD! YOU SAID HE WAS TRIGGERED!
YEAH, SOME OF US COMMITTED INCEST FOR YOUR BIG MASTER PLAN!
GIVE US A LOOK AT THE PHONE...!
YOU CAST OFF...I'LL START THE ENGINE...
LOOK: IF YOU WANT TO BELIEVE THOMAS AND DANIELLA'S SHIT WHILE OUR QUITE LITERAL MOTHERFUCKER KNOCKS US OFF ONE BY ONE, THAT'S YOUR AFFAIR. BUT NOT ME.
I AM NOT WASTING TIME SHOWING YOU MY PHONE. I AM GOING HUNTING DADDY. SO SERIOUSLY, OKAY?
WHO'S WITH M--

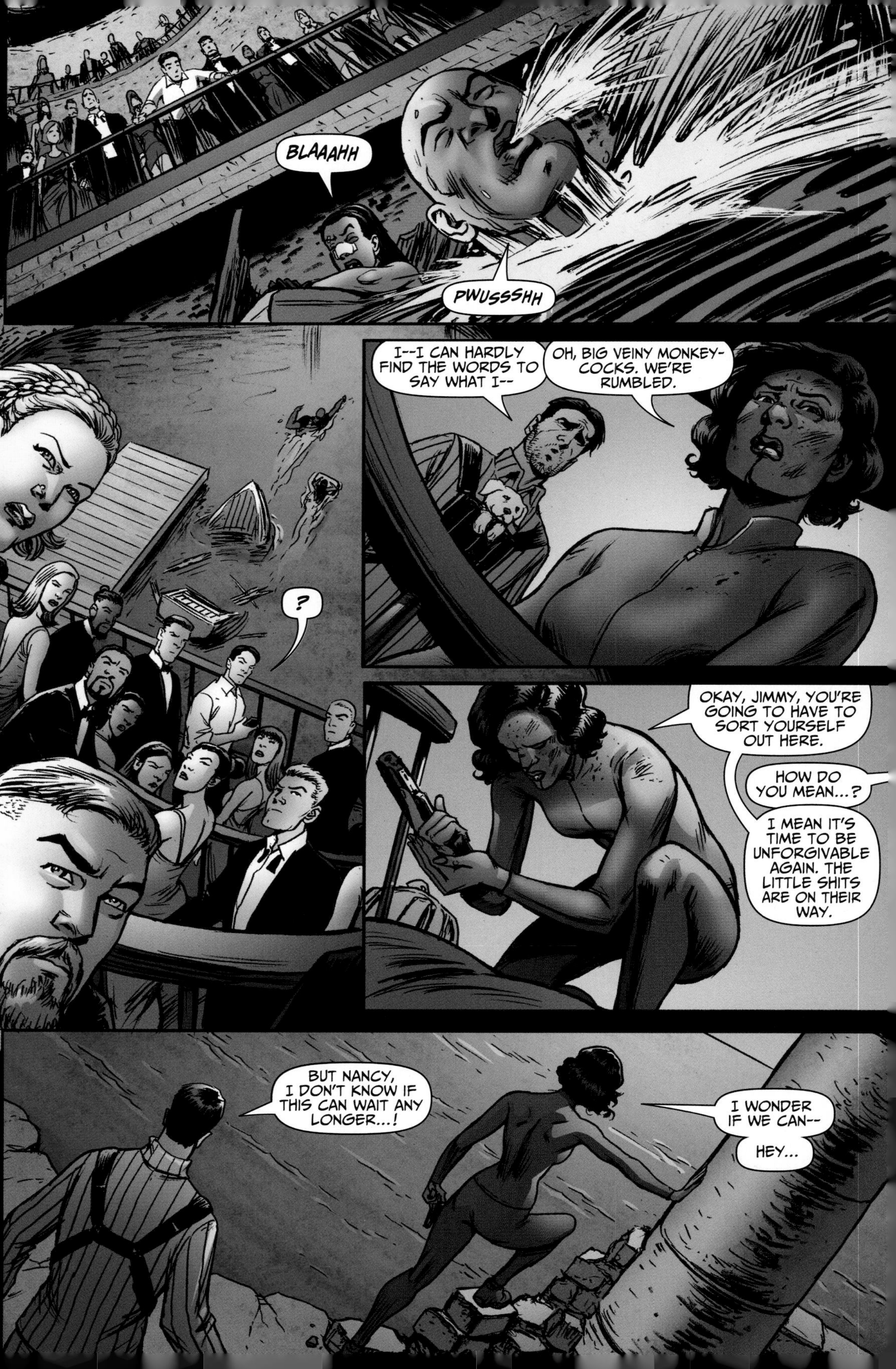
BLAAAHH
PWUSSSHH
?
I--I CAN HARDLY FIND THE WORDS TO SAY WHAT I--
OH, BIG VEINY MONKEY-COCKS. WE'RE RUMBLED.
OKAY, JIMMY, YOU'RE GOING TO HAVE TO SORT YOURSELF OUT HERE.
HOW DO YOU MEAN...?
I MEAN IT'S TIME TO BE UNFORGIVABLE AGAIN. THE LITTLE SHITS ARE ON THEIR WAY.
BUT NANCY, I DON'T KNOW IF THIS CAN WAIT ANY LONGER...!
I WONDER IF WE CAN--
HEY...

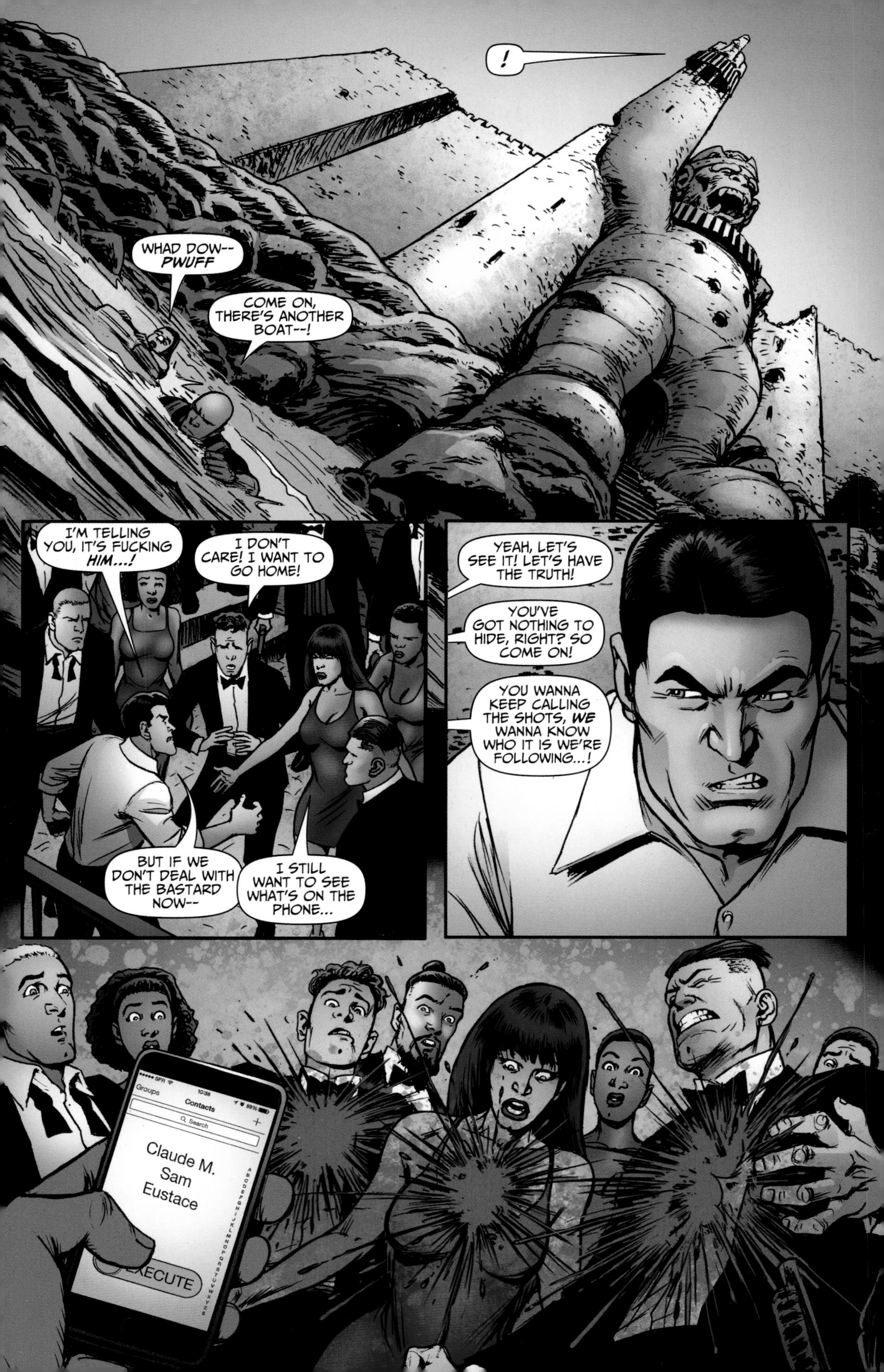
!
WHAD DOW-- PWUFF
COME ON, THERE'S ANOTHER BOAT--!
I'M TELLING YOU, IT'S FUCKING HIM...!
I DON'T CARE! I WANT TO GO HOME!
BUT IF WE DON'T DEAL WITH THE BASTARD NOW--
I STILL WANT TO SEE WHAT'S ON THE PHONE...
YEAH, LET'S SEE IT! LET'S HAVE THE TRUTH!
YOU'VE GOT NOTHING TO HIDE, RIGHT? SO COME ON!
YOU WANNA KEEP CALLING THE SHOTS, WE WANNA KNOW WHO IT IS WE'RE FOLLOWING...!
Groups
Contacts
Search
Claude M.
Sam
Eustace
EXECUTE

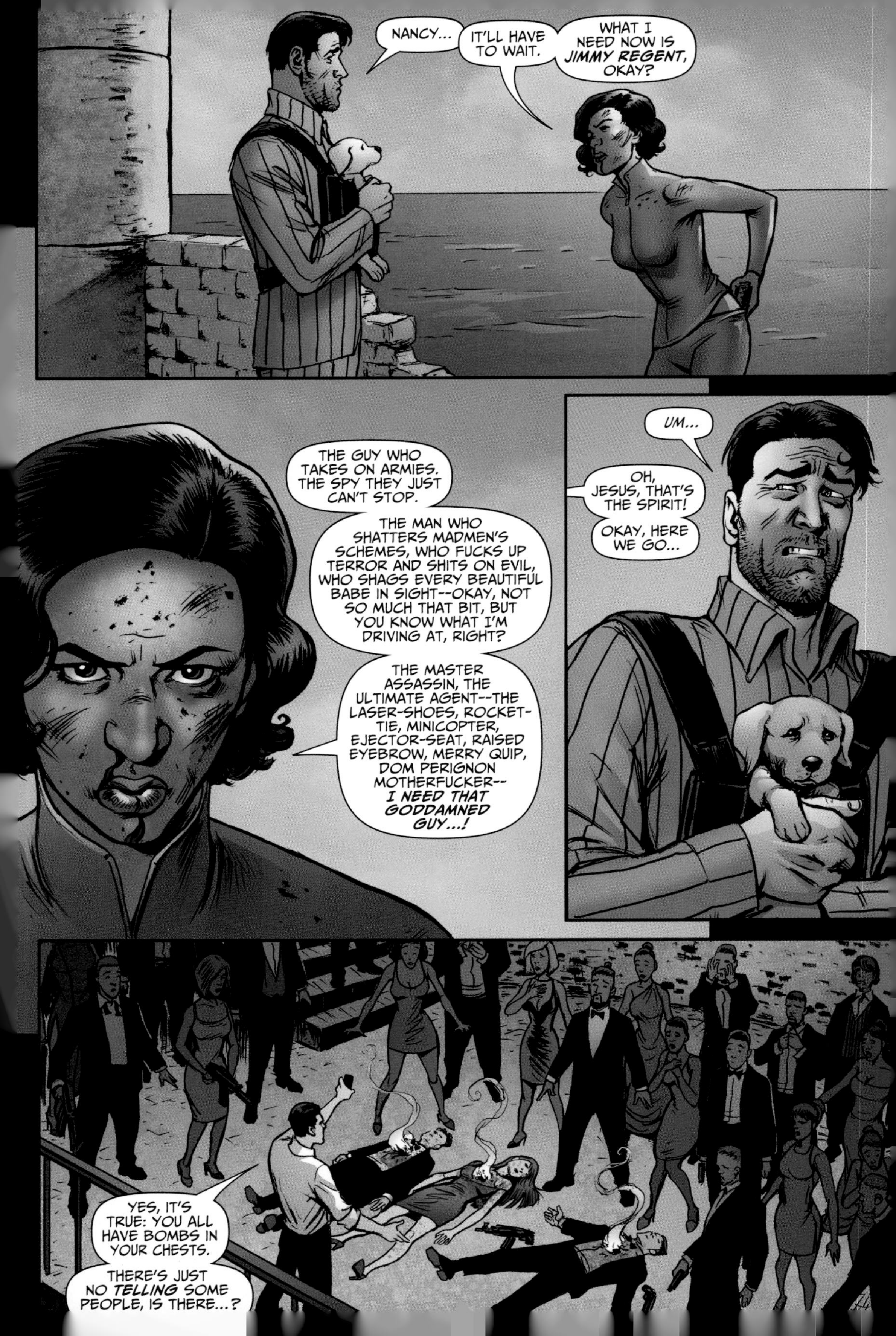
NANCY...
IT'LL HAVE TO WAIT.
WHAT I NEED NOW IS JIMMY REGENT, OKAY?
THE GUY WHO TAKES ON ARMIES. THE SPY THEY JUST CAN'T STOP.
THE MAN WHO SHATTERS MADMEN'S SCHEMES, WHO FUCKS UP TERROR AND SHITS ON EVIL, WHO SHAGS EVERY BEAUTIFUL BABE IN SIGHT--OKAY, NOT SO MUCH THAT BIT, BUT YOU KNOW WHAT I'M DRIVING AT, RIGHT?
THE MASTER ASSASSIN, THE ULTIMATE AGENT--THE LASER-SHOES, ROCKET-TIE, MINICOPTER, EJECTOR-SEAT, RAISED EYEBROW, MERRY QUIP, DOM PERIGNON MOTHERFUCKER-- I NEED THAT GODDAMNED GUY...!
UM...
OH, JESUS, THAT'S THE SPIRIT!
OKAY, HERE WE GO...
YES, IT'S TRUE: YOU ALL HAVE BOMBS IN YOUR CHESTS.
THERE'S JUST NO TELLING SOME PEOPLE, IS THERE...?

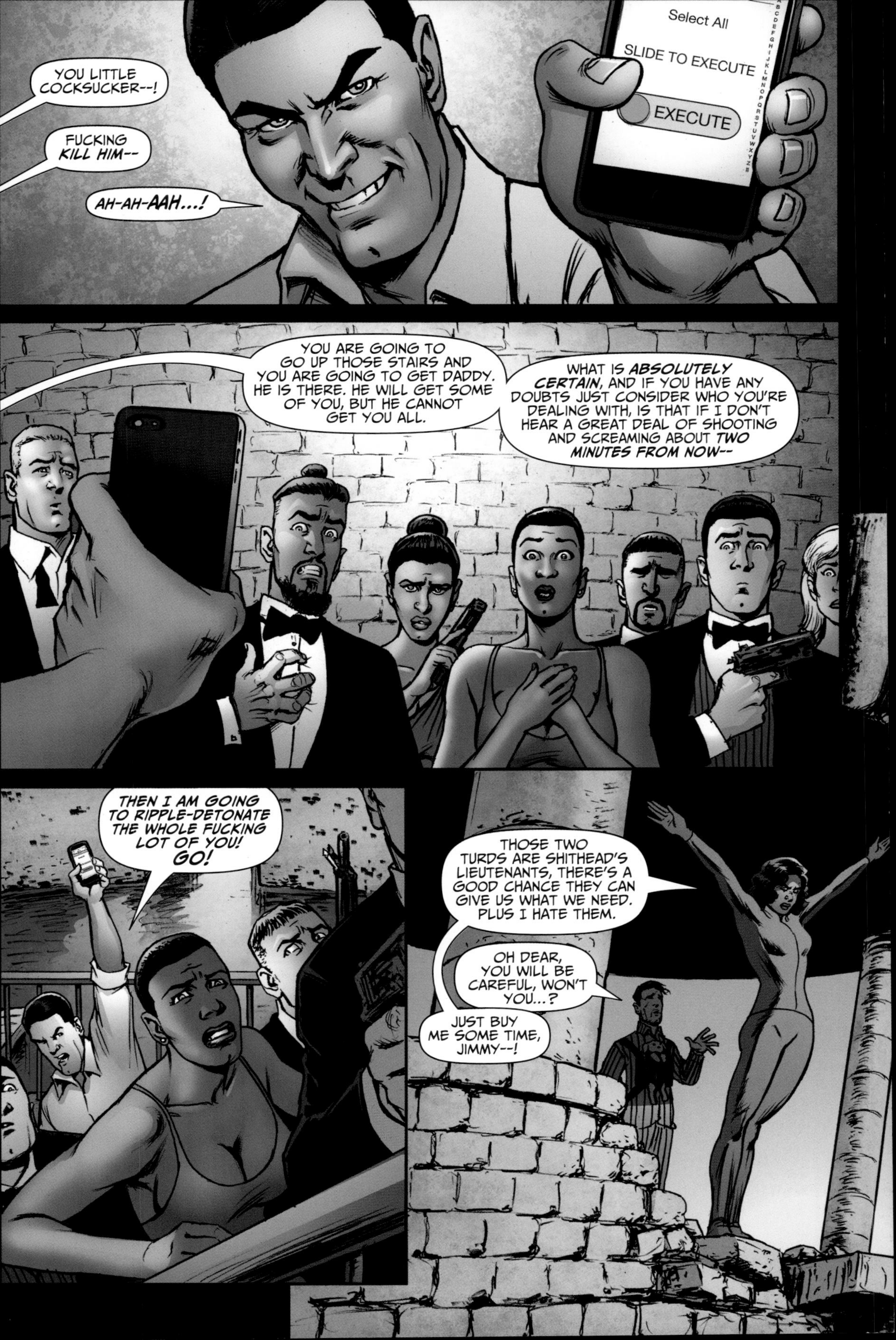
Select All
SLIDE TO EXECUTE
EXECUTE
YOU LITTLE COCKSUCKER--!
FUCKING KILL HIM--
AH-AH-AAH...!
YOU ARE GOING TO GO UP THOSE STAIRS AND YOU ARE GOING TO GET DADDY. HE IS THERE. HE WILL GET SOME OF YOU, BUT HE CANNOT GET YOU ALL.
WHAT IS ABSOLUTELY CERTAIN, AND IF YOU HAVE ANY DOUBTS JUST CONSIDER WHO YOU'RE DEALING WITH, IS THAT IF I DON'T HEAR A GREAT DEAL OF SHOOTING AND SCREAMING ABOUT TWO MINUTES FROM NOW--
THEN I AM GOING TO RIPPLE-DETONATE THE WHOLE FUCKING LOT OF YOU! GO!
THOSE TWO TURDS ARE SHITHEAD'S LIEUTENANTS, THERE'S A GOOD CHANCE THEY CAN GIVE US WHAT WE NEED. PLUS I HATE THEM.
OH DEAR, YOU WILL BE CAREFUL, WON'T YOU...?
JUST BUY ME SOME TIME, JIMMY--!

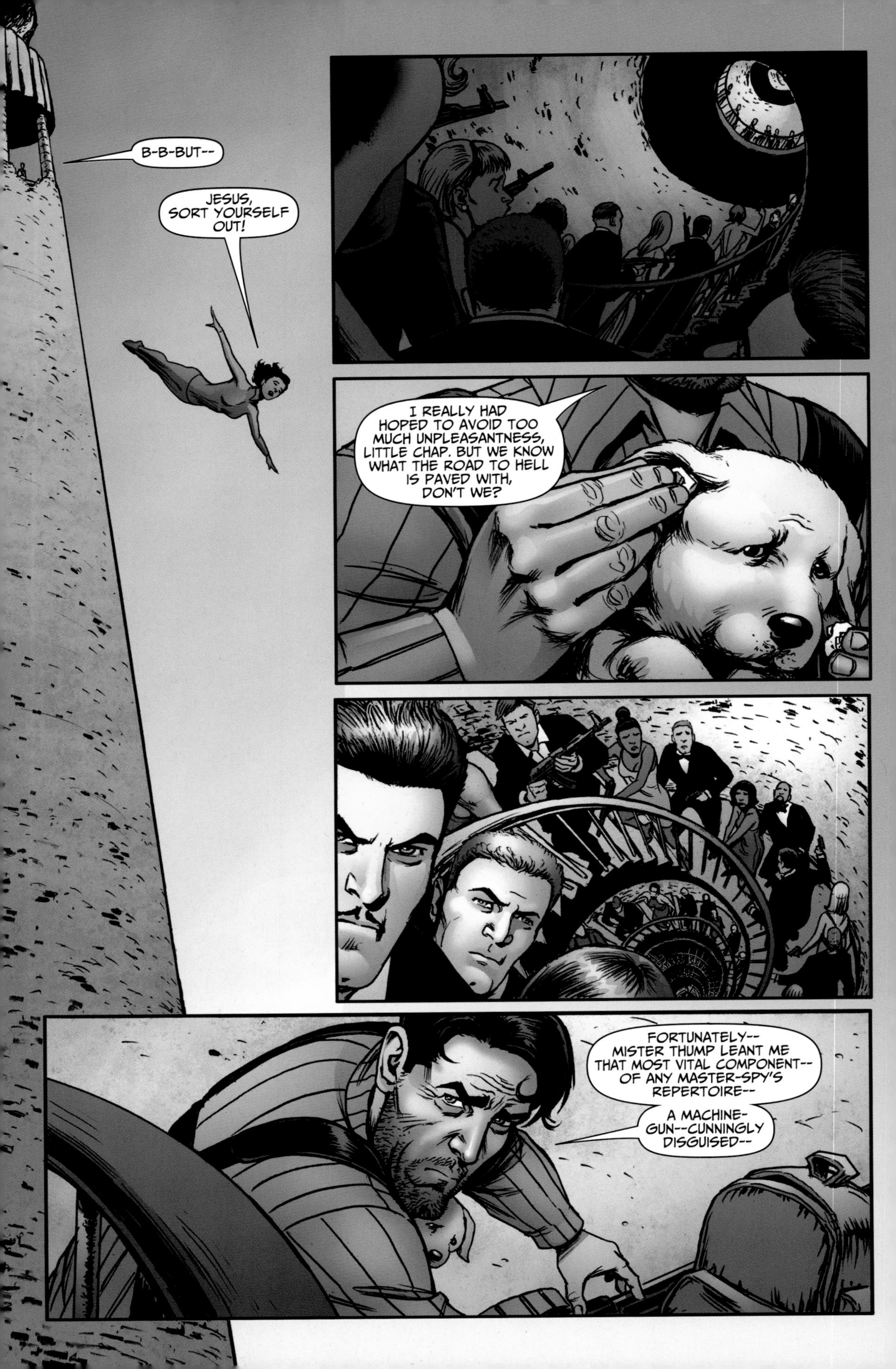
B-B-BUT--
JESUS, SORT YOURSELF OUT!
I REALLY HAD HOPED TO AVOID TOO MUCH UNPLEASANTNESS, LITTLE CHAP. BUT WE KNOW WHAT THE ROAD TO HELL IS PAVED WITH, DON'T WE?
FORTUNATELY-- MISTER THUMP LEANT ME THAT MOST VITAL COMPONENT-- OF ANY MASTER-SPY'S REPERTOIRE--
A MACHINE-GUN--CUNNINGLY DISGUISED--

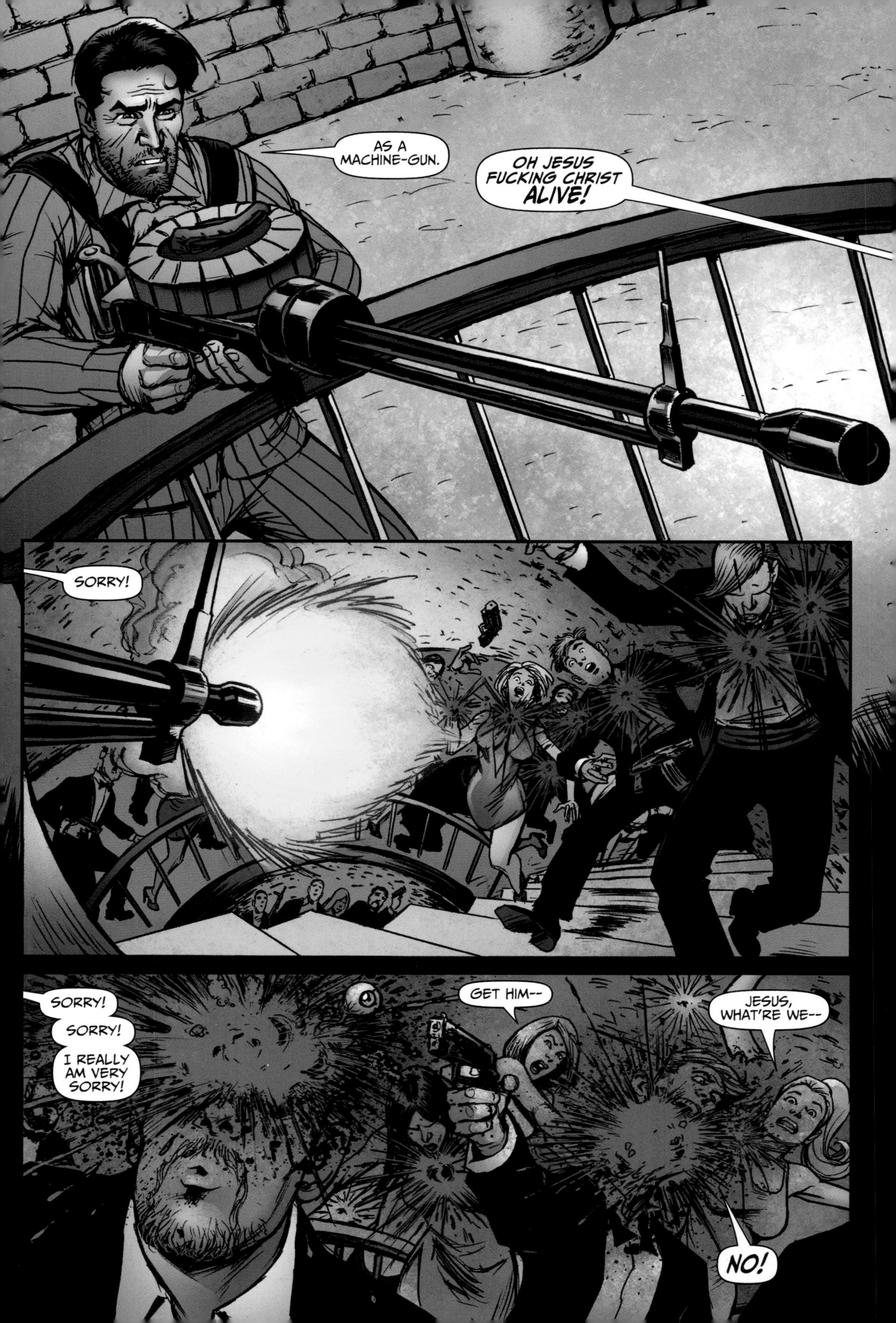
AS A MACHINE-GUN.
OH JESUS FUCKING CHRIST ALIVE!
SORRY!
SORRY!
SORRY!
I REALLY AM VERY SORRY!
GET HIM--
JESUS, WHAT'RE WE--
NO!

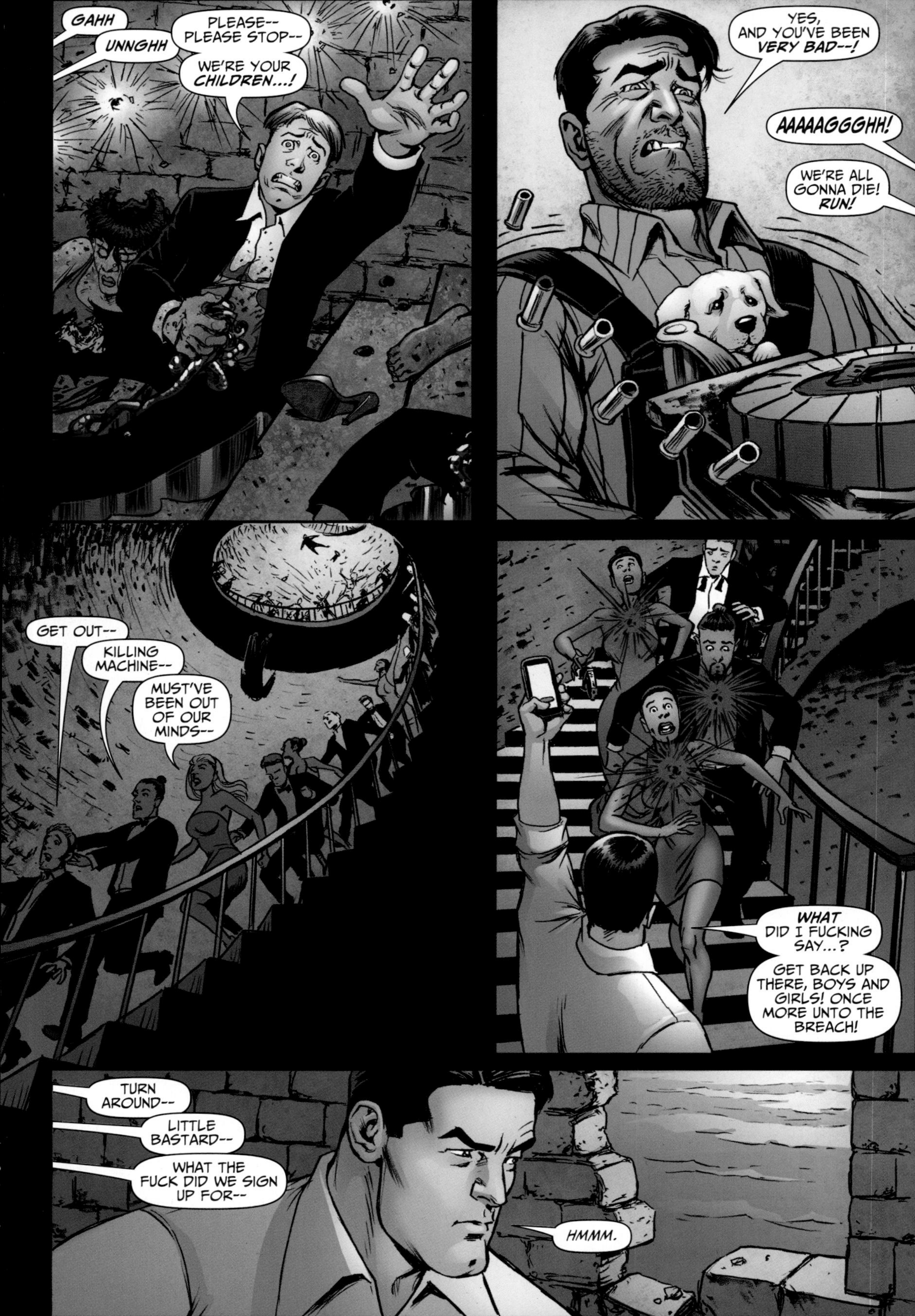
GAHH
UNNGHH
PLEASE-- PLEASE STOP--
WE'RE YOUR CHILDREN...!
YES, AND YOU'VE BEEN VERY BAD--!
AAAAAGGGHH!
WE'RE ALL GONNA DIE! RUN!
GET OUT--
KILLING MACHINE--
MUST'VE BEEN OUT OF OUR MINDS--
WHAT DID I FUCKING SAY...?
GET BACK UP THERE, BOYS AND GIRLS! ONCE MORE UNTO THE BREACH!
TURN AROUND--
LITTLE BASTARD--
WHAT THE FUCK DID WE SIGN UP FOR--
HMMM.

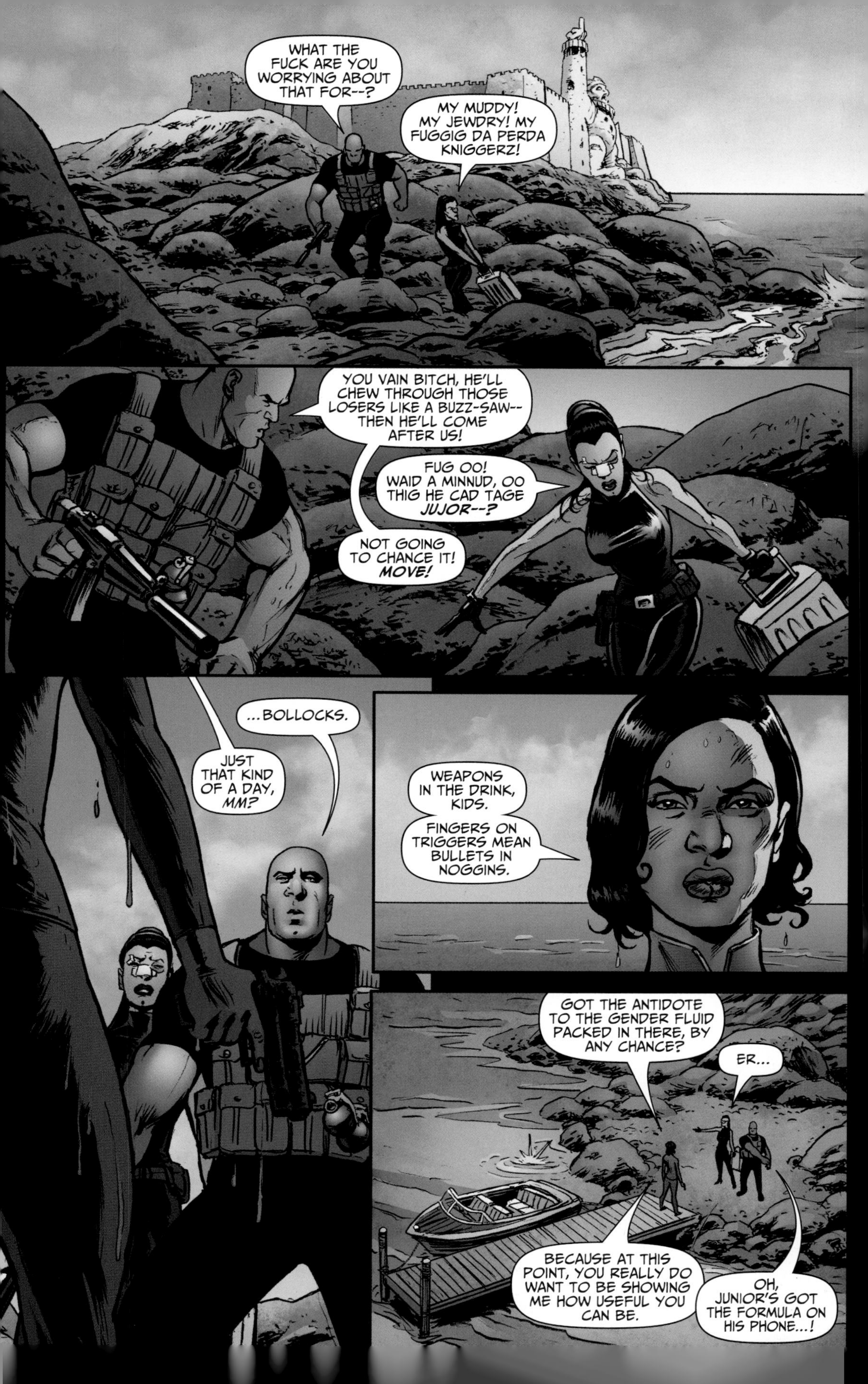
WHAT THE FUCK ARE YOU WORRYING ABOUT THAT FOR--?
MY MUDDY! MY JEWDRY! MY FUGGIG DA PERDA KNIGGERZ!
YOU VAIN BITCH, HE'LL CHEW THROUGH THOSE LOSERS LIKE A BUZZ-SAW-- THEN HE'LL COME AFTER US!
FUG OO! WAID A MINNUD, OO THIG HE CAD TAGE JUJOR--?
NOT GOING TO CHANCE IT! MOVE!
JUST THAT KIND OF A DAY, MM?
...BOLLOCKS.
WEAPONS IN THE DRINK, KIDS.
FINGERS ON TRIGGERS MEAN BULLETS IN NOGGINS.
GOT THE ANTIDOTE TO THE GENDER FLUID PACKED IN THERE, BY ANY CHANCE?
ER...
BECAUSE AT THIS POINT, YOU REALLY DO WANT TO BE SHOWING ME HOW USEFUL YOU CAN BE.
OH, JUNIOR'S GOT THE FORMULA ON HIS PHONE...!

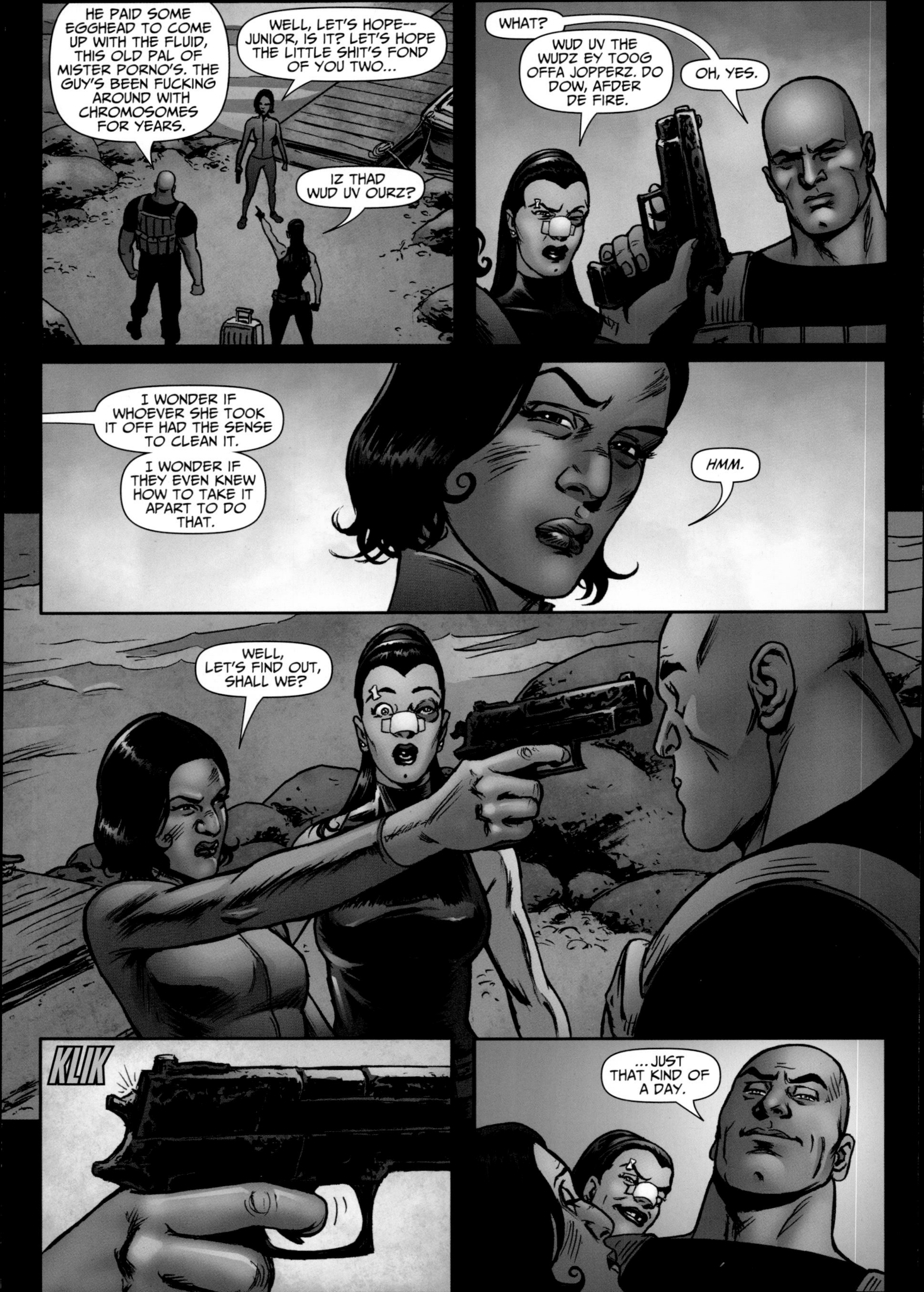
HE PAID SOME EGGHEAD TO COME UP WITH THE FLUID, THIS OLD PAL OF MISTER PORNO'S. THE GUY'S BEEN FUCKING AROUND WITH CHROMOSOMES FOR YEARS.
WELL, LET'S HOPE-- JUNIOR, IS IT? LET'S HOPE THE LITTLE SHIT'S FOND OF YOU TWO...
IZ THAD WUD UV OURZ?
WHAT?
WUD UV THE WUDZ EY TOOG OFFA JOPPERZ. DO DOW, AFDER DE FIRE.
OH, YES.
I WONDER IF WHOEVER SHE TOOK IT OFF HAD THE SENSE TO CLEAN IT.
I WONDER IF THEY EVEN KNEW HOW TO TAKE IT APART TO DO THAT.
HMM.
WELL, LET'S FIND OUT, SHALL WE?
KLIK
... JUST THAT KIND OF A DAY.

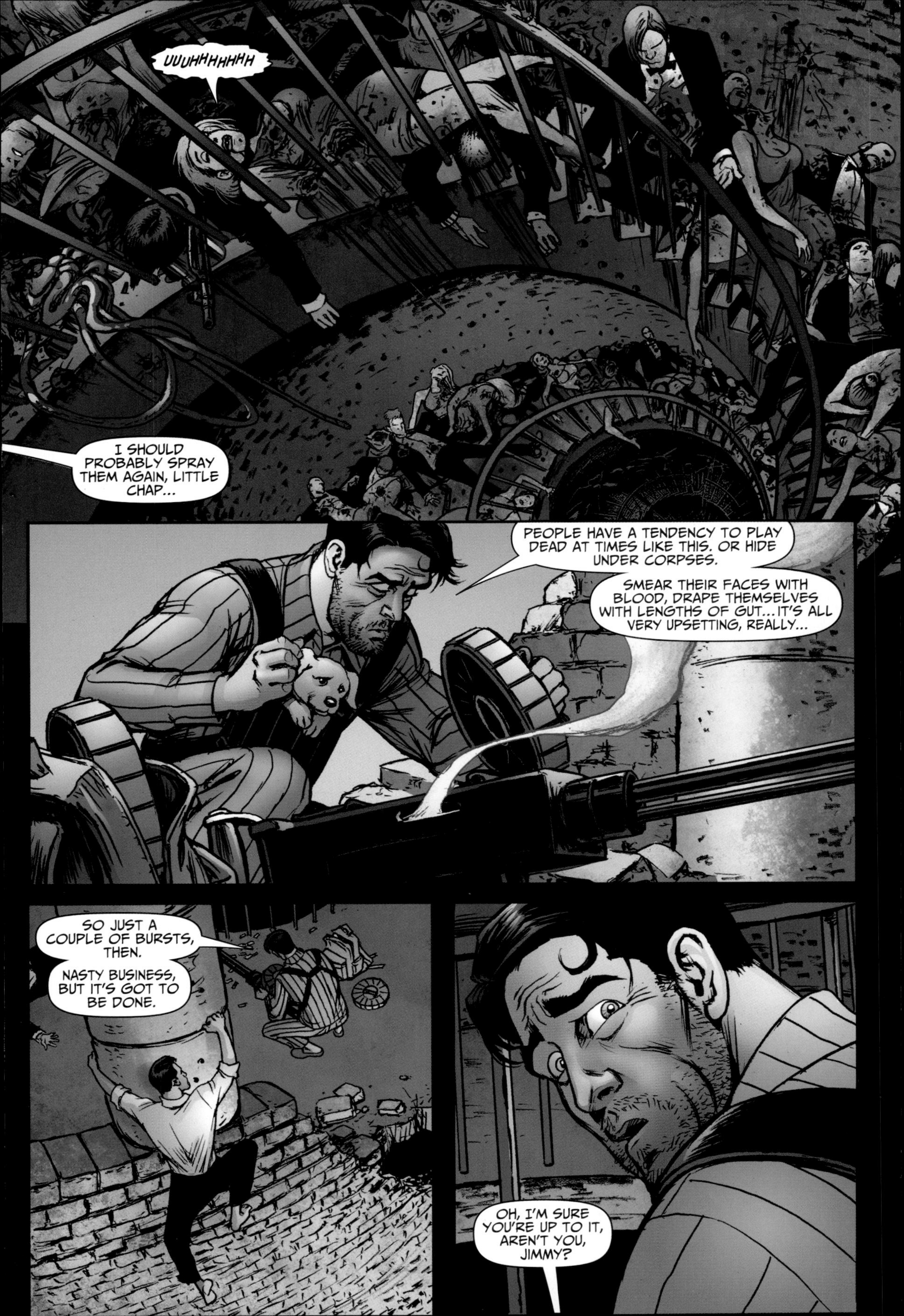
UUUHHHHHHH
I SHOULD PROBABLY SPRAY THEM AGAIN, LITTLE CHAP...
PEOPLE HAVE A TENDENCY TO PLAY DEAD AT TIMES LIKE THIS. OR HIDE UNDER CORPSES.
SMEAR THEIR FACES WITH BLOOD, DRAPE THEMSELVES WITH LENGTHS OF GUT... IT'S ALL VERY UPSETTING, REALLY...
SO JUST A COUPLE OF BURSTS, THEN.
NASTY BUSINESS, BUT IT'S GOT TO BE DONE.
OH, I'M SURE YOU'RE UP TO IT, AREN'T YOU, JIMMY?

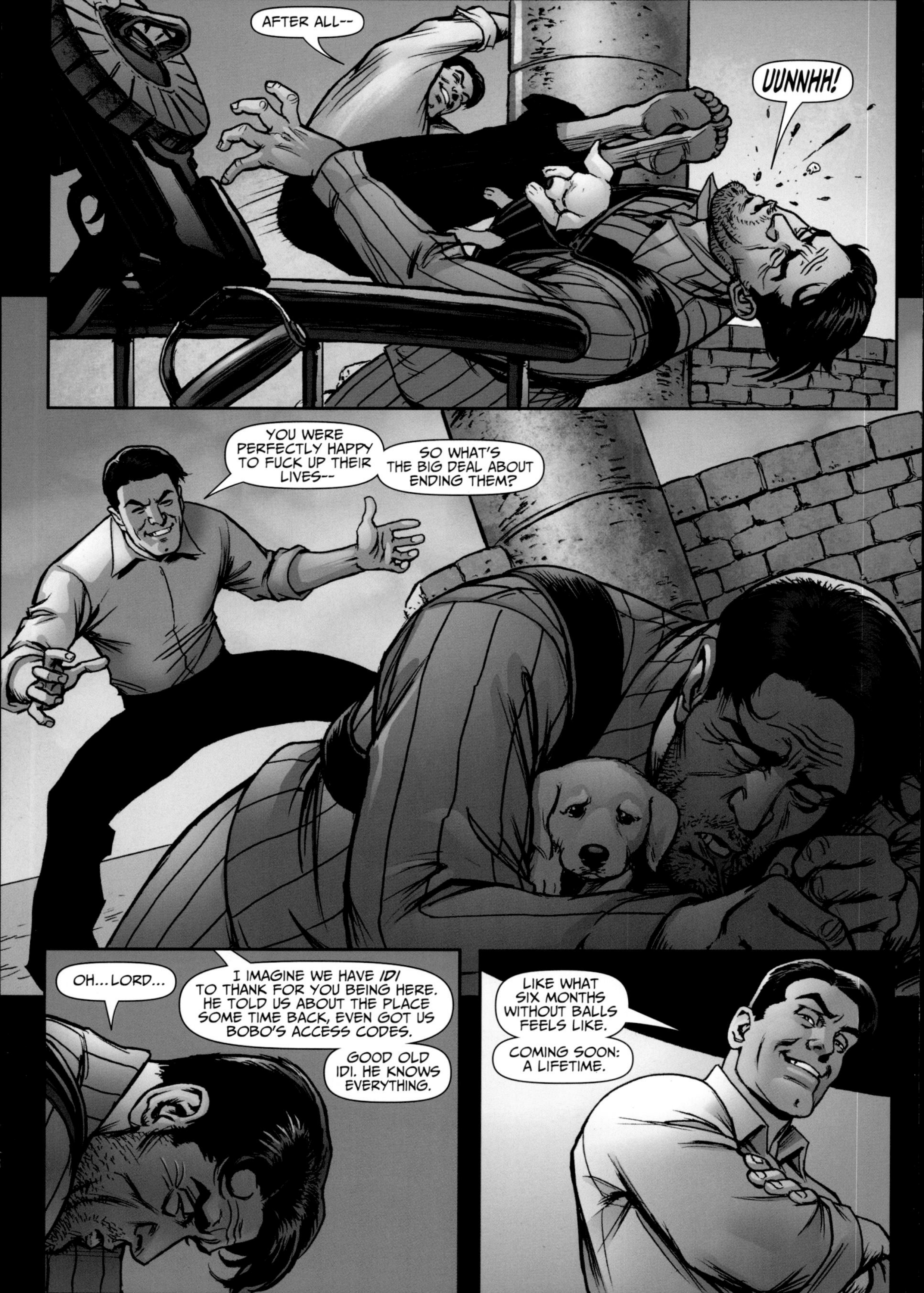
AFTER ALL--
UUNNHH!
YOU WERE PERFECTLY HAPPY TO FUCK UP THEIR LIVES--
SO WHAT'S THE BIG DEAL ABOUT ENDING THEM?
OH... LORD...
I IMAGINE WE HAVE *IDI* TO THANK FOR YOU BEING HERE. HE TOLD US ABOUT THE PLACE SOME TIME BACK, EVEN GOT US BOBO'S ACCESS CODES.
GOOD OLD IDI. HE KNOWS EVERYTHING.
LIKE WHAT SIX MONTHS WITHOUT BALLS FEELS LIKE.
COMING SOON: A LIFETIME.

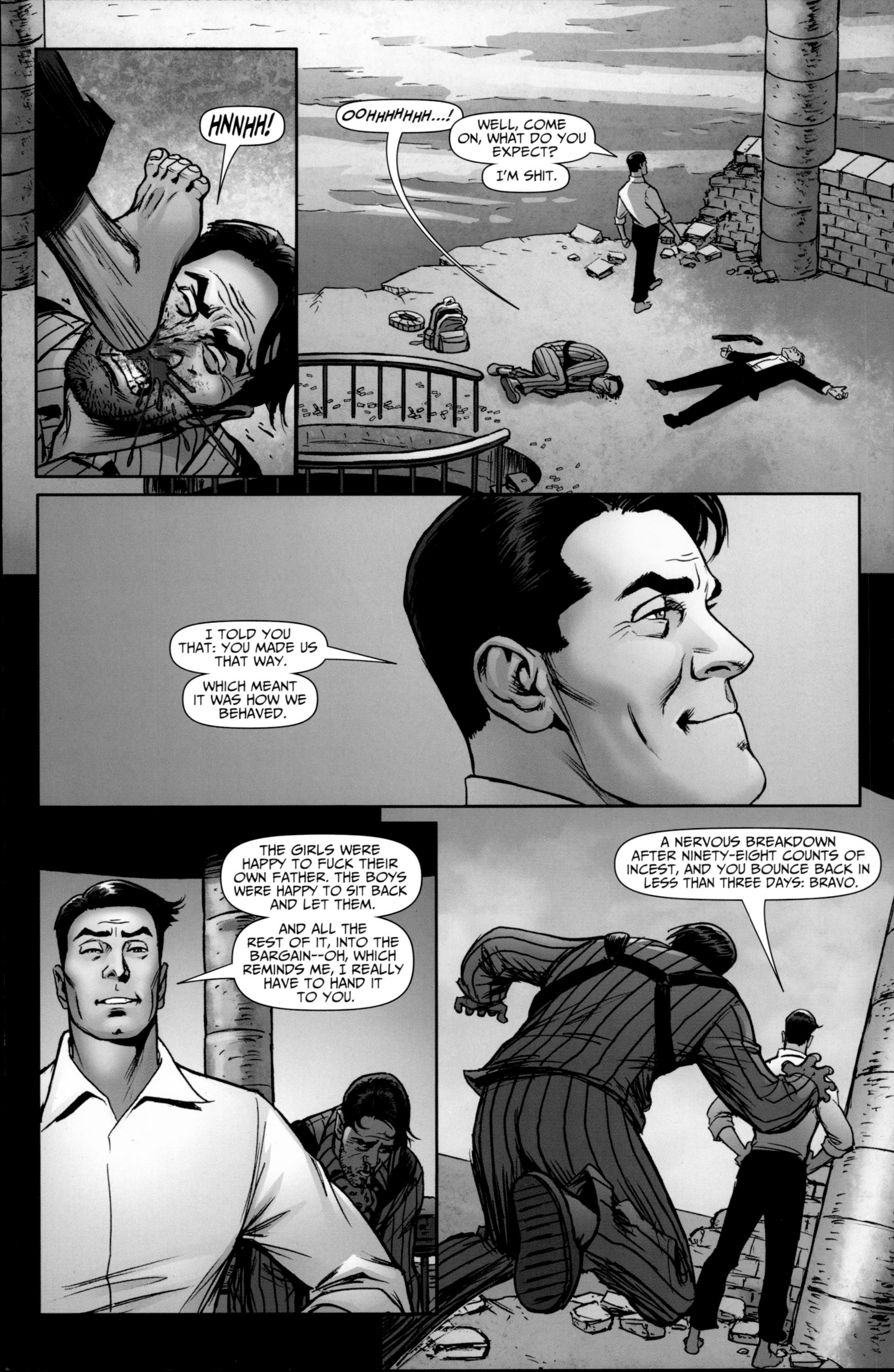
HNNHH!
OOHHHHHHH...!
WELL, COME ON, WHAT DO YOU EXPECT?
I'M SHIT.
I TOLD YOU THAT: YOU MADE US THAT WAY.
WHICH MEANT IT WAS HOW WE BEHAVED.
THE GIRLS WERE HAPPY TO FUCK THEIR OWN FATHER. THE BOYS WERE HAPPY TO SIT BACK AND LET THEM.
AND ALL THE REST OF IT, INTO THE BARGAIN--OH, WHICH REMINDS ME, I REALLY HAVE TO HAND IT TO YOU.
A NERVOUS BREAKDOWN AFTER NINETY-EIGHT COUNTS OF INCEST, AND YOU BOUNCE BACK IN LESS THAN THREE DAYS: BRAVO.

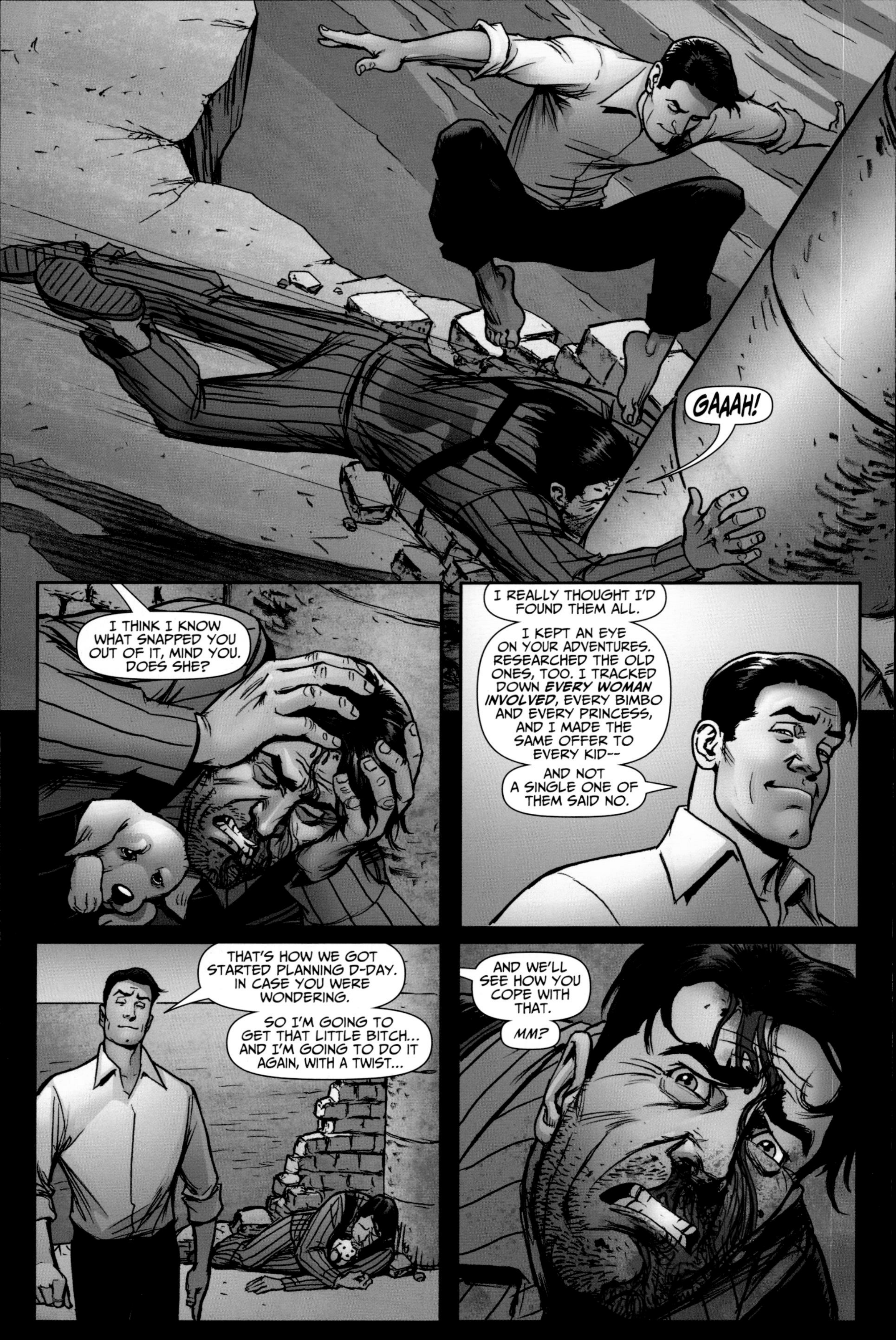
GAAAH!
I THINK I KNOW WHAT SNAPPED YOU OUT OF IT, MIND YOU. DOES SHE?
I REALLY THOUGHT I'D FOUND THEM ALL.
I KEPT AN EYE ON YOUR ADVENTURES. RESEARCHED THE OLD ONES, TOO. I TRACKED DOWN EVERY WOMAN INVOLVED, EVERY BIMBO AND EVERY PRINCESS, AND I MADE THE SAME OFFER TO EVERY KID--
AND NOT A SINGLE ONE OF THEM SAID NO.
THAT'S HOW WE GOT STARTED PLANNING D-DAY. IN CASE YOU WERE WONDERING.
SO I'M GOING TO GET THAT LITTLE BITCH... AND I'M GOING TO DO IT AGAIN, WITH A TWIST...
AND WE'LL SEE HOW YOU COPE WITH THAT.
MM?

9

YOU'VE GOT HER EYES

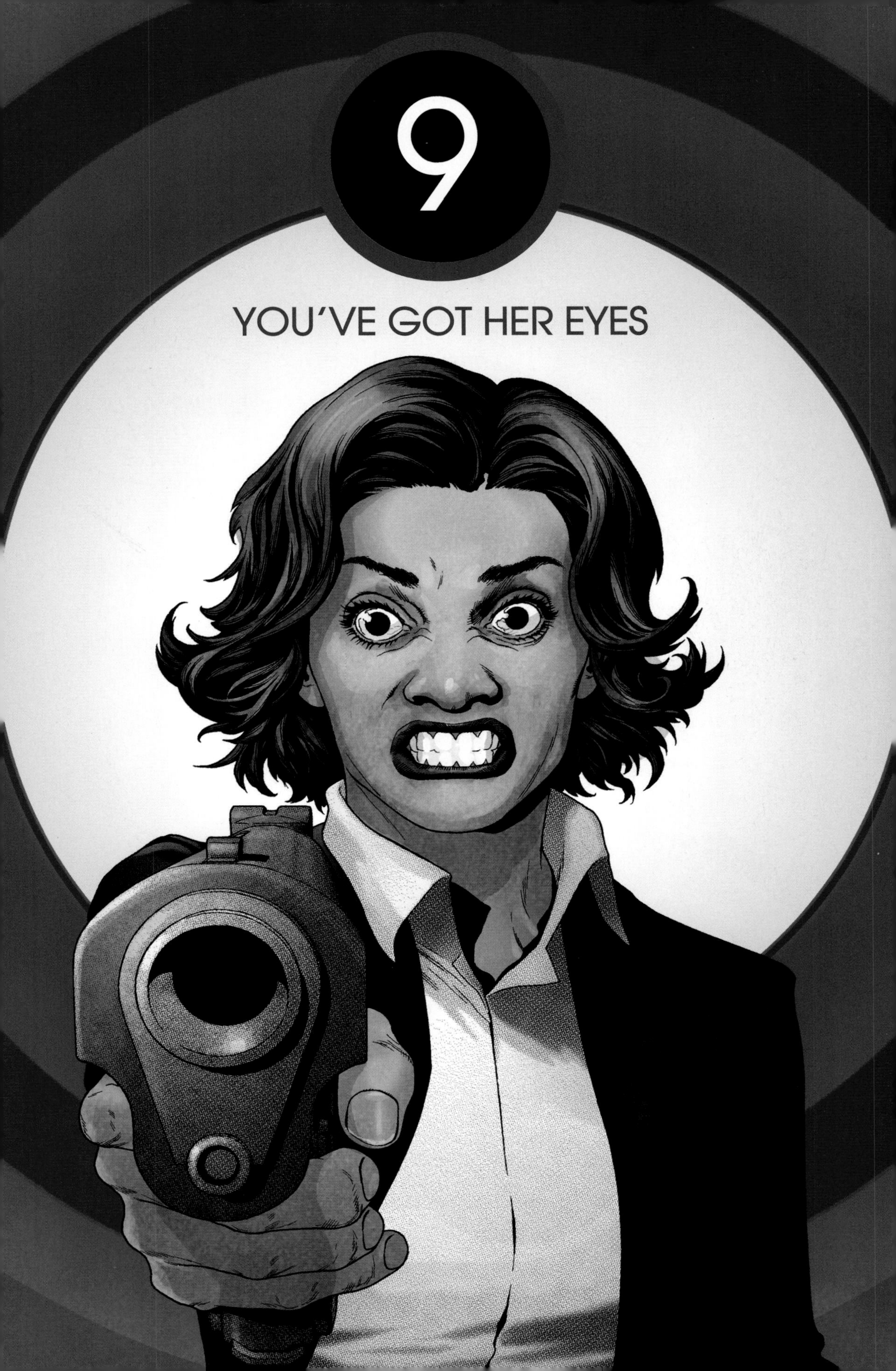

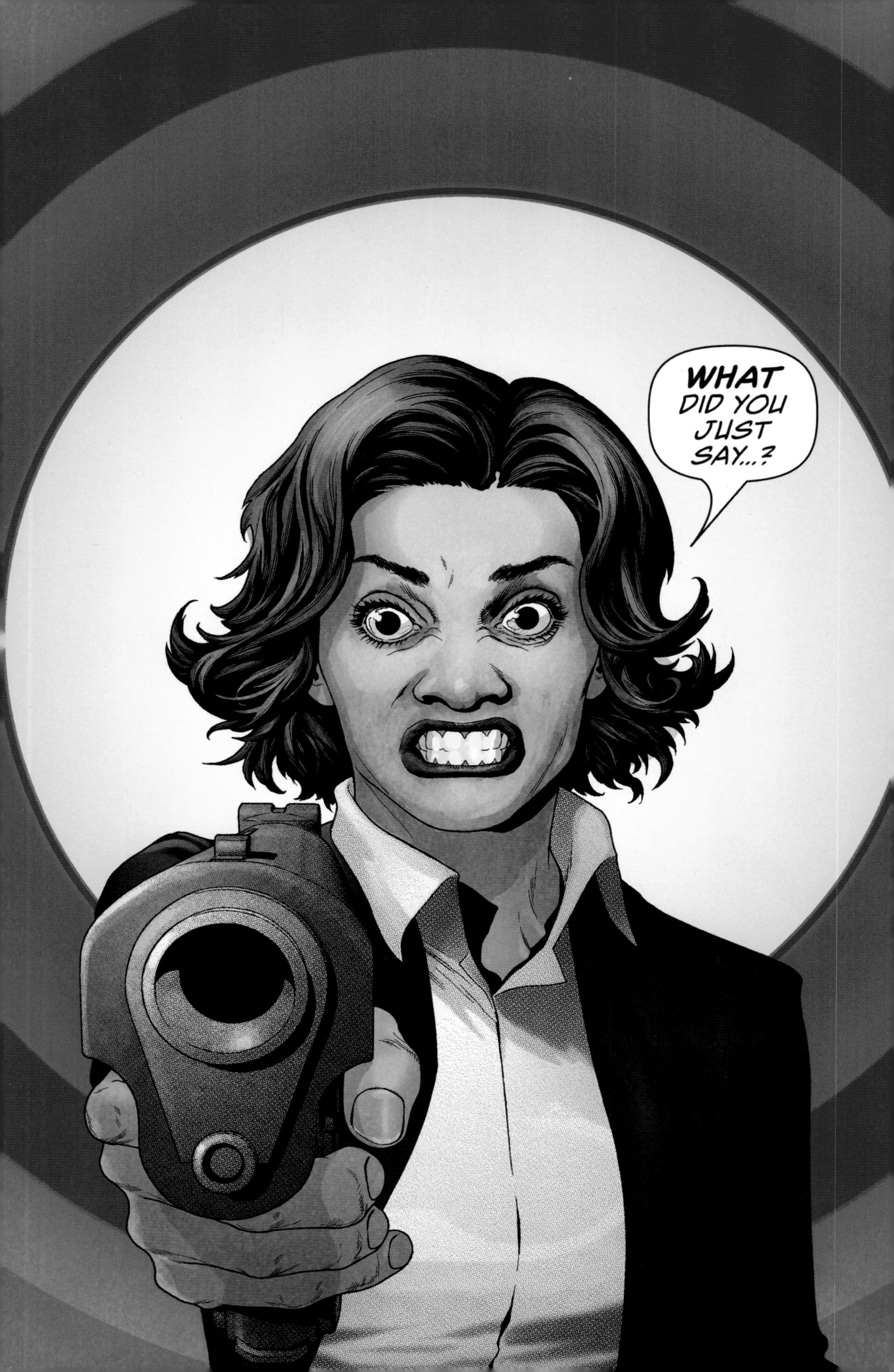
WHAT DID YOU JUST SAY...?

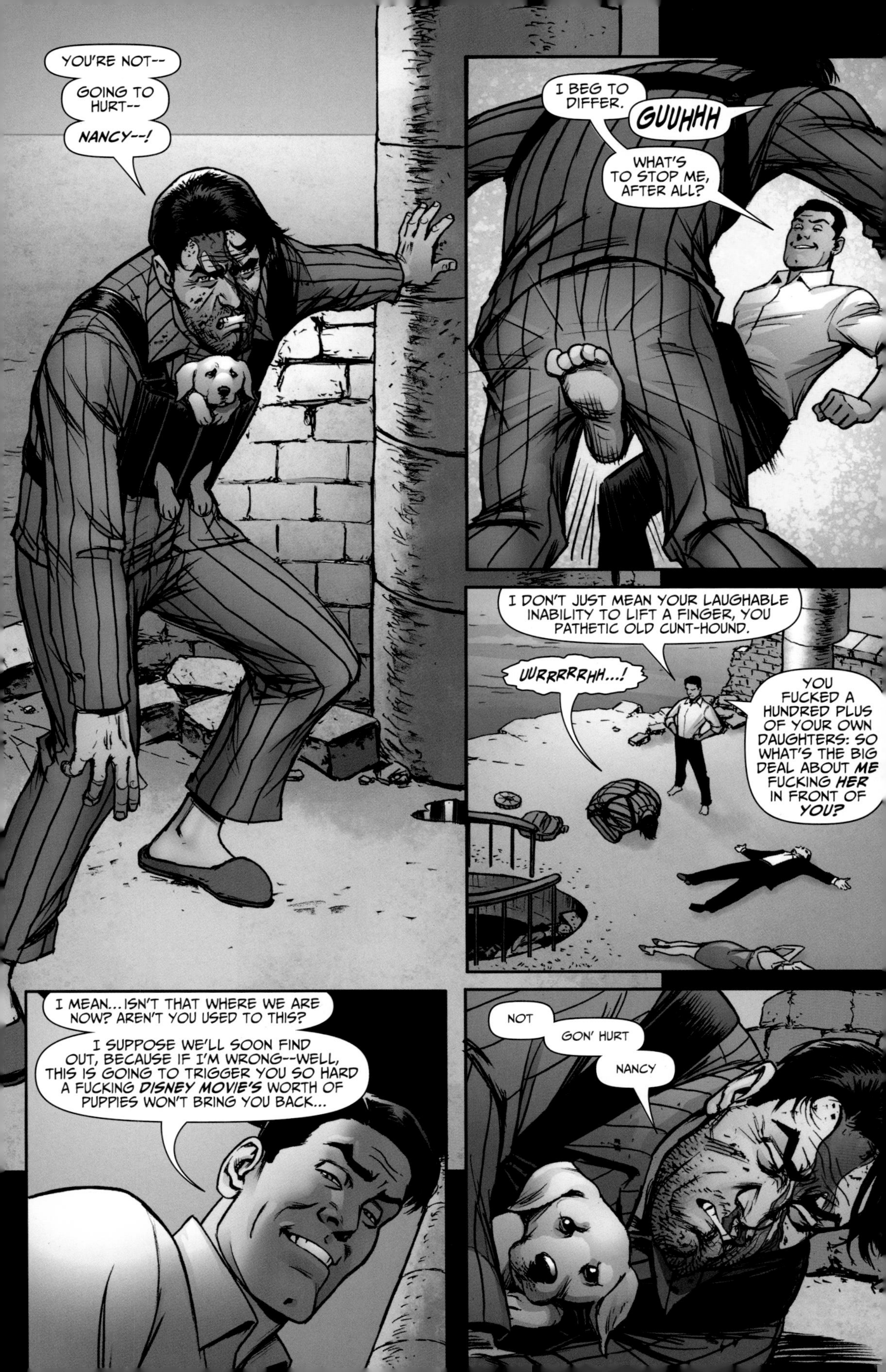
YOU'RE NOT--
GOING TO HURT--
NANCY--!
I BEG TO DIFFER.
GUUHHH
WHAT'S TO STOP ME, AFTER ALL?
I DON'T JUST MEAN YOUR LAUGHABLE INABILITY TO LIFT A FINGER, YOU PATHETIC OLD CUNT-HOUND.
UURRRRRHH...!
YOU FUCKED A HUNDRED PLUS OF YOUR OWN DAUGHTERS: SO WHAT'S THE BIG DEAL ABOUT ME FUCKING HER IN FRONT OF YOU?
I MEAN...ISN'T THAT WHERE WE ARE NOW? AREN'T YOU USED TO THIS?
I SUPPOSE WE'LL SOON FIND OUT, BECAUSE IF I'M WRONG--WELL, THIS IS GOING TO TRIGGER YOU SO HARD A FUCKING DISNEY MOVIE'S WORTH OF PUPPIES WON'T BRING YOU BACK...
NOT
GON' HURT
NANCY

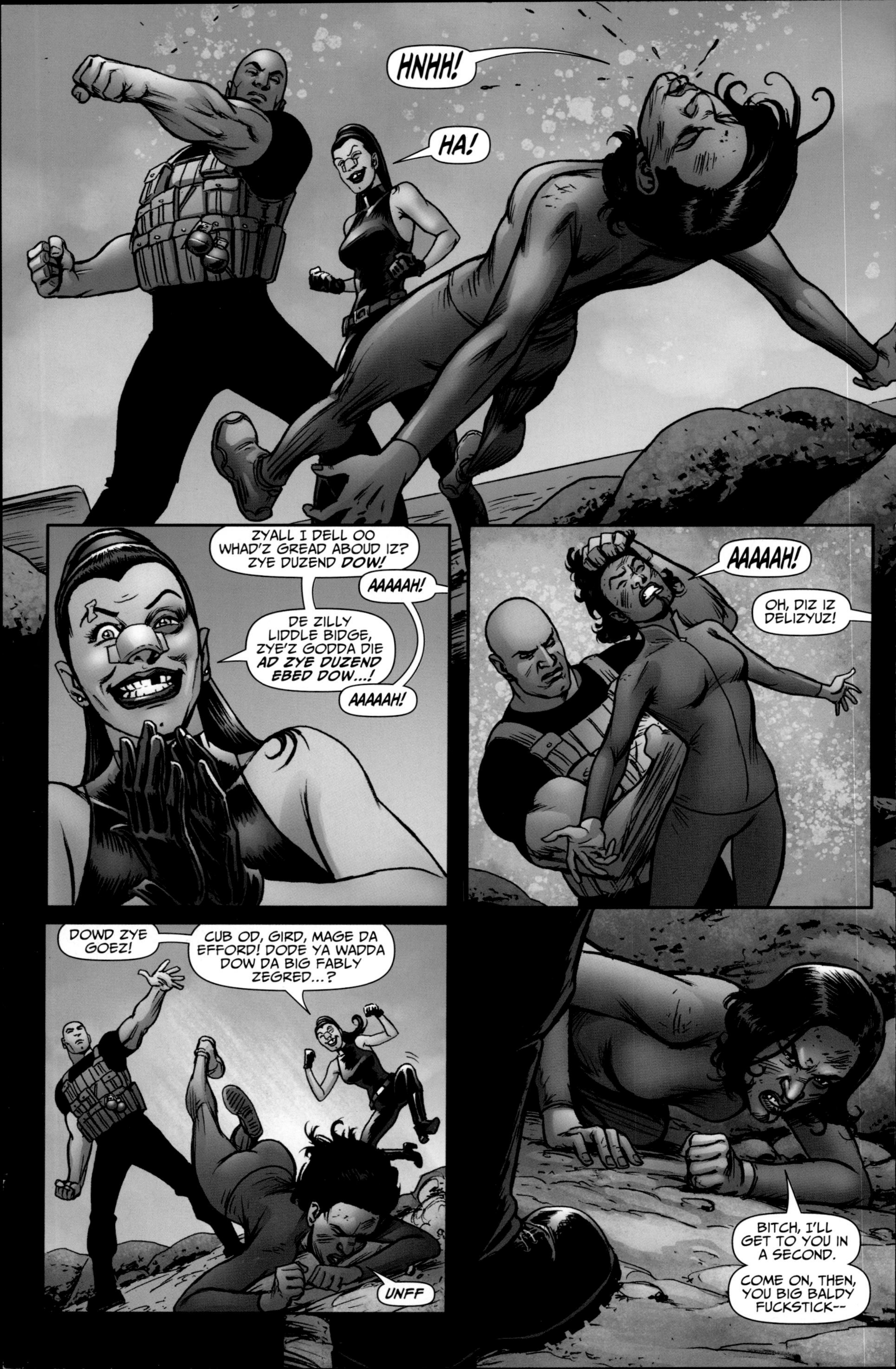
HNHH!
HA!
ZYALL I DELL OO WHAD'Z GREAD ABOUD IZ? ZYE DUZEND DOW!
AAAAAH!
DE ZILLY LIDDLE BIDGE, ZYE'Z GODDA DIE AD ZYE DUZEND EBED DOW...!
AAAAAH!
AAAAAH!
OH, DIZ IZ DELIZYUZ!
DOWD ZYE GOEZ!
CUB OD, GIRD, MAGE DA EFFORD! DODE YA WADDA DOW DA BIG FABLY ZEGRED...?
UNFF
BITCH, I'LL GET TO YOU IN A SECOND.
COME ON, THEN, YOU BIG BALDY FUCKSTICK--

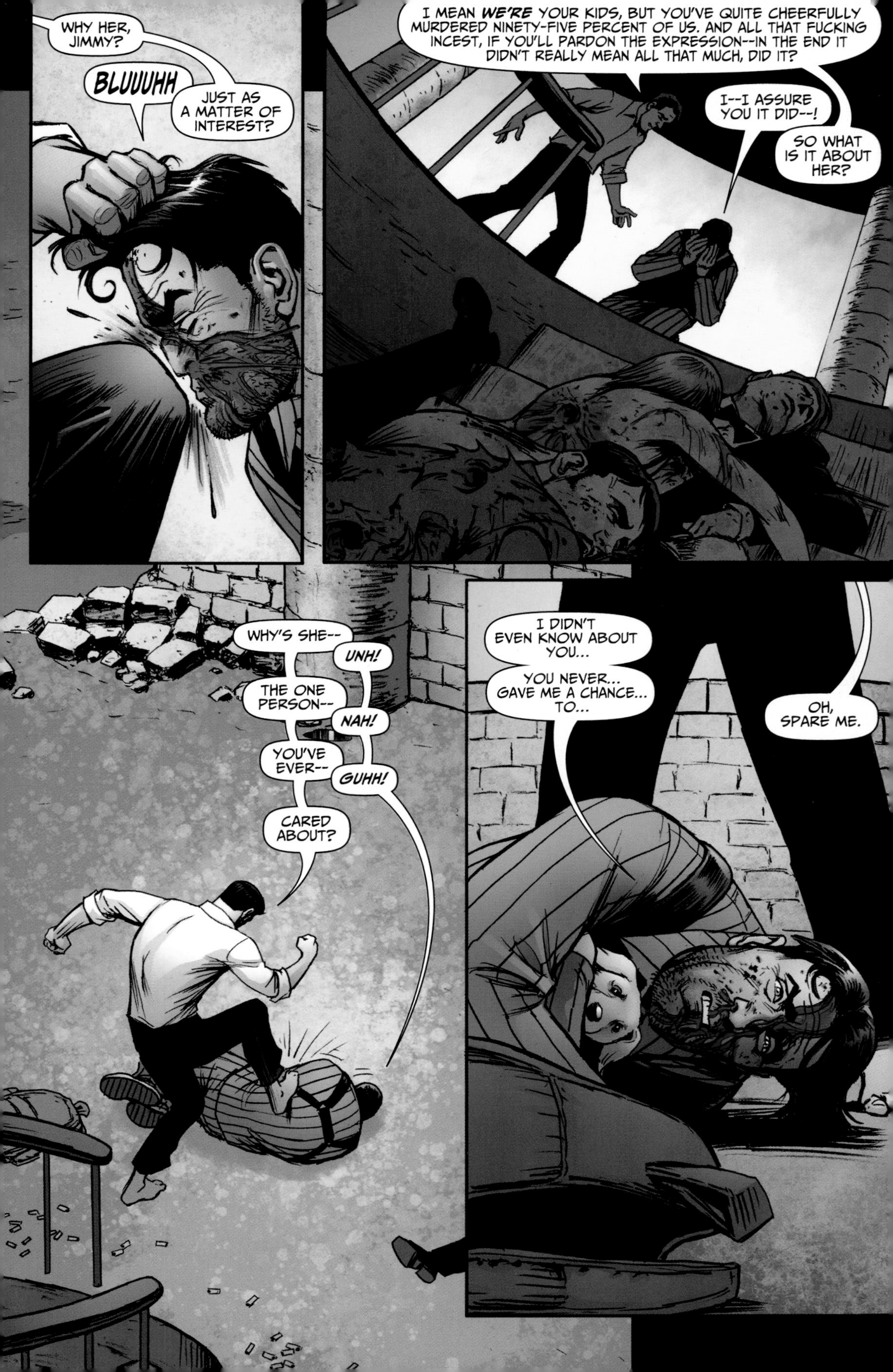
WHY HER, JIMMY?
BLUUUHH
JUST AS A MATTER OF INTEREST?
I MEAN WE'RE YOUR KIDS, BUT YOU'VE QUITE CHEERFULLY MURDERED NINETY-FIVE PERCENT OF US. AND ALL THAT FUCKING INCEST, IF YOU'LL PARDON THE EXPRESSION--IN THE END IT DIDN'T REALLY MEAN ALL THAT MUCH, DID IT?
I--I ASSURE YOU IT DID--!
SO WHAT IS IT ABOUT HER?
WHY'S SHE--
UNH!
THE ONE PERSON--
NAH!
YOU'VE EVER--
GUHH!
CARED ABOUT?
I DIDN'T EVEN KNOW ABOUT YOU...
YOU NEVER... GAVE ME A CHANCE... TO...
OH, SPARE ME.

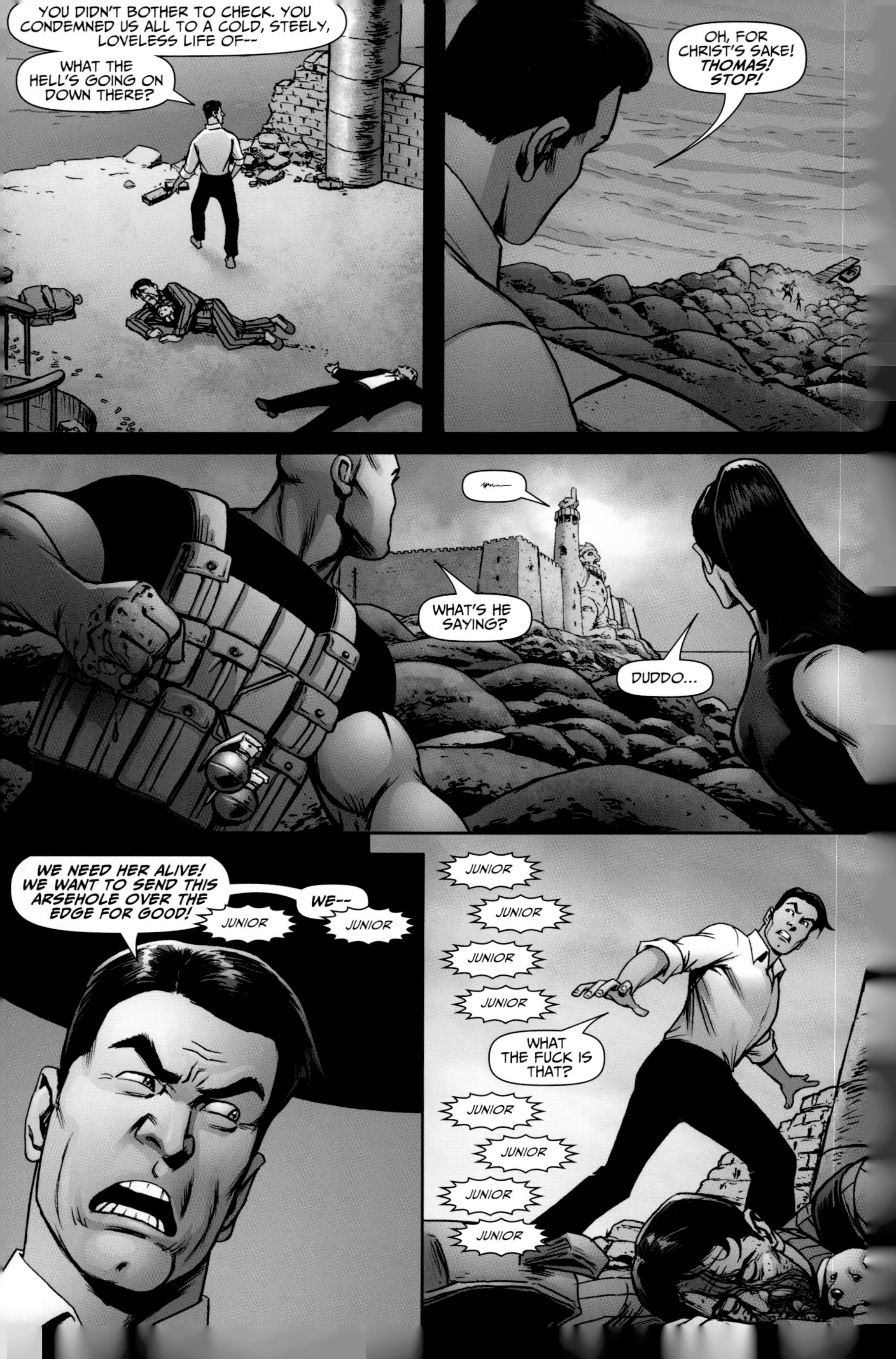
YOU DIDN'T BOTHER TO CHECK. YOU CONDEMNED US ALL TO A COLD, STEELY, LOVELESS LIFE OF--
WHAT THE HELL'S GOING ON DOWN THERE?
OH, FOR CHRIST'S SAKE! THOMAS! STOP!
WHAT'S HE SAYING?
DUDDO...
WE NEED HER ALIVE! WE WANT TO SEND THIS ARSEHOLE OVER THE EDGE FOR GOOD!
JUNIOR
WE--
JUNIOR
JUNIOR
JUNIOR
JUNIOR
JUNIOR
WHAT THE FUCK IS THAT?
JUNIOR
JUNIOR
JUNIOR
JUNIOR

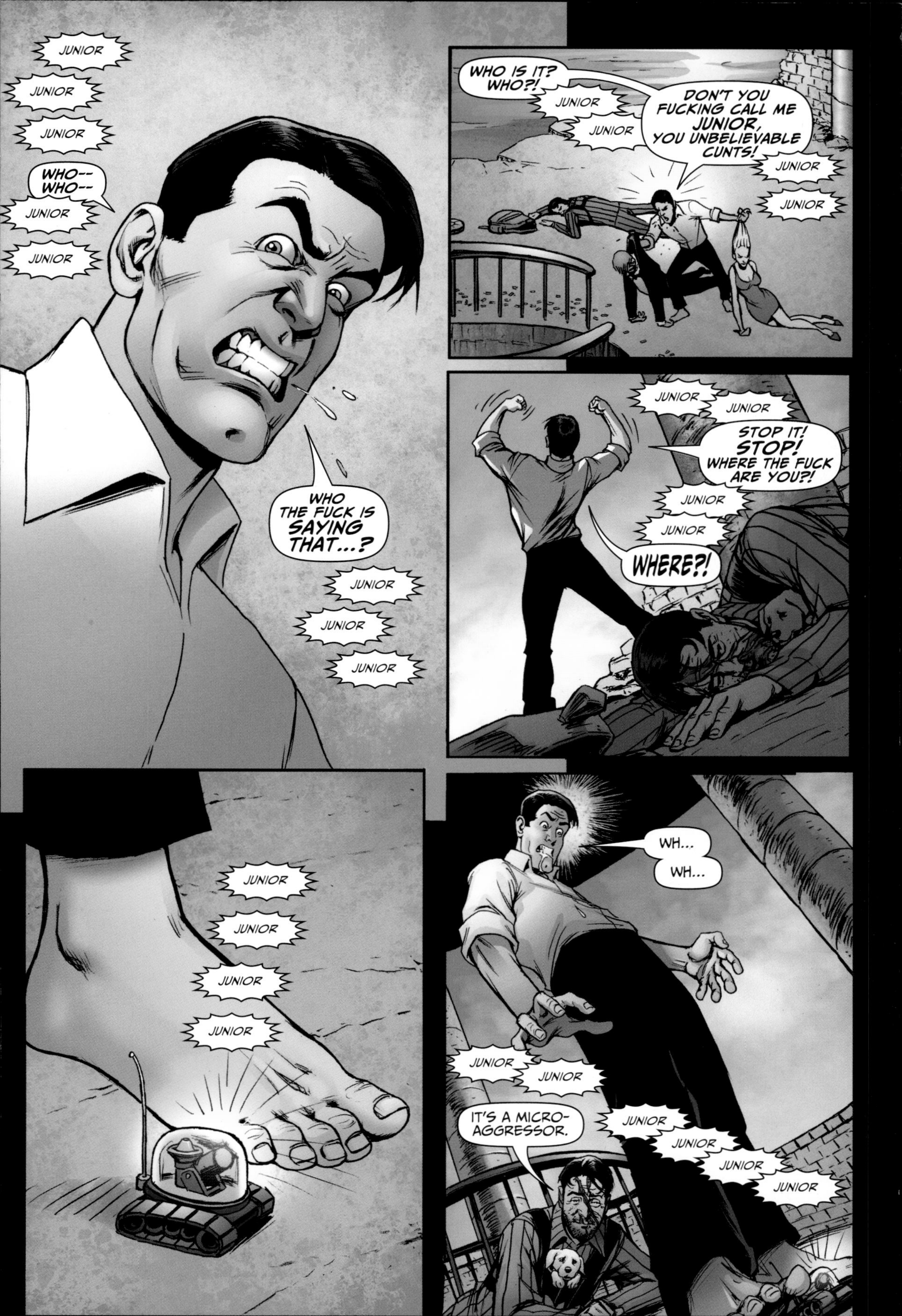
JUNIOR
JUNIOR
JUNIOR
WHO-- WHO--
JUNIOR
JUNIOR
WHO THE FUCK IS SAYING THAT...?
JUNIOR
JUNIOR
JUNIOR
WHO IS IT? WHO?!
JUNIOR
JUNIOR
DON'T YOU FUCKING CALL ME JUNIOR, YOU UNBELIEVABLE CUNTS!
JUNIOR
JUNIOR
JUNIOR
JUNIOR
STOP IT! STOP! WHERE THE FUCK ARE YOU?!
JUNIOR
JUNIOR
WHERE?!
JUNIOR
JUNIOR
JUNIOR
JUNIOR
WH...
WH...
JUNIOR
JUNIOR
IT'S A MICRO-AGGRESSOR.
JUNIOR
JUNIOR
JUNIOR
JUNIOR

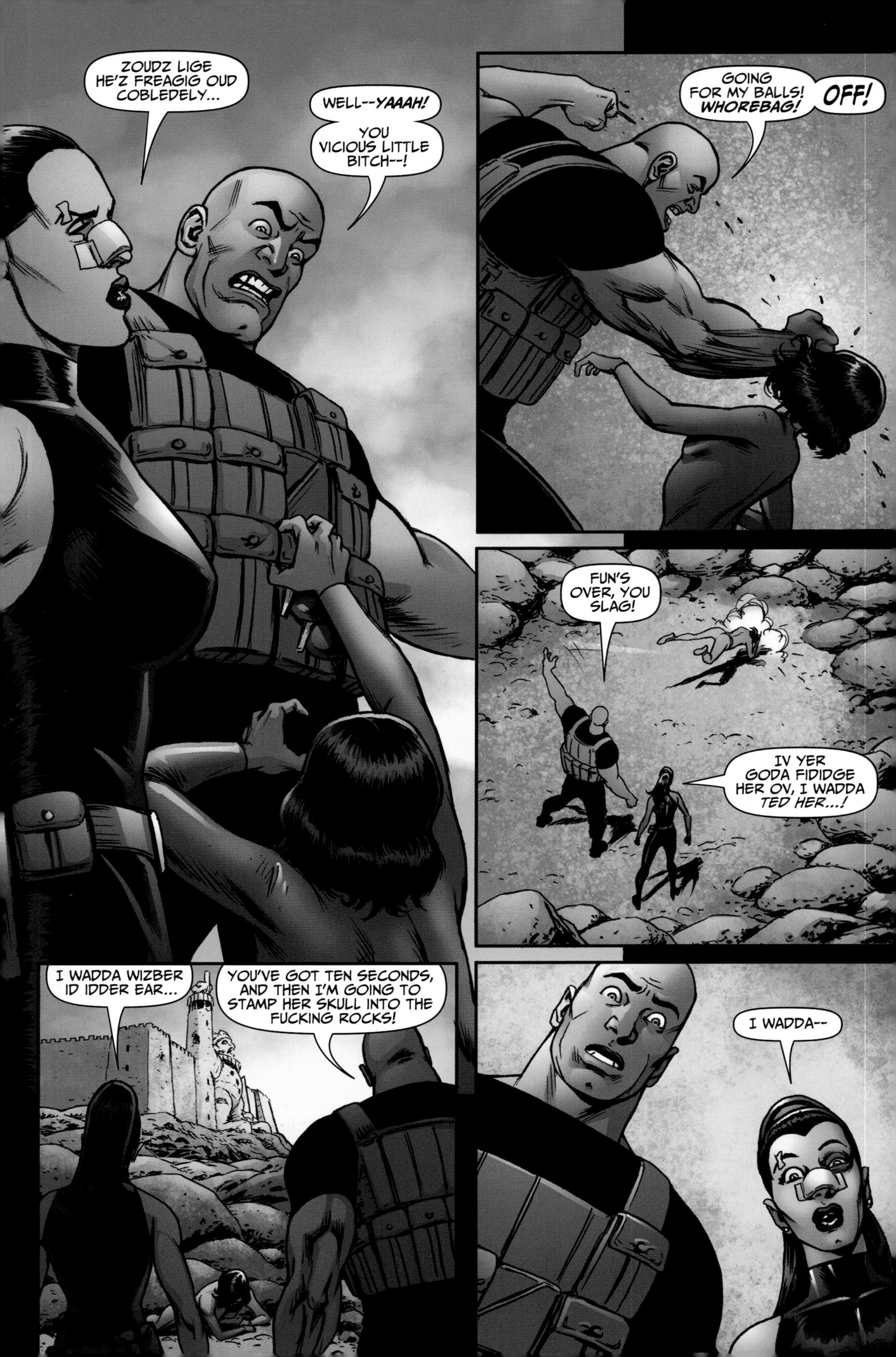
ZOUDZ LIGE HE'Z FREAGIG OUD COBLEDELY...
WELL--*YAAAH!*
YOU VICIOUS LITTLE BITCH--!
GOING FOR MY BALLS! *WHOREBAG!*
OFF!
FUN'S OVER, YOU SLAG!
IV YER GODA FIDIDGE HER OV, I WADDA *TED HER*...!
I WADDA WIZBER ID IDDER EAR...
YOU'VE GOT TEN SECONDS, AND THEN I'M GOING TO STAMP HER SKULL INTO THE FUCKING ROCKS!
I WADDA--

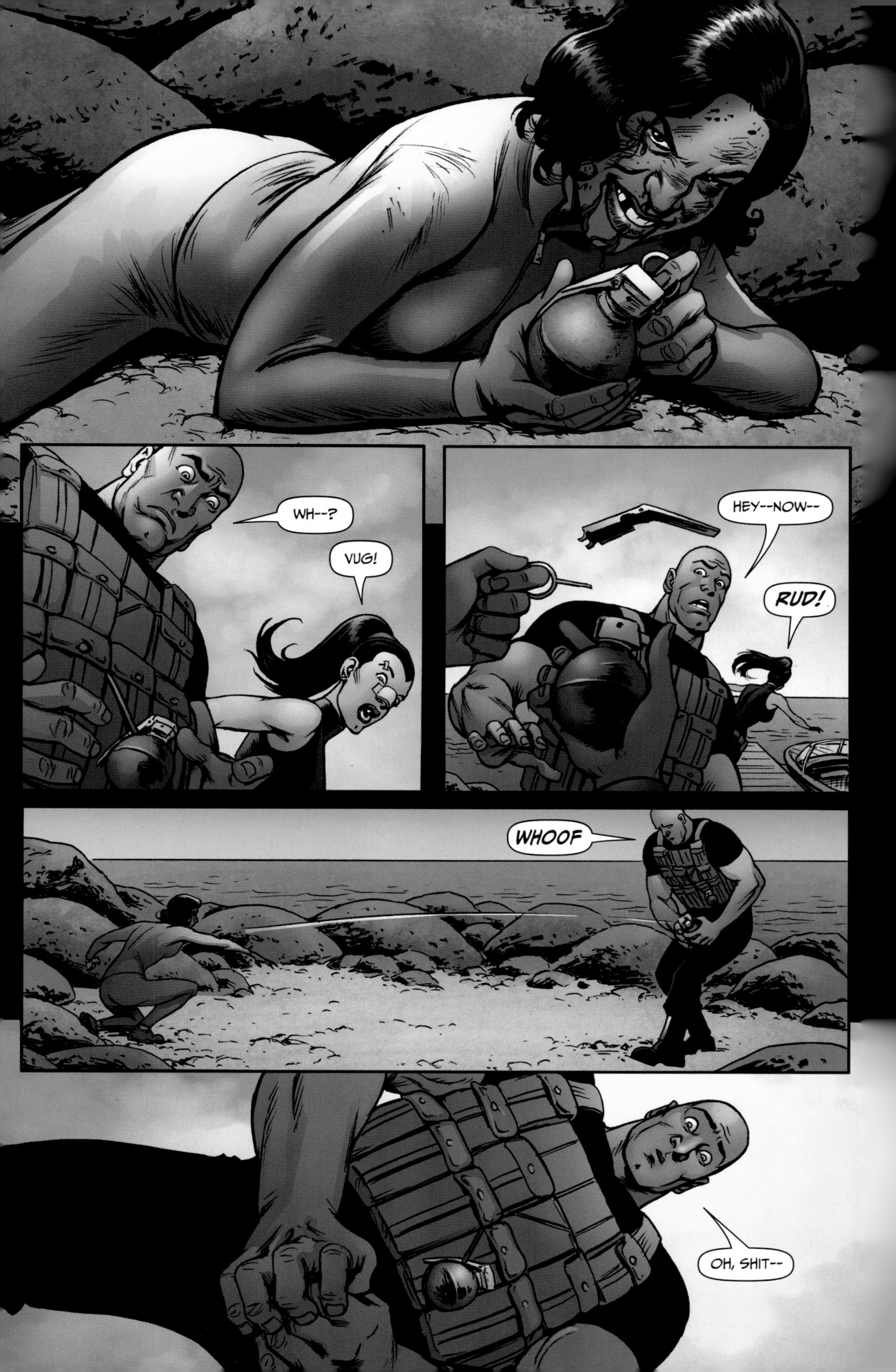
WH--?
VUG!
HEY--NOW--
RUD!
WHOOF
OH, SHIT--

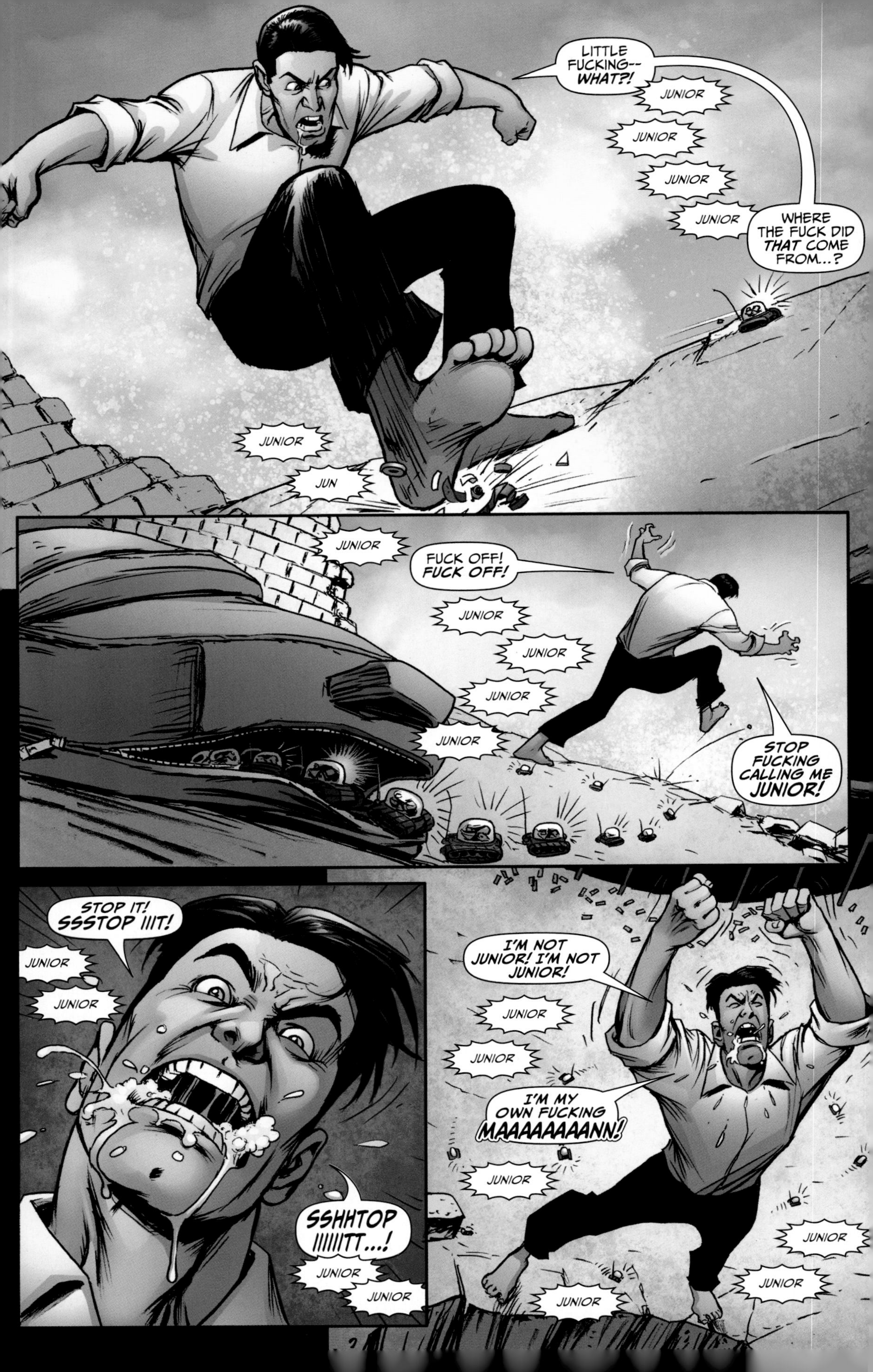
LITTLE FUCKING-- WHAT?!
JUNIOR
JUNIOR
JUNIOR
JUNIOR
WHERE THE FUCK DID THAT COME FROM..?
JUNIOR
JUN
JUNIOR
FUCK OFF! FUCK OFF!
JUNIOR
JUNIOR
JUNIOR
JUNIOR
STOP FUCKING CALLING ME JUNIOR!
STOP IT! SSSTOP IIIT!
JUNIOR
JUNIOR
SSHHTOP IIIIIITT...!
JUNIOR
JUNIOR
I'M NOT JUNIOR! I'M NOT JUNIOR!
JUNIOR
JUNIOR
I'M MY OWN FUCKING MAAAAAAAANN!
JUNIOR
JUNIOR
JUNIOR
JUNIOR

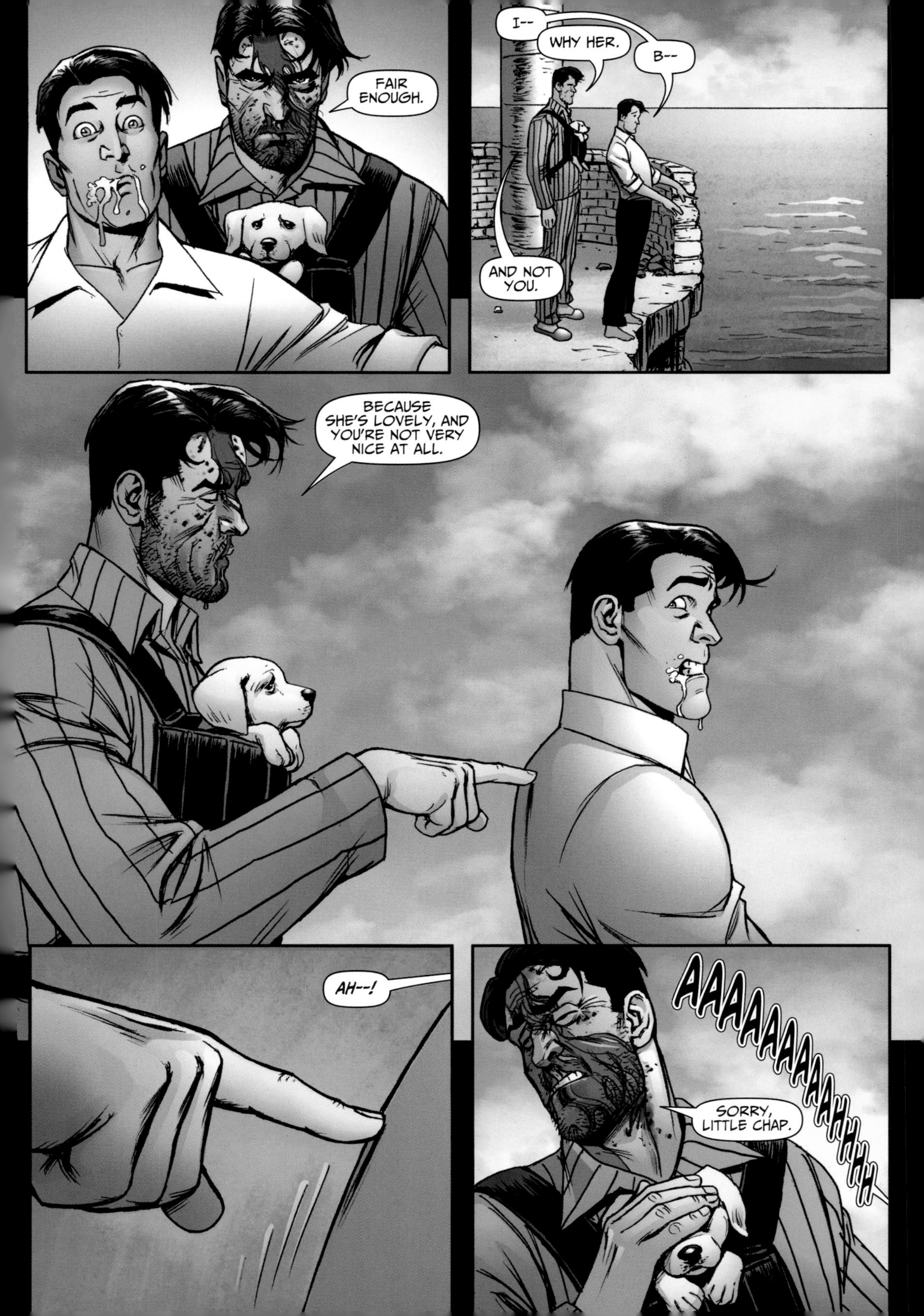
FAIR ENOUGH.
I--
WHY HER.
B--
AND NOT YOU.
BECAUSE SHE'S LOVELY, AND YOU'RE NOT VERY NICE AT ALL.
AH--!
AAAAAAAAAAAHHHH
SORRY, LITTLE CHAP.

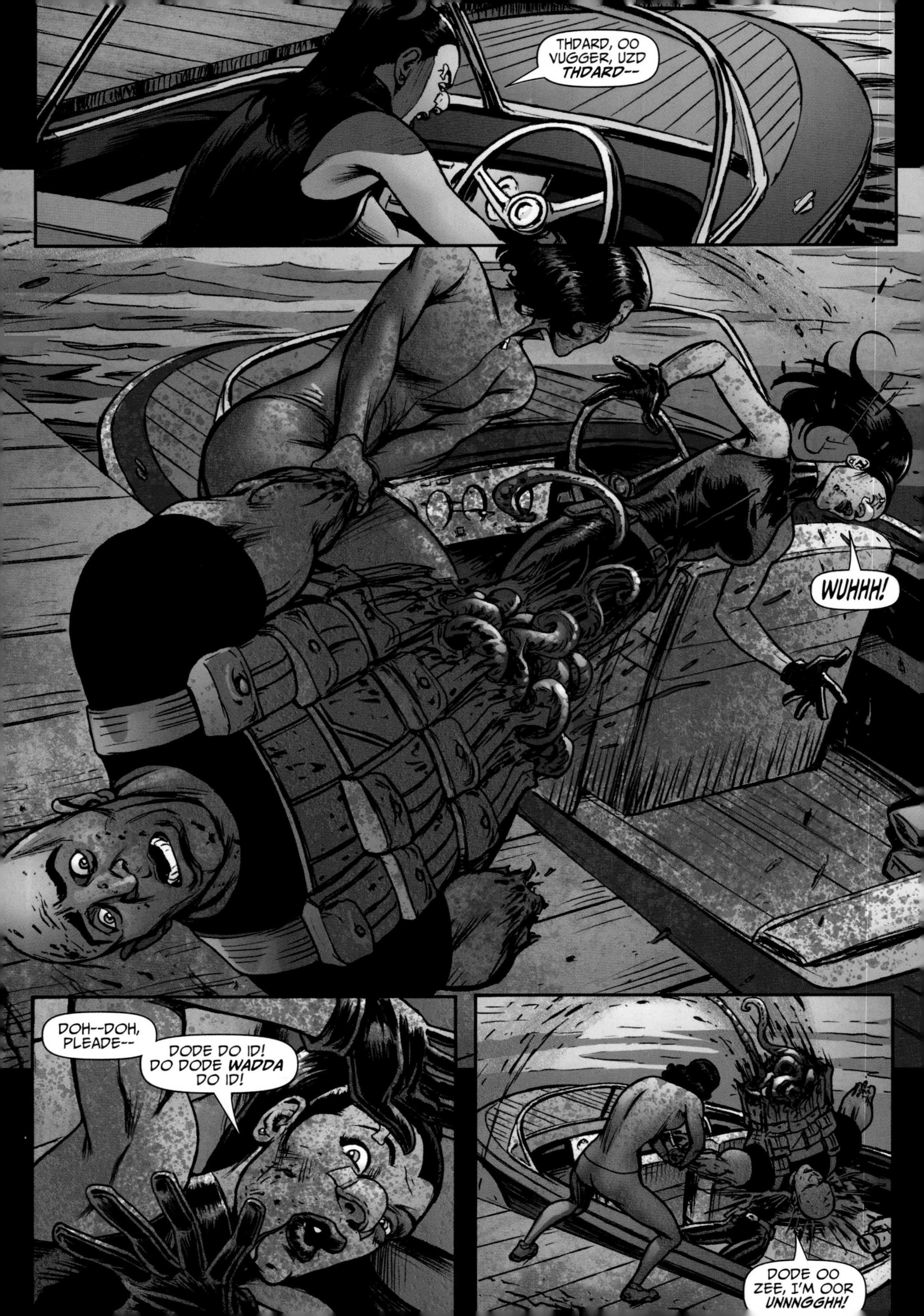
THDARD, OO VUGGER, UZD THDARD--
WUHHH!
DOH--DOH, PLEADE--
DODE DO ID! DO DODE WADDA DO ID!
DODE OO ZEE, I'M OOR UNNNGGHH!

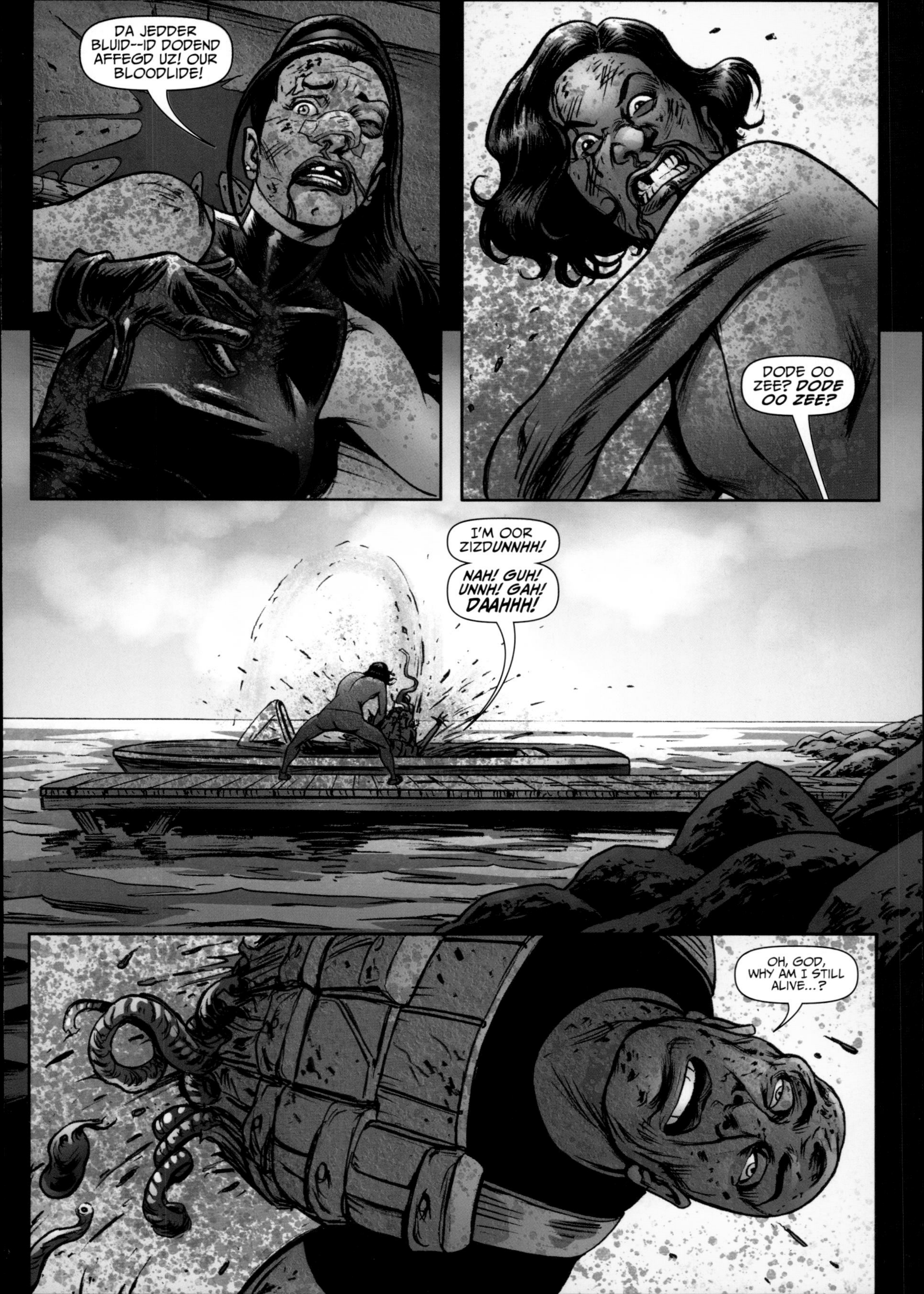
DA JEDDER BLUID--ID DODEND AFFEGD UZ! OUR BLOODLIDE!
DODE OO ZEE? DODE OO ZEE?
I'M OOR ZIZDUNNHH!
NAH! GUH! UNNH! GAH! DAAHHH!
OH, GOD, WHY AM I STILL ALIVE...?

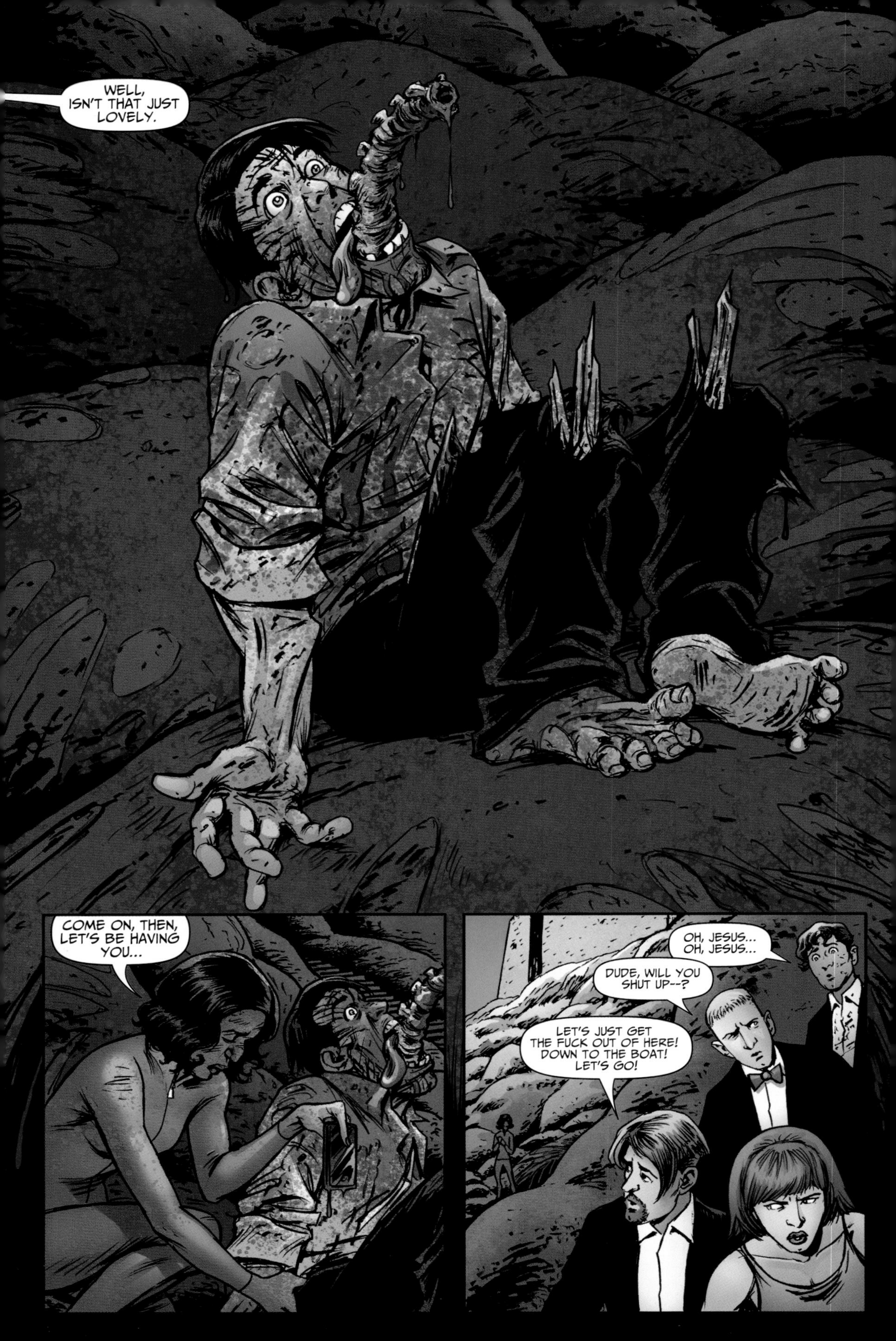
WELL, ISN'T THAT JUST LOVELY.
COME ON, THEN, LET'S BE HAVING YOU...
OH, JESUS... OH, JESUS...
DUDE, WILL YOU SHUT UP--?
LET'S JUST GET THE FUCK OUT OF HERE! DOWN TO THE BOAT! LET'S GO!

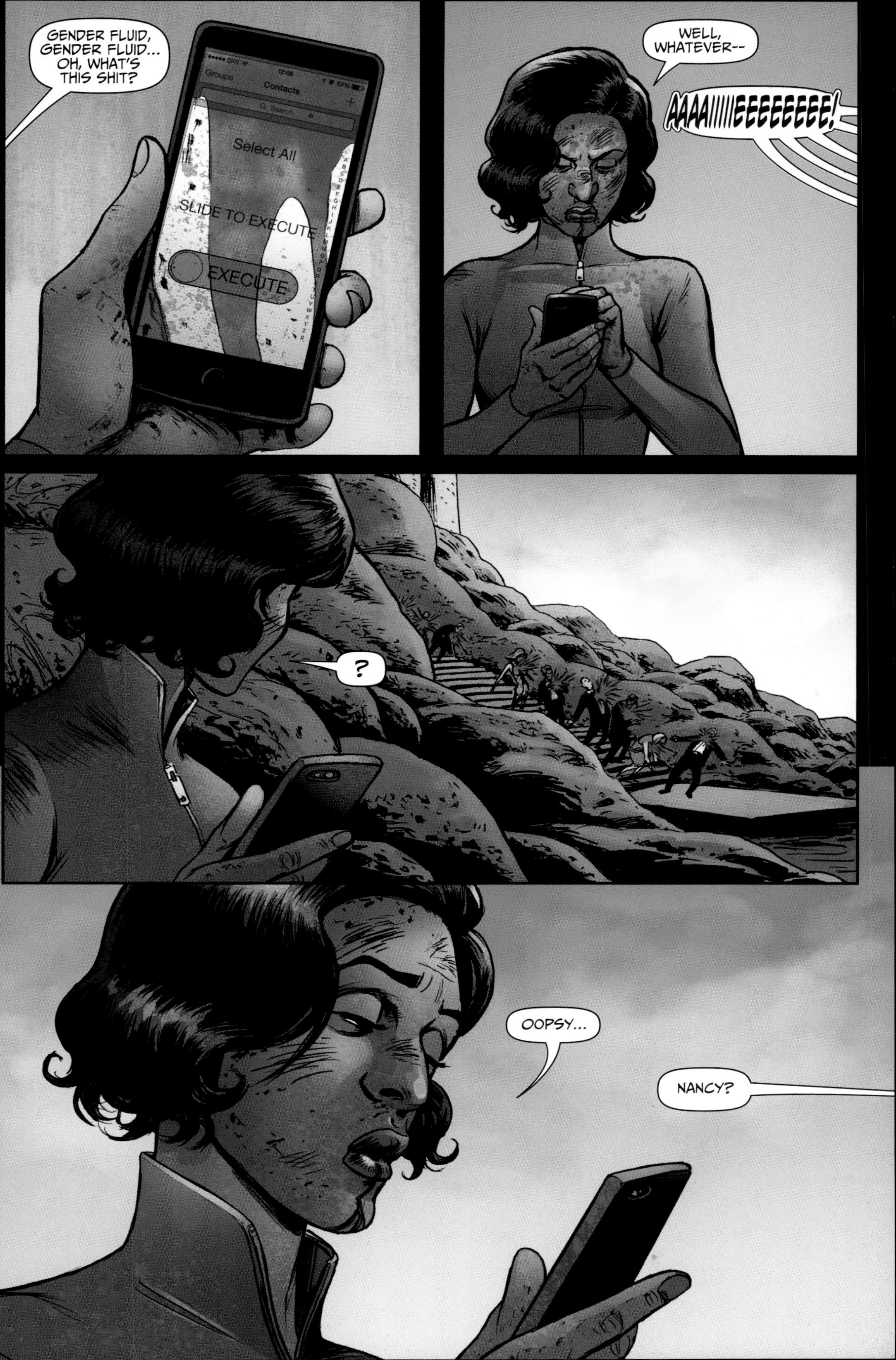
GENDER FLUID, GENDER FLUID... OH, WHAT'S THIS SHIT?
Groups
Contacts
Search
Select All
SLIDE TO EXECUTE
EXECUTE
WELL, WHATEVER--
AAAAIIIIIIEEEEEEEEE!
?
OOPSY...
NANCY?

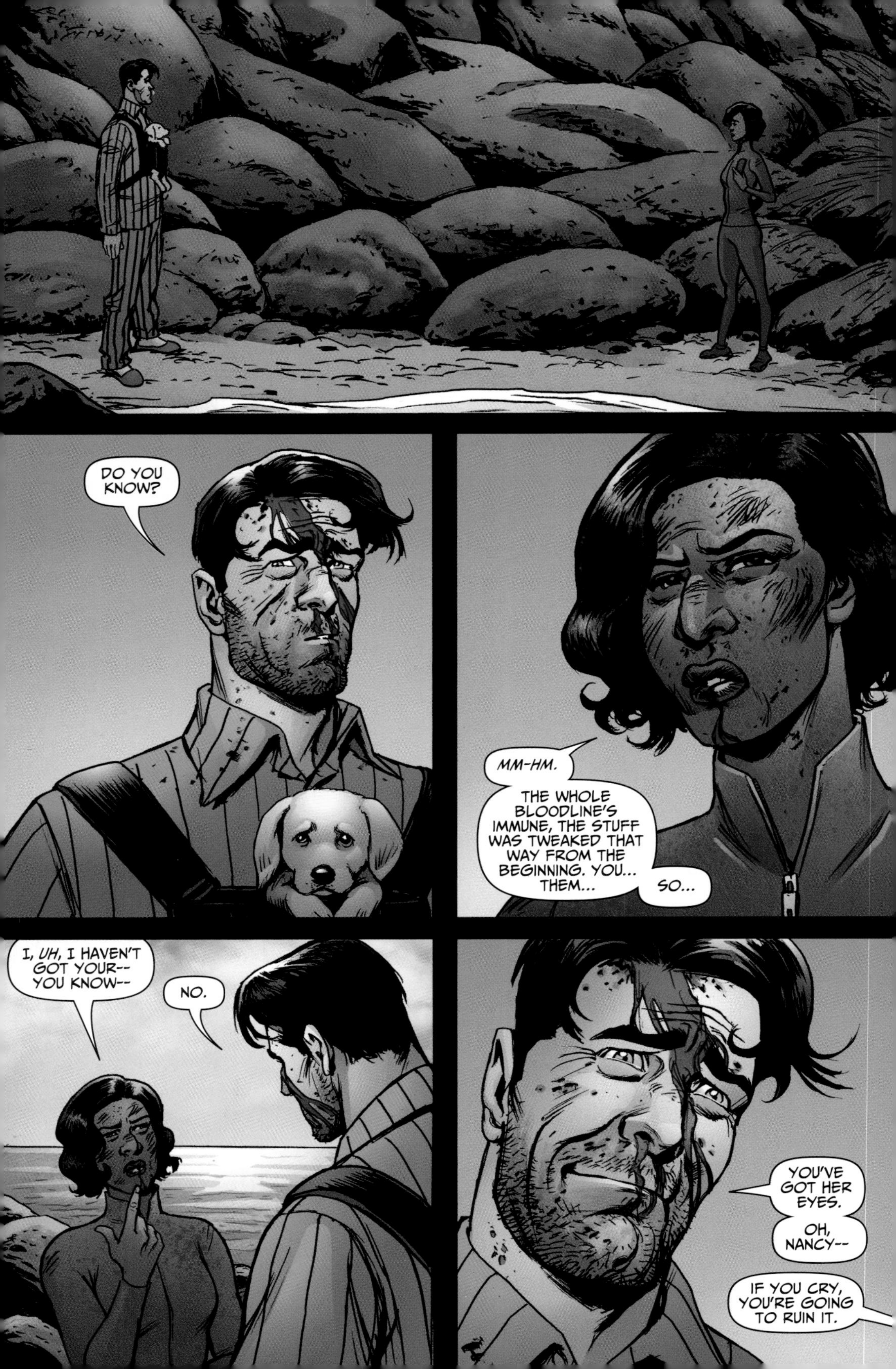

DO YOU KNOW?
MM-HM.
THE WHOLE BLOODLINE'S IMMUNE, THE STUFF WAS TWEAKED THAT WAY FROM THE BEGINNING. YOU... THEM...
SO...
I, UH, I HAVEN'T GOT YOUR-- YOU KNOW--
NO.
YOU'VE GOT HER EYES.
OH, NANCY--
IF YOU CRY, YOU'RE GOING TO RUIN IT.

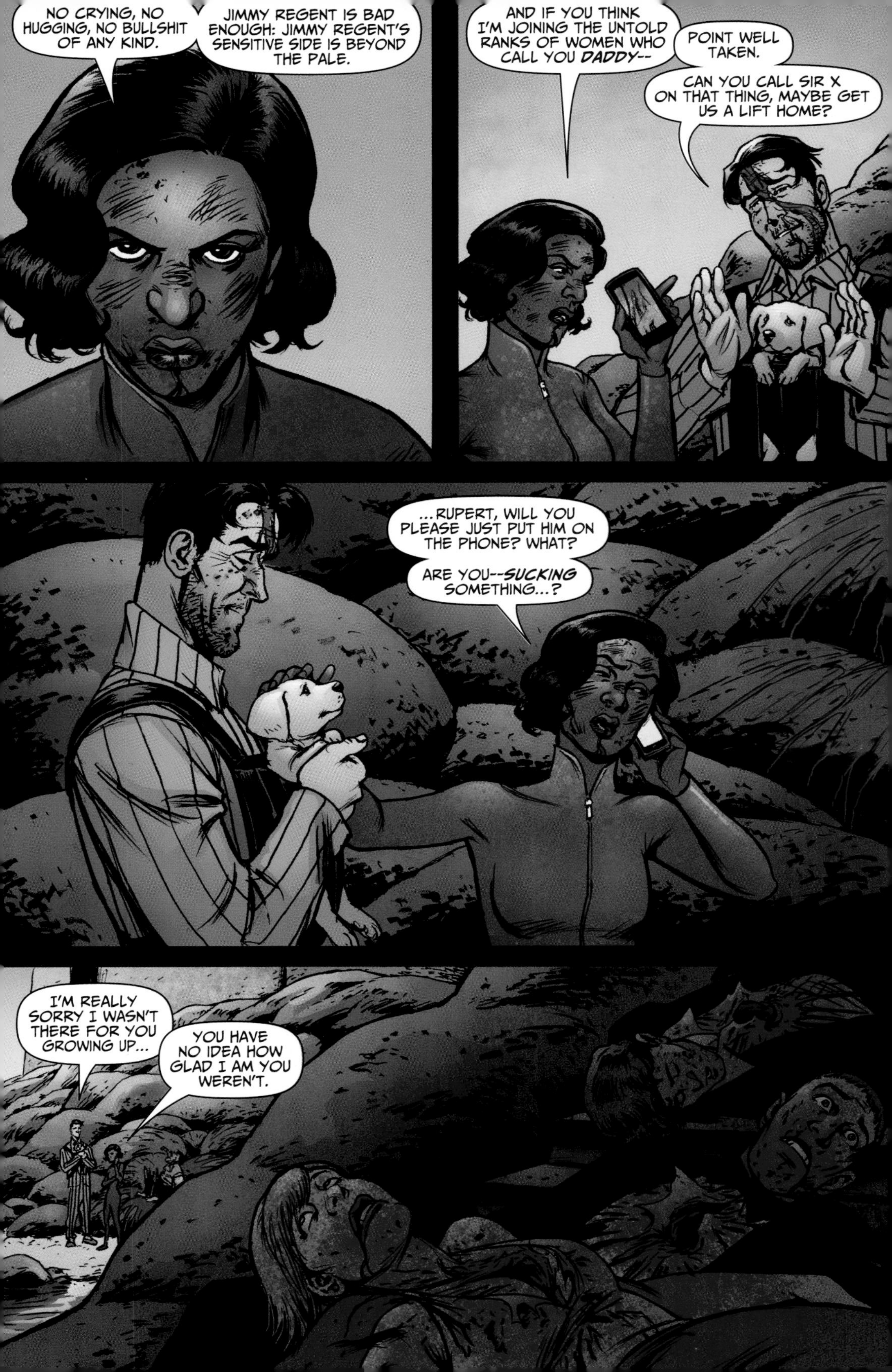

NO CRYING, NO HUGGING, NO BULLSHIT OF ANY KIND.
JIMMY REGENT IS BAD ENOUGH: JIMMY REGENT'S SENSITIVE SIDE IS BEYOND THE PALE.
AND IF YOU THINK I'M JOINING THE UNTOLD RANKS OF WOMEN WHO CALL YOU *DADDY*--
POINT WELL TAKEN.
CAN YOU CALL SIR X ON THAT THING, MAYBE GET US A LIFT HOME?
...RUPERT, WILL YOU PLEASE JUST PUT HIM ON THE PHONE? WHAT?
ARE YOU--*SUCKING* SOMETHING...?
I'M REALLY SORRY I WASN'T THERE FOR YOU GROWING UP...
YOU HAVE NO IDEA HOW GLAD I AM YOU WEREN'T.

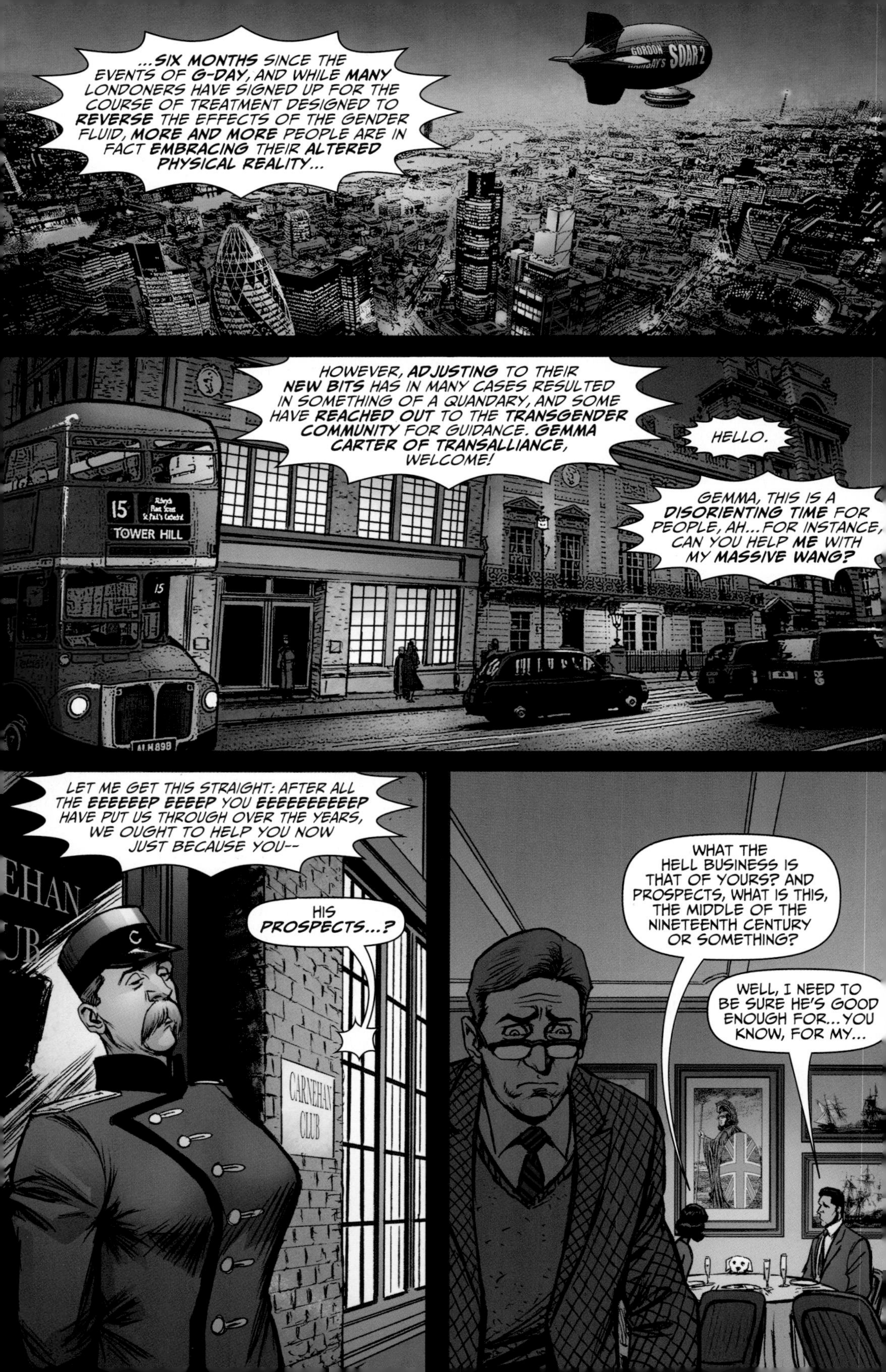
GORDON
...AY'S SOAR 2
...SIX MONTHS SINCE THE EVENTS OF G-DAY, AND WHILE MANY LONDONERS HAVE SIGNED UP FOR THE COURSE OF TREATMENT DESIGNED TO REVERSE THE EFFECTS OF THE GENDER FLUID, MORE AND MORE PEOPLE ARE IN FACT EMBRACING THEIR ALTERED PHYSICAL REALITY...
HOWEVER, ADJUSTING TO THEIR NEW BITS HAS IN MANY CASES RESULTED IN SOMETHING OF A QUANDARY, AND SOME HAVE REACHED OUT TO THE TRANSGENDER COMMUNITY FOR GUIDANCE. GEMMA CARTER OF TRANSALLIANCE, WELCOME!
15
TOWER HILL
HELLO.
GEMMA, THIS IS A DISORIENTING TIME FOR PEOPLE, AH...FOR INSTANCE, CAN YOU HELP ME WITH MY MASSIVE WANG?
LET ME GET THIS STRAIGHT: AFTER ALL THE EEEEEEP EEEEP YOU EEEEEEEEEP HAVE PUT US THROUGH OVER THE YEARS, WE OUGHT TO HELP YOU NOW JUST BECAUSE YOU--
HIS PROSPECTS...?
CARNEHAN CLUB
WHAT THE HELL BUSINESS IS THAT OF YOURS? AND PROSPECTS, WHAT IS THIS, THE MIDDLE OF THE NINETEENTH CENTURY OR SOMETHING?
WELL, I NEED TO BE SURE HE'S GOOD ENOUGH FOR...YOU KNOW, FOR MY...

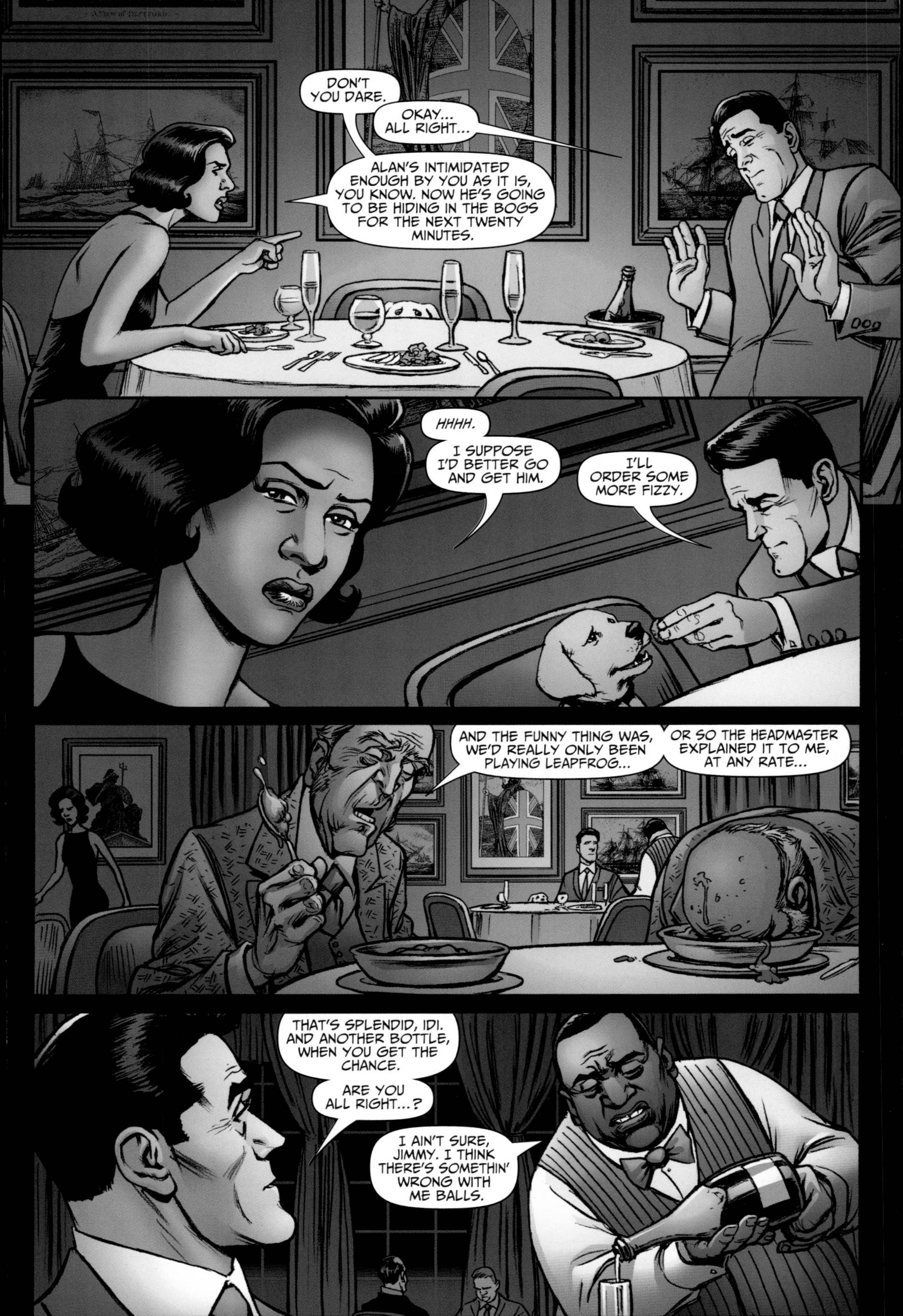

DON'T YOU DARE.
OKAY... ALL RIGHT...
ALAN'S INTIMIDATED ENOUGH BY YOU AS IT IS, YOU KNOW. NOW HE'S GOING TO BE HIDING IN THE BOGS FOR THE NEXT TWENTY MINUTES.
HHHH.
I SUPPOSE I'D BETTER GO AND GET HIM.
I'LL ORDER SOME MORE FIZZY.
AND THE FUNNY THING WAS, WE'D REALLY ONLY BEEN PLAYING LEAPFROG...
OR SO THE HEADMASTER EXPLAINED IT TO ME, AT ANY RATE...
THAT'S SPLENDID, IDI. AND ANOTHER BOTTLE, WHEN YOU GET THE CHANCE.
ARE YOU ALL RIGHT...?
I AIN'T SURE, JIMMY. I THINK THERE'S SOMETHIN' WRONG WITH ME BALLS.

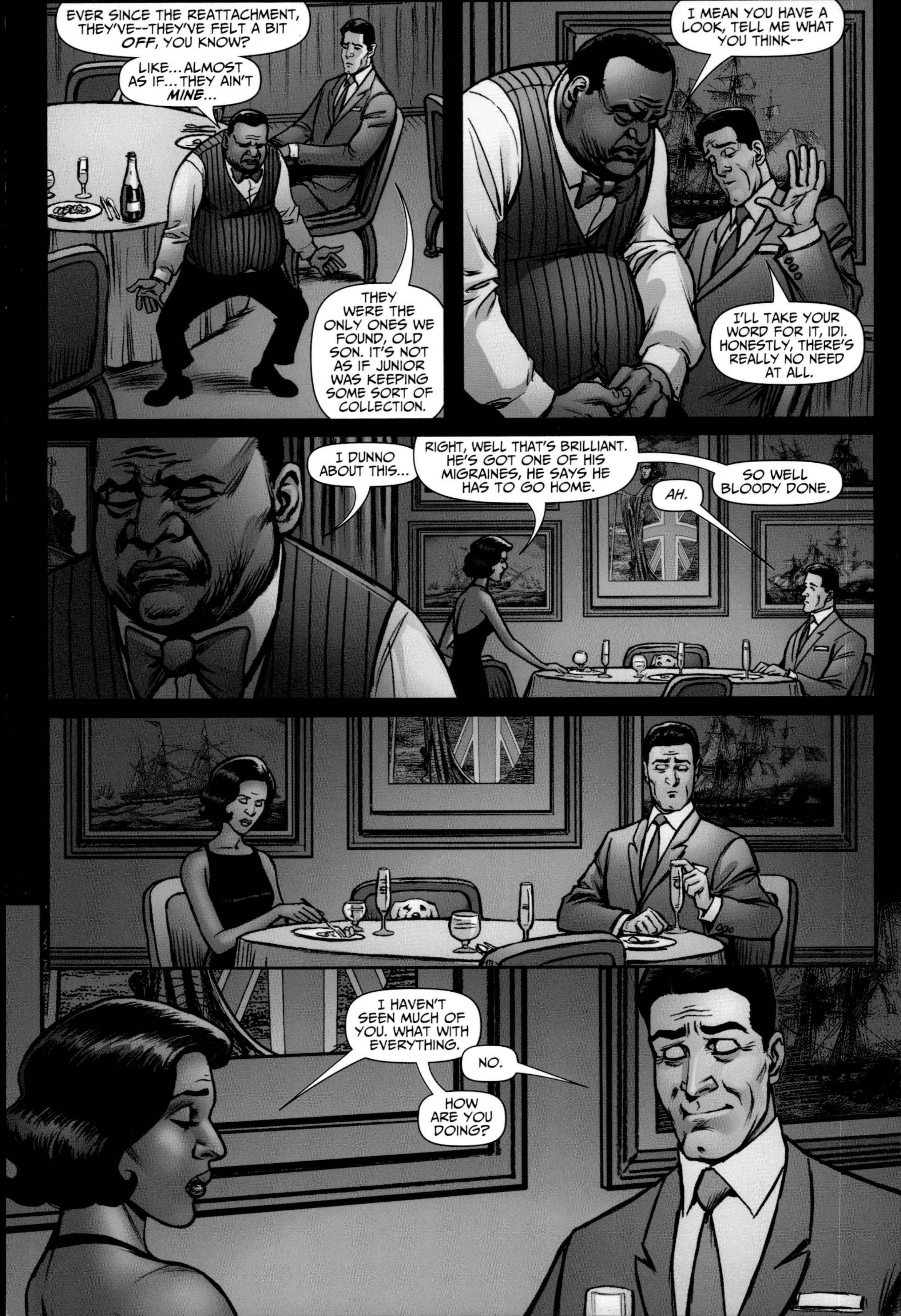

EVER SINCE THE REATTACHMENT, THEY'VE--THEY'VE FELT A BIT *OFF*, YOU KNOW?
LIKE...ALMOST AS IF...THEY AIN'T *MINE*...
THEY WERE THE ONLY ONES WE FOUND, OLD SON. IT'S NOT AS IF JUNIOR WAS KEEPING SOME SORT OF COLLECTION.
I MEAN YOU HAVE A LOOK, TELL ME WHAT YOU THINK--
I'LL TAKE YOUR WORD FOR IT, IDI. HONESTLY, THERE'S REALLY NO NEED AT ALL.
I DUNNO ABOUT THIS...
RIGHT, WELL THAT'S BRILLIANT. HE'S GOT ONE OF HIS MIGRAINES, HE SAYS HE HAS TO GO HOME.
AH.
SO WELL BLOODY DONE.
I HAVEN'T SEEN MUCH OF YOU. WHAT WITH EVERYTHING.
NO.
HOW ARE YOU DOING?

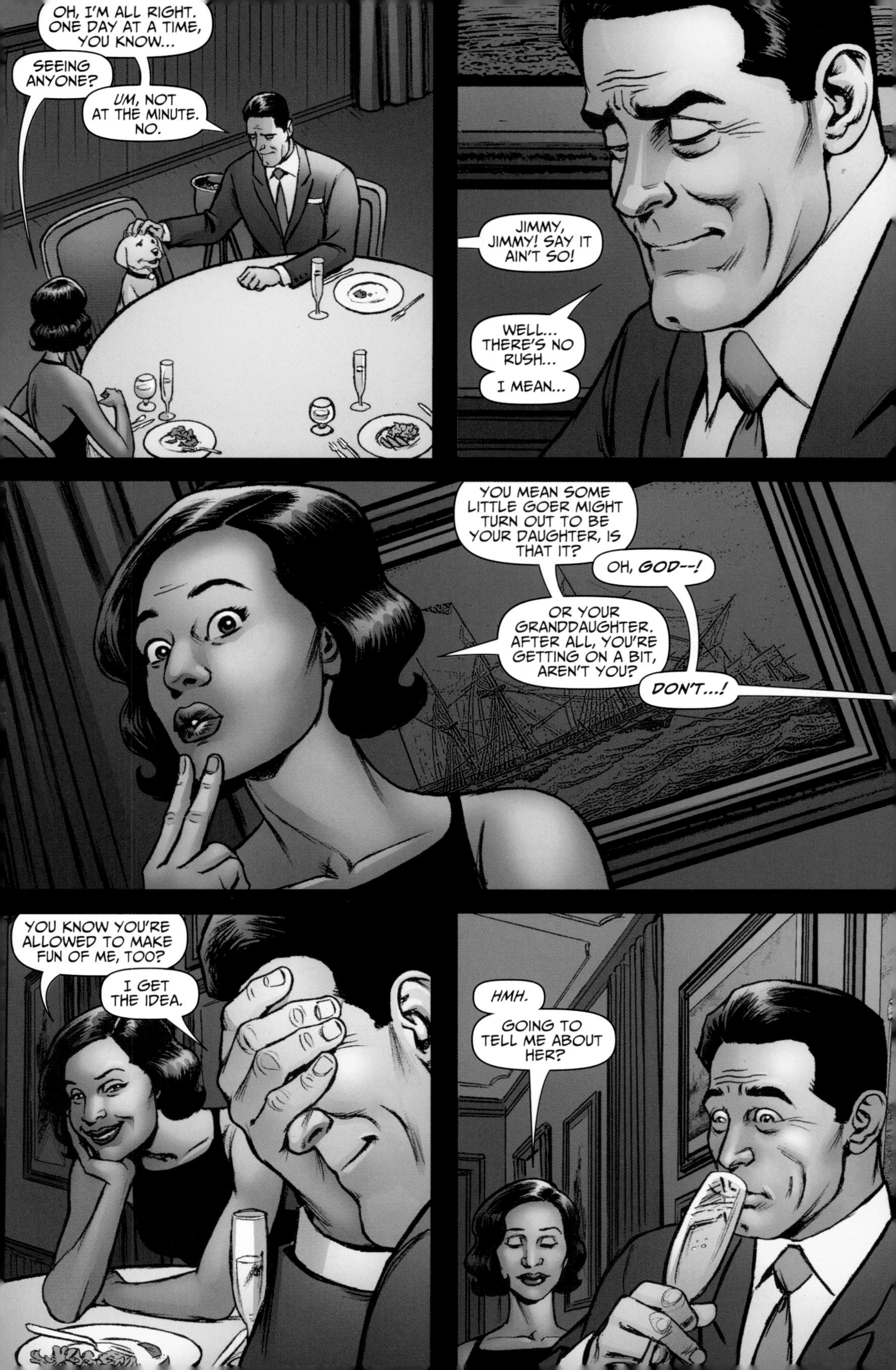
OH, I'M ALL RIGHT. ONE DAY AT A TIME, YOU KNOW...
SEEING ANYONE?
UM, NOT AT THE MINUTE. NO.
JIMMY, JIMMY! SAY IT AIN'T SO!
WELL... THERE'S NO RUSH...
I MEAN...
YOU MEAN SOME LITTLE GOER MIGHT TURN OUT TO BE YOUR DAUGHTER, IS THAT IT?
OH, GOD--!
OR YOUR GRANDDAUGHTER. AFTER ALL, YOU'RE GETTING ON A BIT, AREN'T YOU?
DON'T...!
YOU KNOW YOU'RE ALLOWED TO MAKE FUN OF ME, TOO?
I GET THE IDEA.
HMH.
GOING TO TELL ME ABOUT HER?

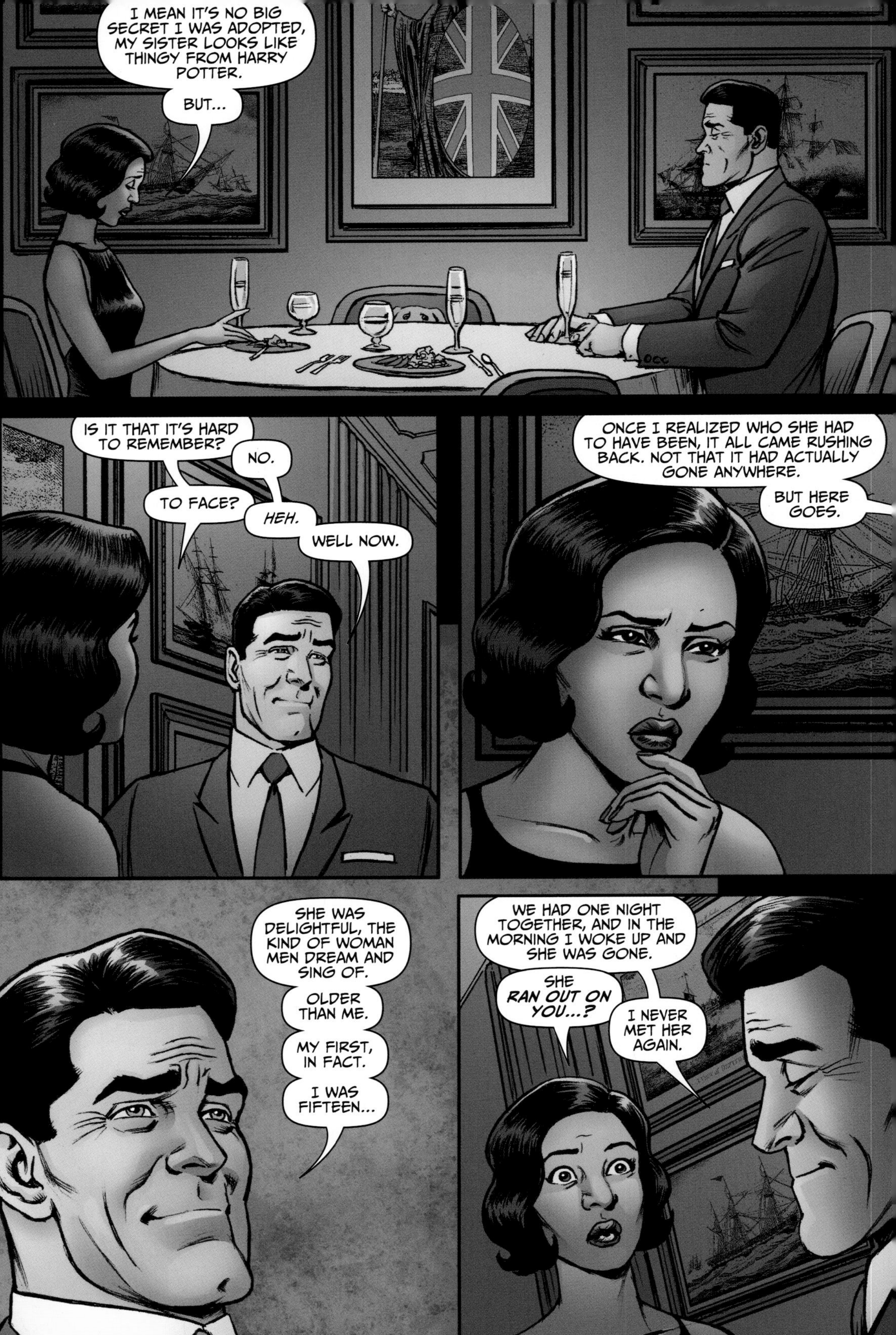
I MEAN IT'S NO BIG SECRET I WAS ADOPTED, MY SISTER LOOKS LIKE THINGY FROM HARRY POTTER.
BUT...
IS IT THAT IT'S HARD TO REMEMBER?
NO.
TO FACE?
HEH.
WELL NOW.
ONCE I REALIZED WHO SHE HAD TO HAVE BEEN, IT ALL CAME RUSHING BACK. NOT THAT IT HAD ACTUALLY GONE ANYWHERE.
BUT HERE GOES.
SHE WAS DELIGHTFUL, THE KIND OF WOMAN MEN DREAM AND SING OF.
OLDER THAN ME.
MY FIRST, IN FACT.
I WAS FIFTEEN...
WE HAD ONE NIGHT TOGETHER, AND IN THE MORNING I WOKE UP AND SHE WAS GONE.
SHE ***RAN OUT ON YOU...?***
I NEVER MET HER AGAIN.

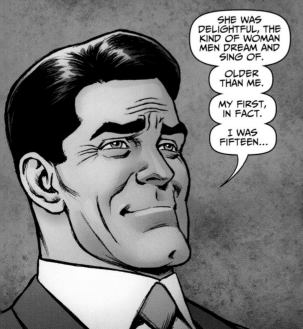

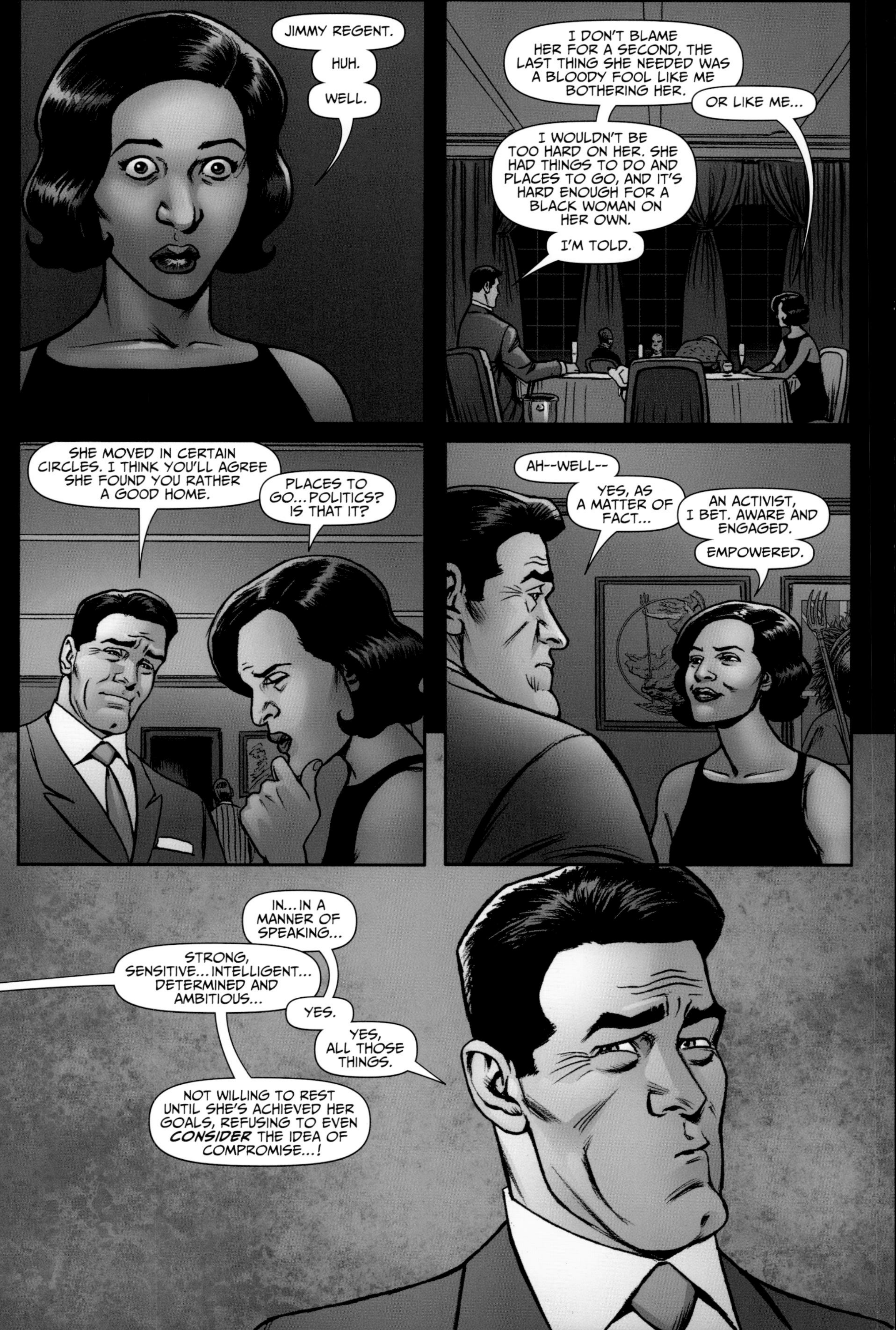
JIMMY REGENT.
HUH.
WELL.
I DON'T BLAME HER FOR A SECOND, THE LAST THING SHE NEEDED WAS A BLOODY FOOL LIKE ME BOTHERING HER.
OR LIKE ME...
I WOULDN'T BE TOO HARD ON HER. SHE HAD THINGS TO DO AND PLACES TO GO, AND IT'S HARD ENOUGH FOR A BLACK WOMAN ON HER OWN.
I'M TOLD.
SHE MOVED IN CERTAIN CIRCLES. I THINK YOU'LL AGREE SHE FOUND YOU RATHER A GOOD HOME.
PLACES TO GO... POLITICS? IS THAT IT?
AH--WELL--
YES, AS A MATTER OF FACT...
AN ACTIVIST, I BET. AWARE AND ENGAGED.
EMPOWERED.
IN... IN A MANNER OF SPEAKING...
STRONG, SENSITIVE... INTELLIGENT... DETERMINED AND AMBITIOUS...
YES.
YES, ALL THOSE THINGS.
NOT WILLING TO REST UNTIL SHE'S ACHIEVED HER GOALS, REFUSING TO EVEN CONSIDER THE IDEA OF COMPROMISE...!

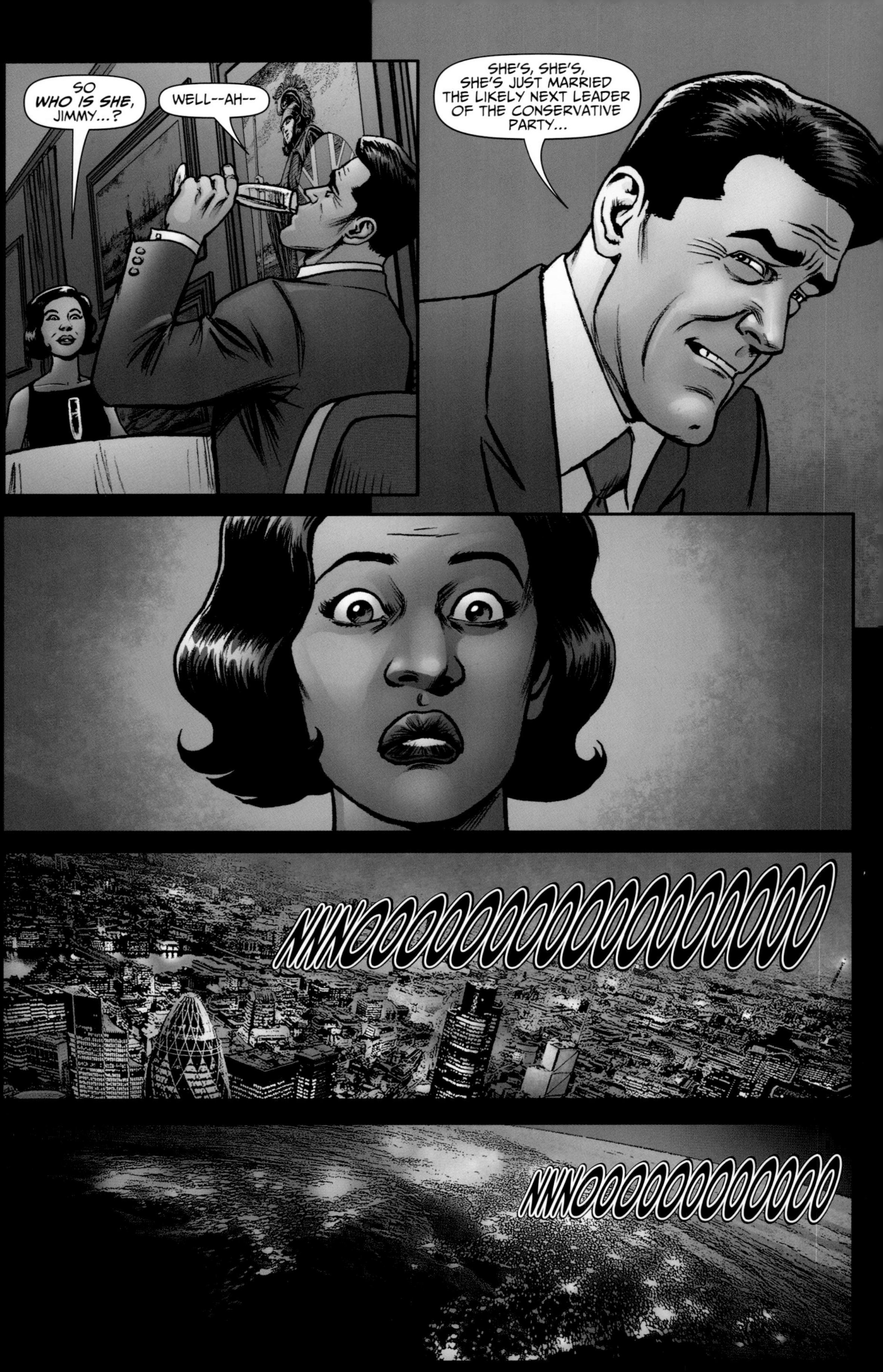
SO *WHO IS SHE,* JIMMY...?
WELL--AH--
SHE'S, SHE'S, SHE'S JUST MARRIED THE LIKELY NEXT LEADER OF THE CONSERVATIVE PARTY...
NNNOOOOOOOOOOOOOOOOOOO
NNNOOOOOOOOOOOOOO

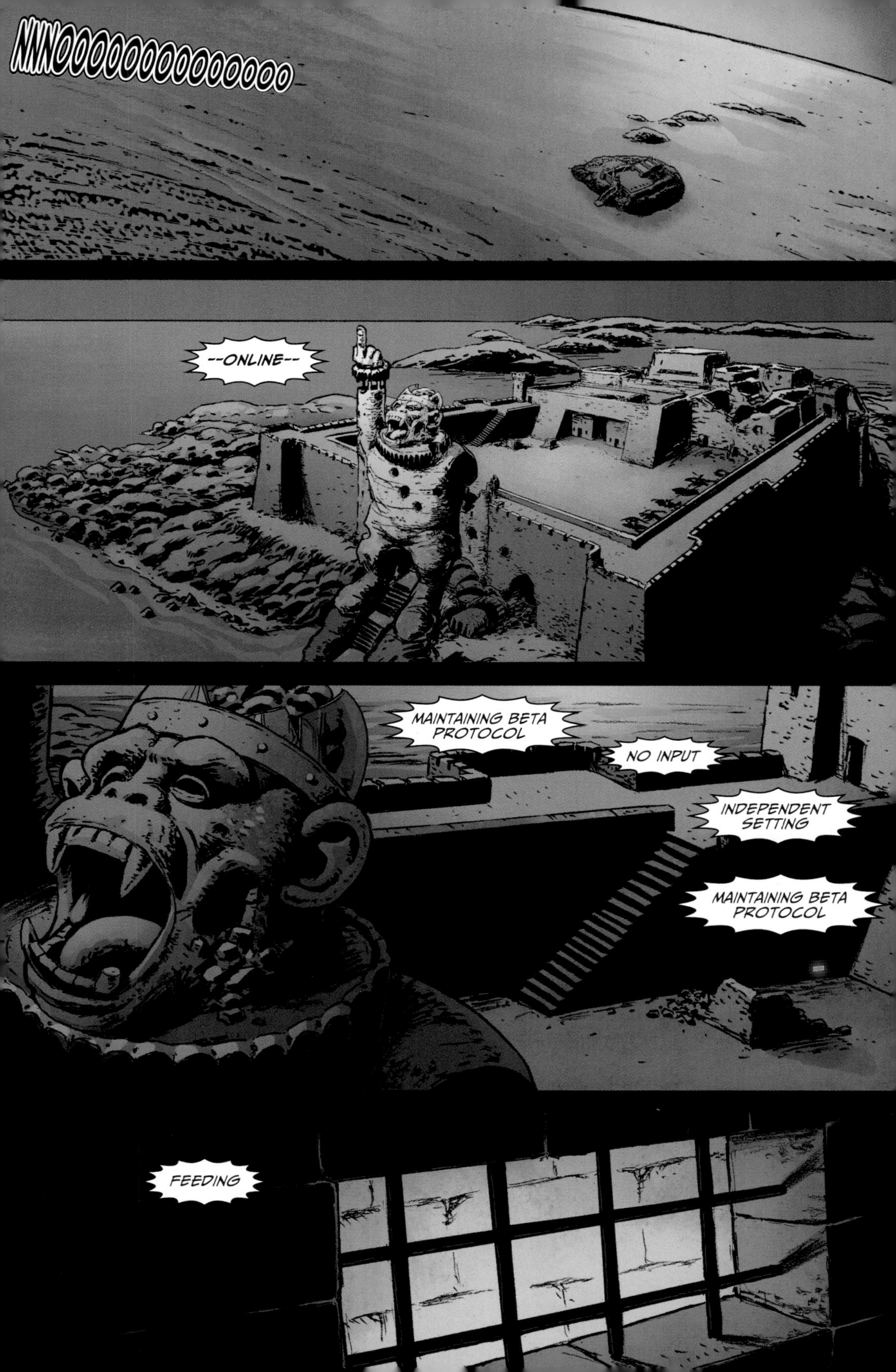
NNNOOOOOOOOOOOOOOO
--ONLINE--
MAINTAINING BETA PROTOCOL
NO INPUT
INDEPENDENT SETTING
MAINTAINING BETA PROTOCOL
FEEDING

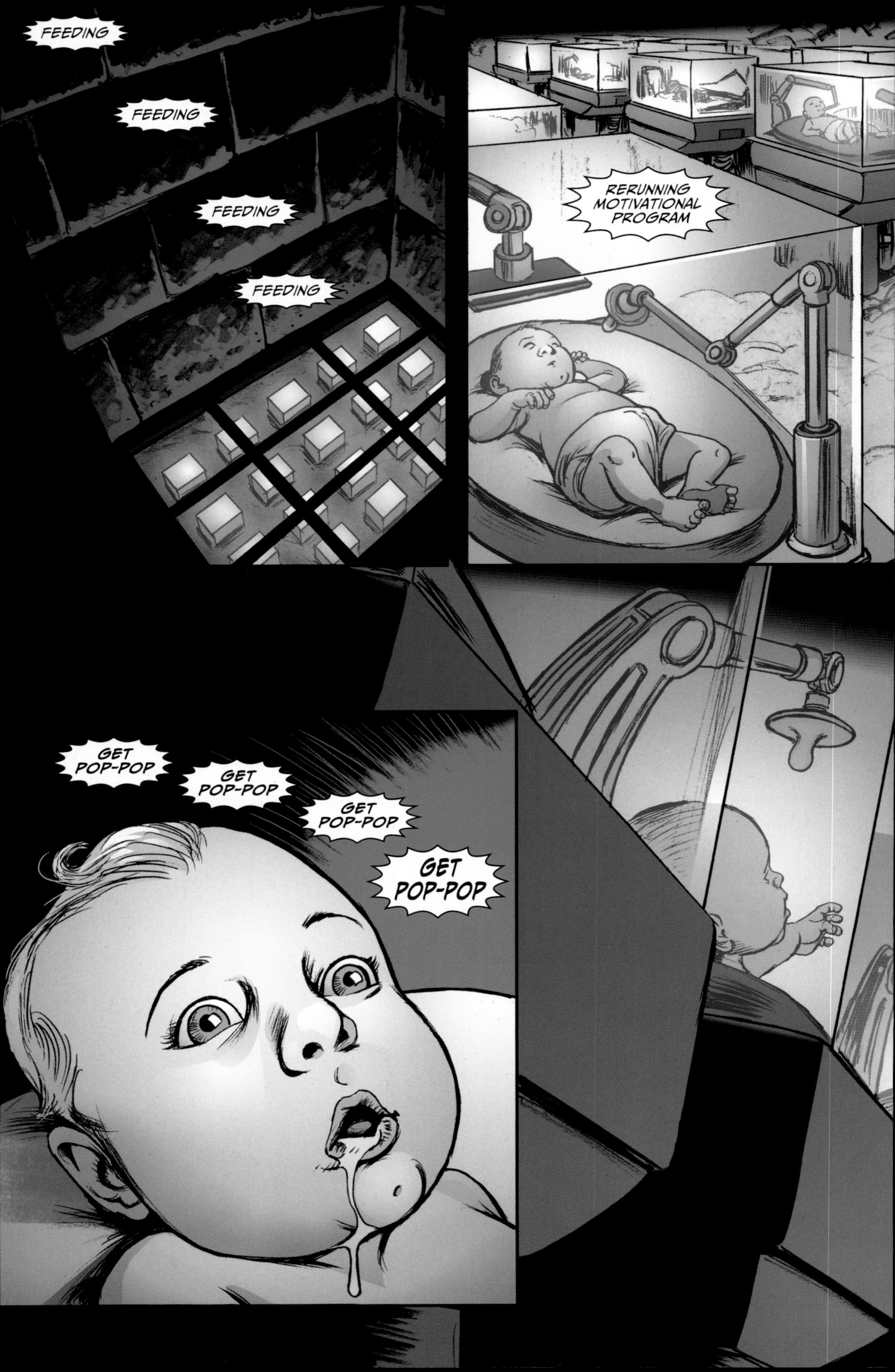
FEEDING
FEEDING
FEEDING
FEEDING
RERUNNING MOTIVATIONAL PROGRAM
GET POP-POP
GET POP-POP
GET POP-POP
GET POP-POP

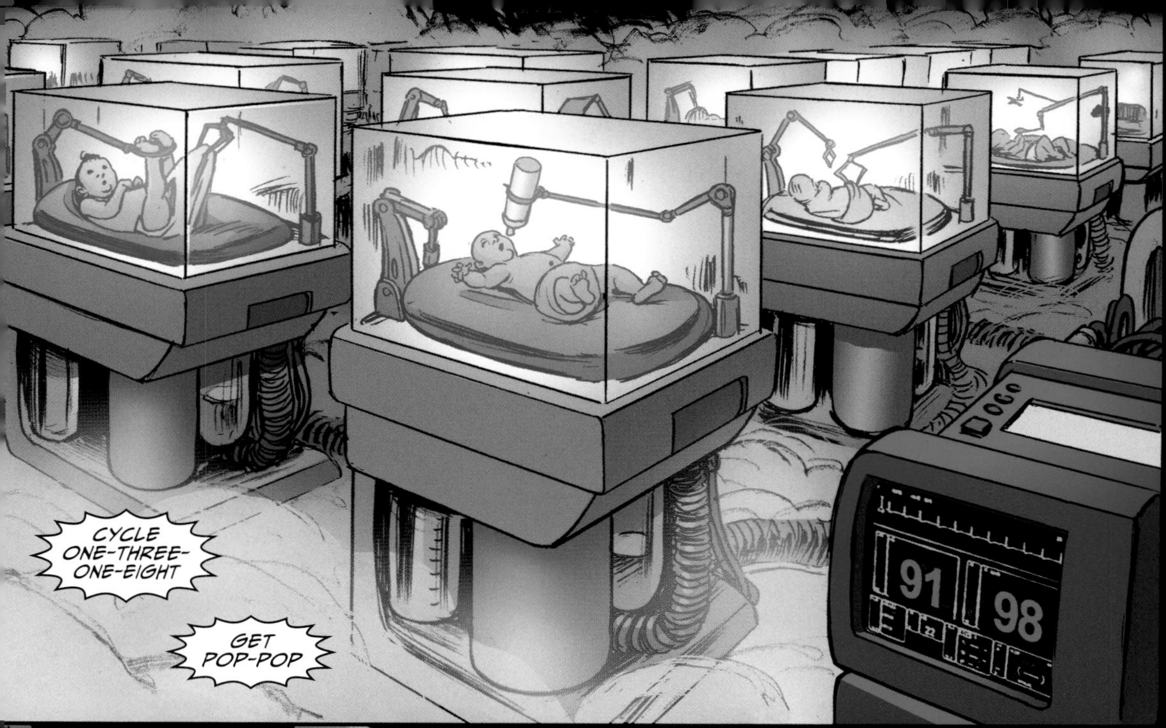
CYCLE ONE-THREE-ONE-EIGHT
GET POP-POP
91
98

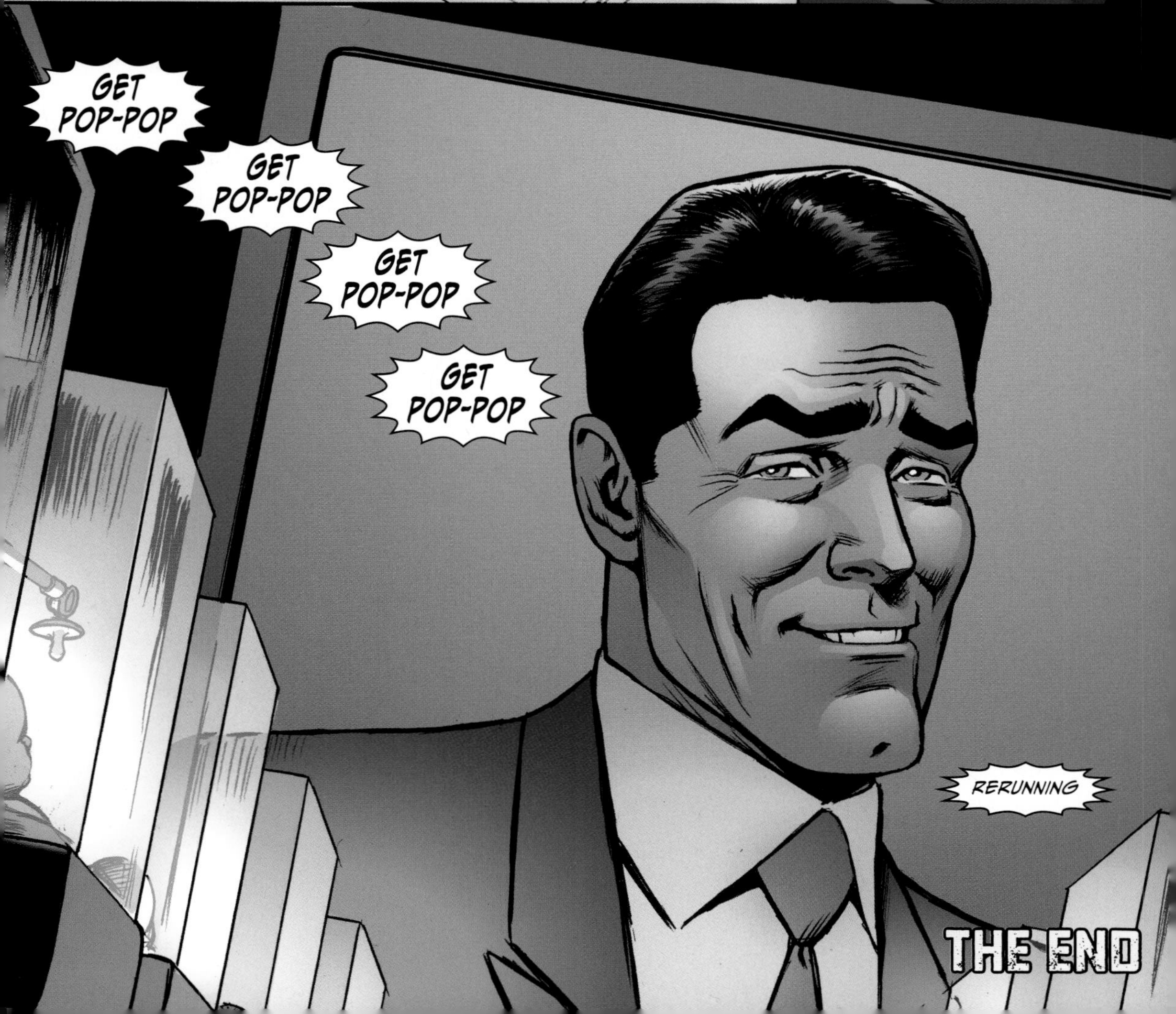
GET POP-POP
GET POP-POP
GET POP-POP
GET POP-POP
RERUNNING
THE END

JIMMY'S BASTARDS

COVER GALLERY

Issue 6 cover
ANDY CLARKE w/ JOSE VILLARRUBIA

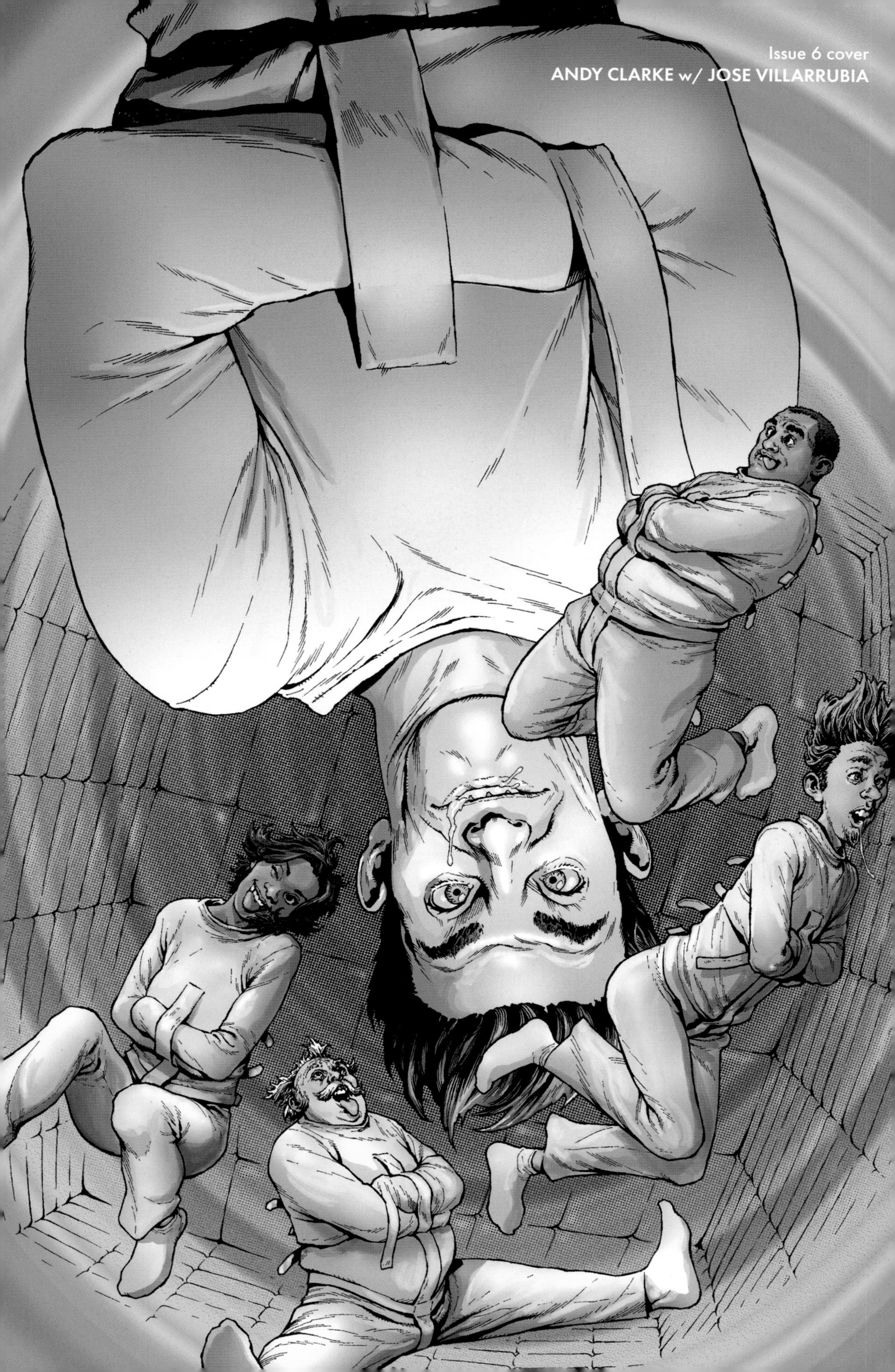

Issue 7 cover
ANDY CLARKE w/ JOSE VILLARRUBIA

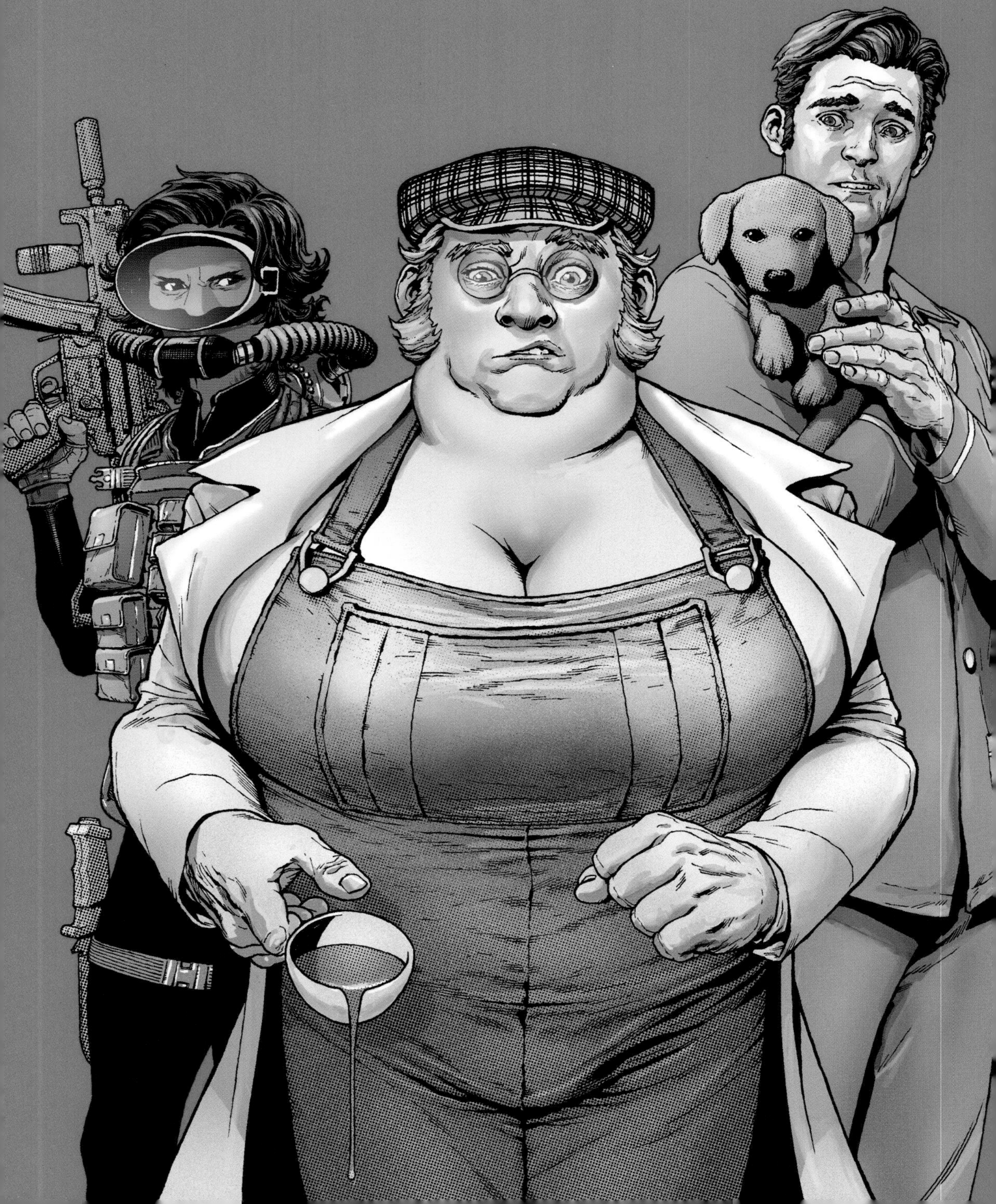

Issue 8 cover
ANDY CLARKE w/ JOSE VILLARRUBIA

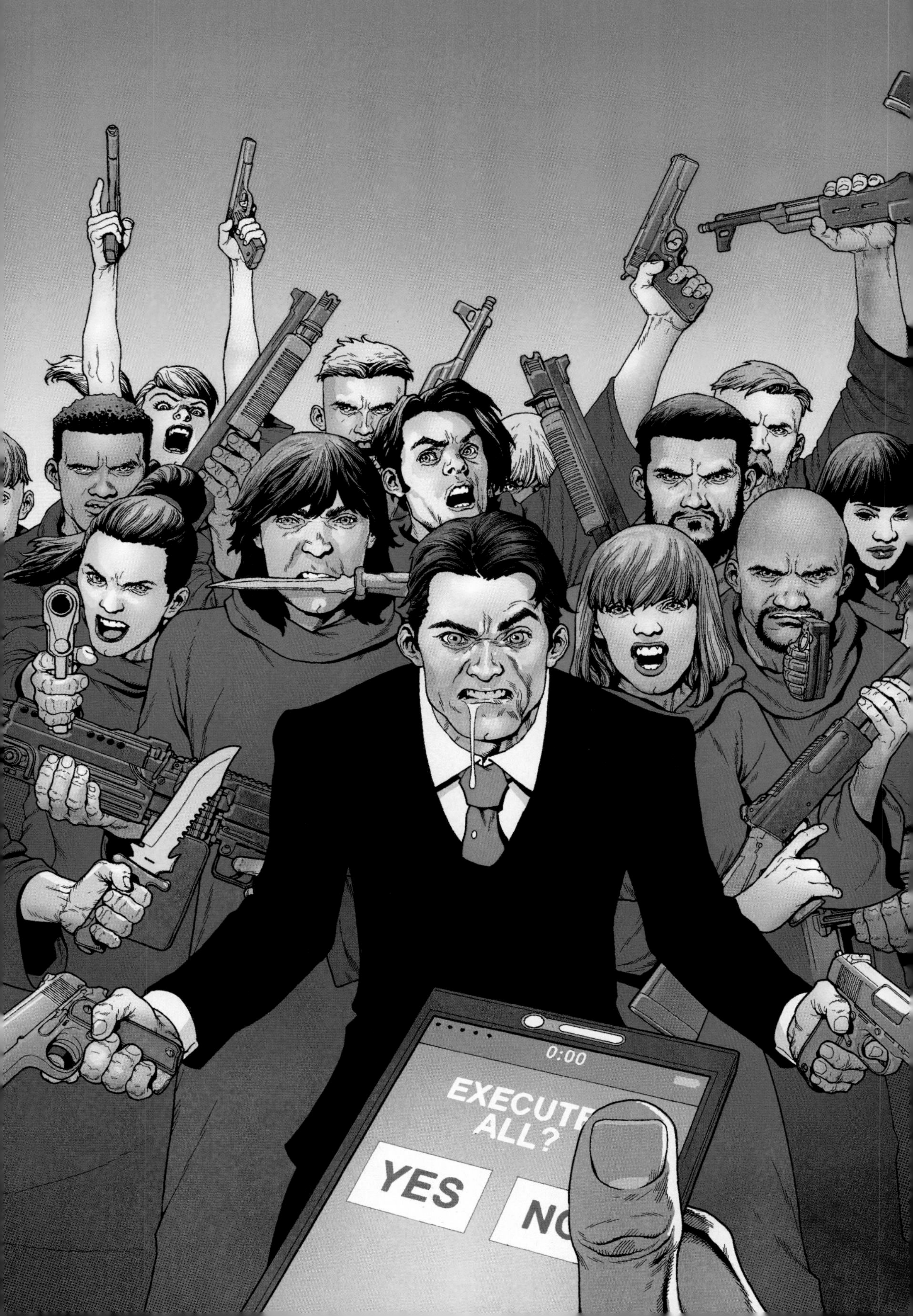
0:00
EXECUTE
ALL?
YES
NO

Issue 9 cover
ANDY CLARKE w/ JOSE VILLARRUBIA

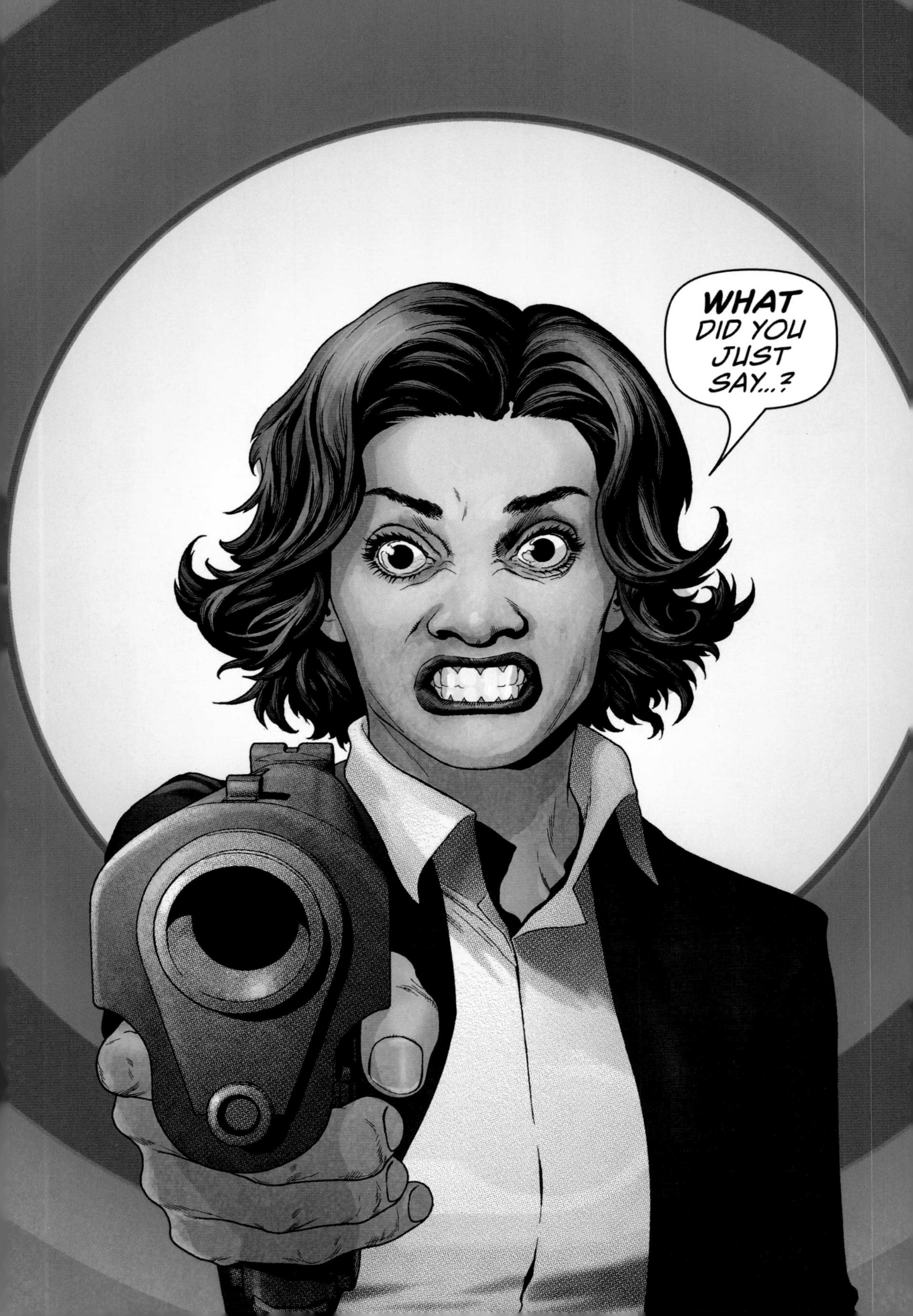
WHAT DID YOU JUST SAY...?

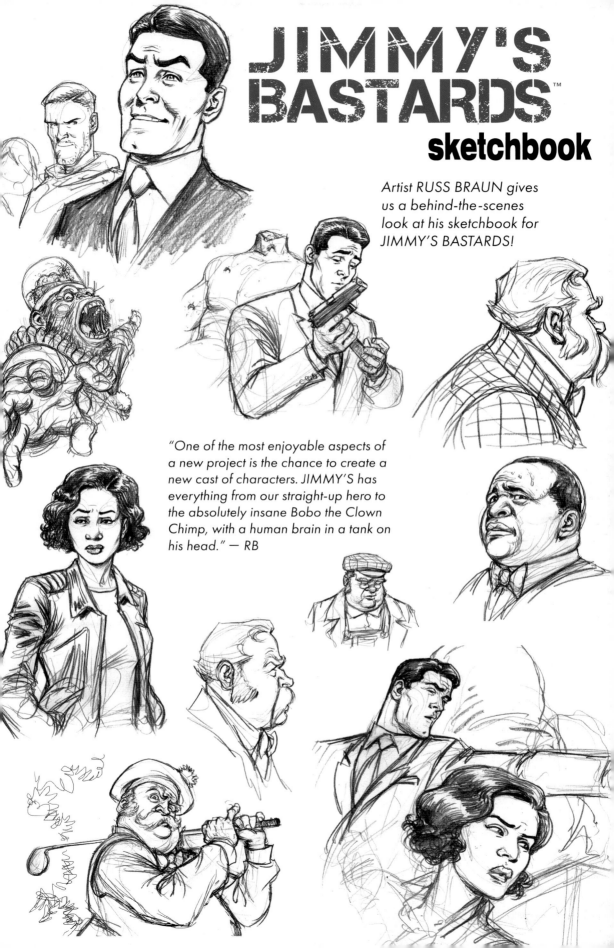

JIMMY'S BASTARDS™

sketchbook

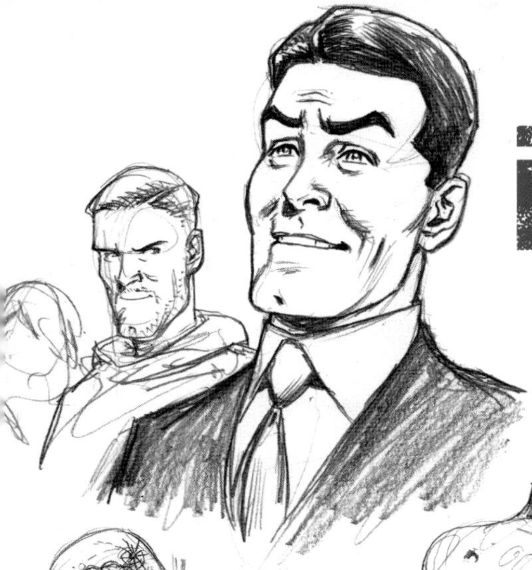

Artist RUSS BRAUN gives us a behind-the-scenes look at his sketchbook for JIMMY'S BASTARDS!

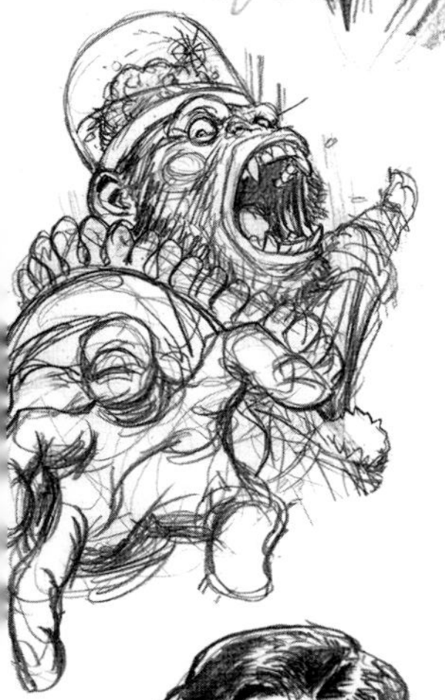

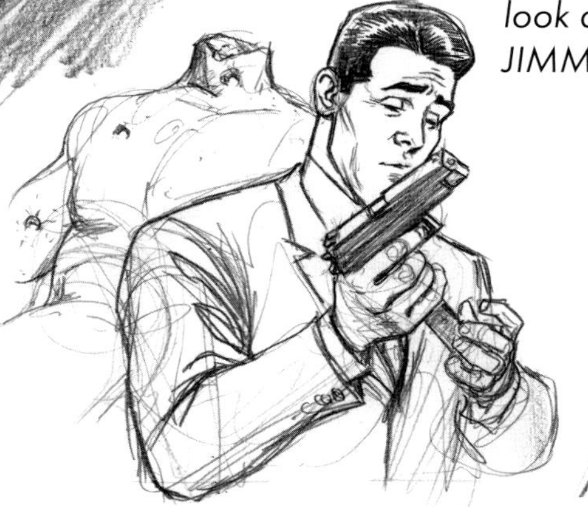

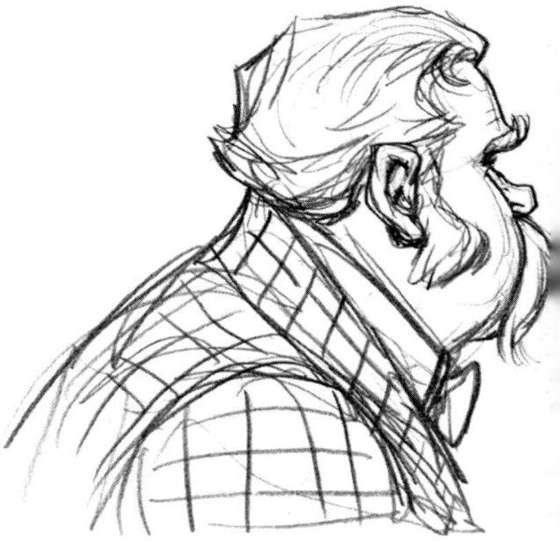

"One of the most enjoyable aspects of a new project is the chance to create a new cast of characters. JIMMY'S has everything from our straight-up hero to the absolutely insane Bobo the Clown Chimp, with a human brain in a tank on his head." — RB

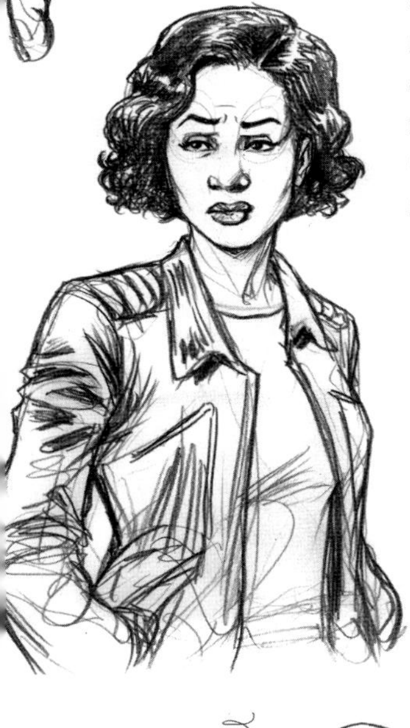

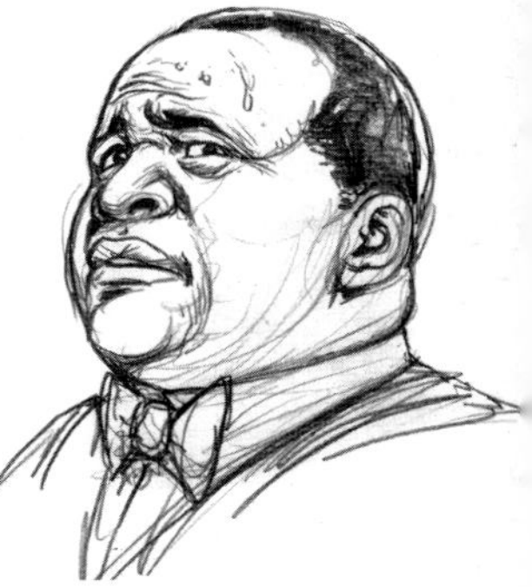

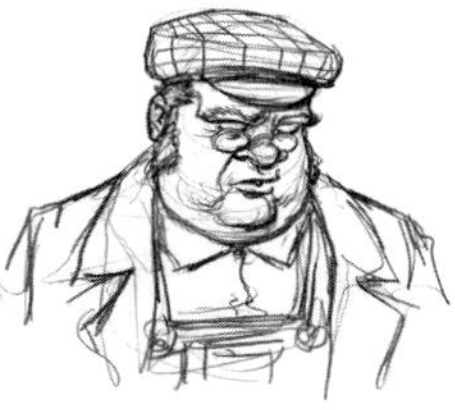

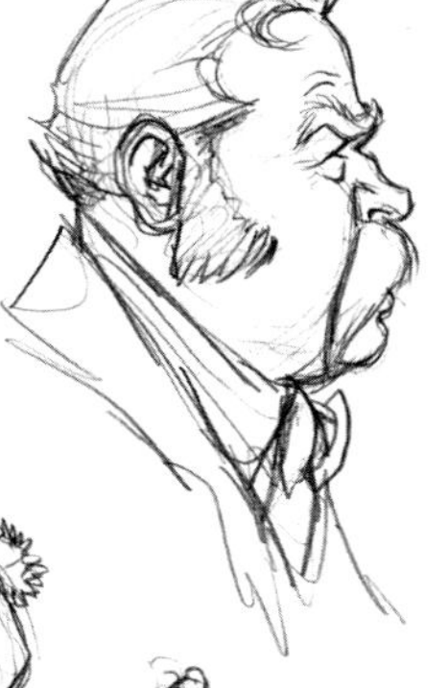

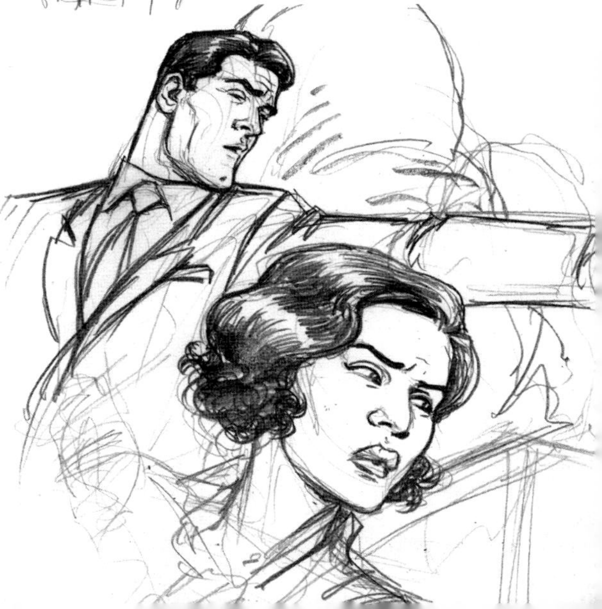

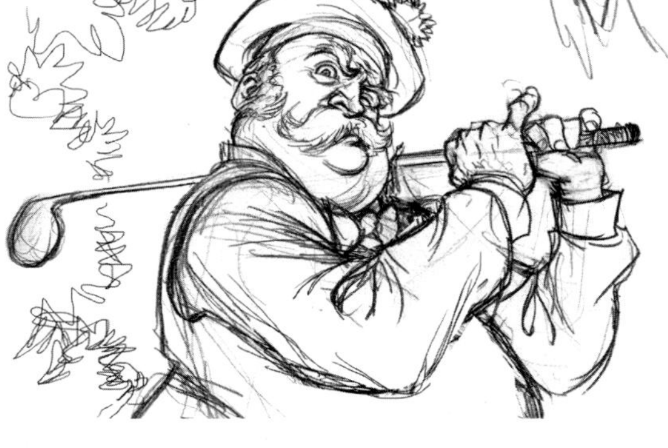

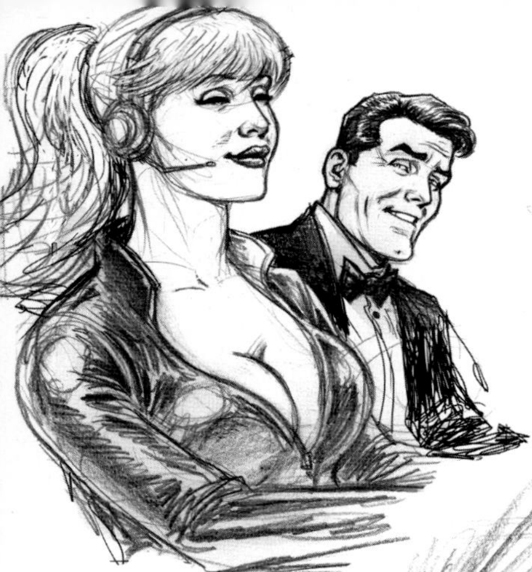

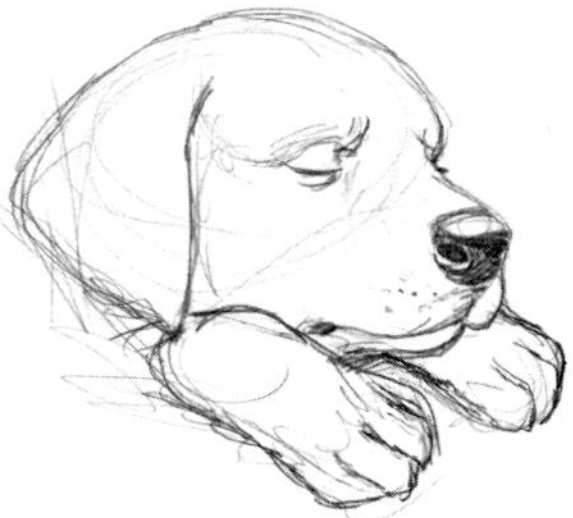

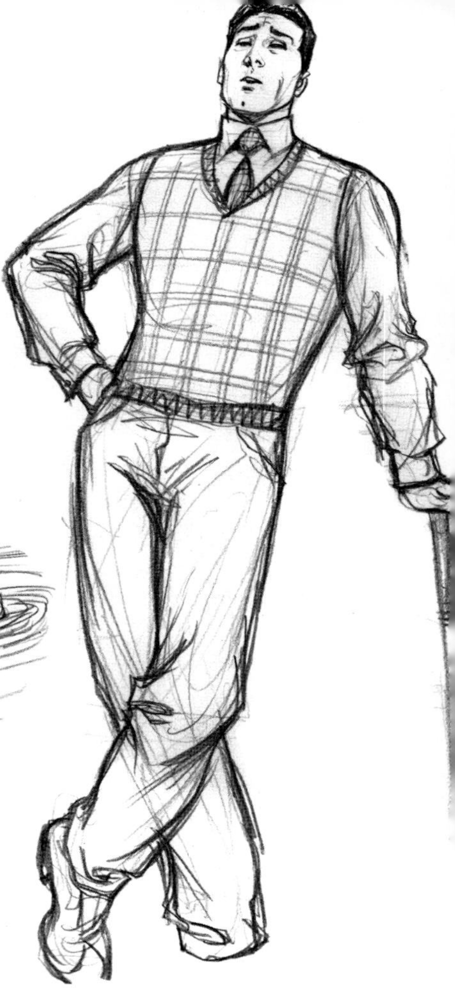

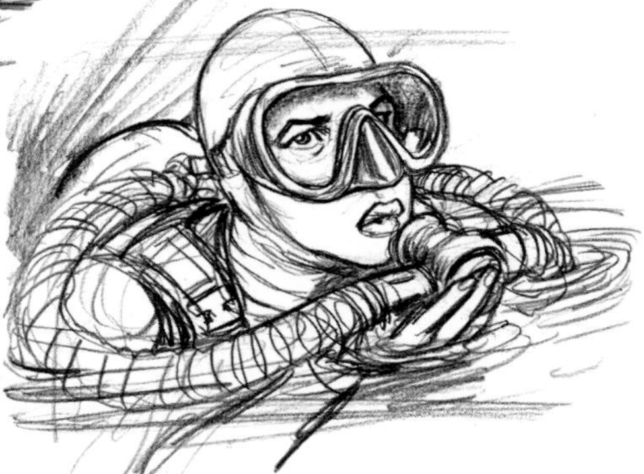

"Jimmy himself is basically a composite of all the Bonds, a healthy dose of Cary Grant wryness and class, and a touch of classic Superman for bone structure. Add on to that the challenge of making Jimmy's offspring all reminiscent of Daddy, with at least his blue eyes and cleft chin, and you can see why I had to keep Jimmy cut from the classic hero cloth."
— RB

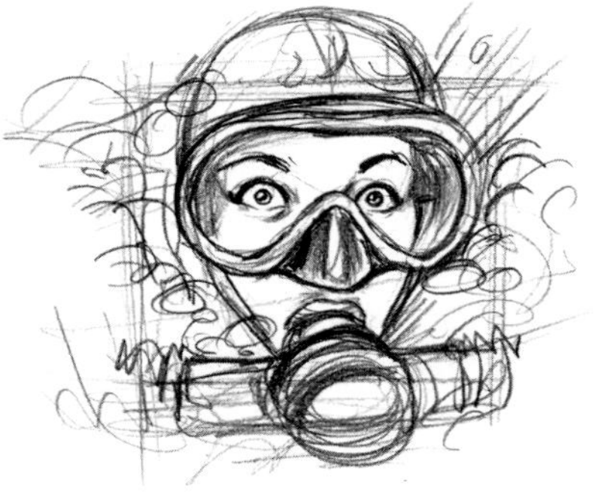

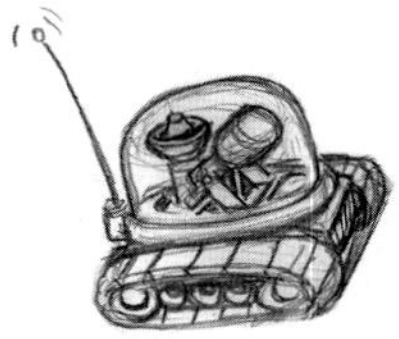

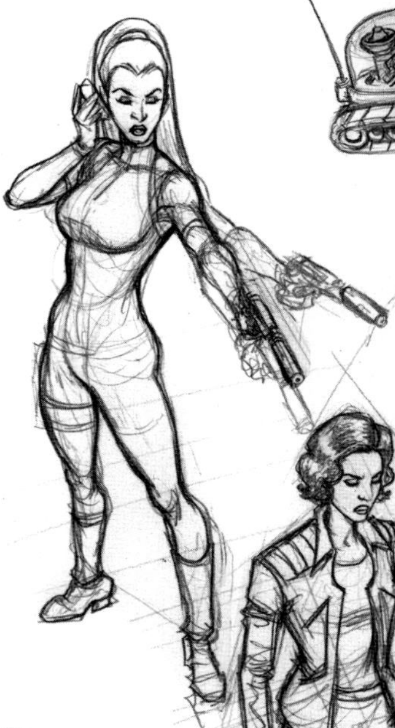

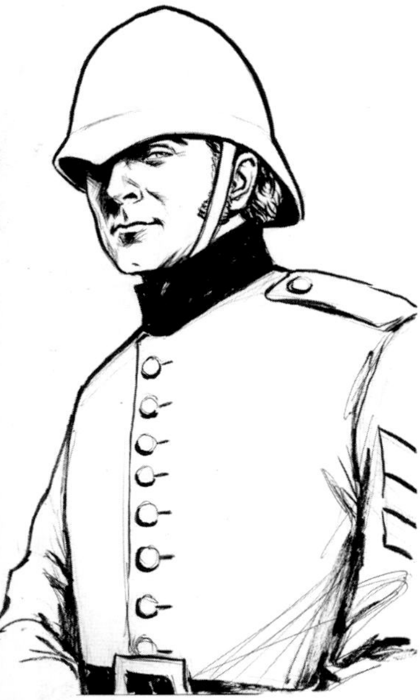

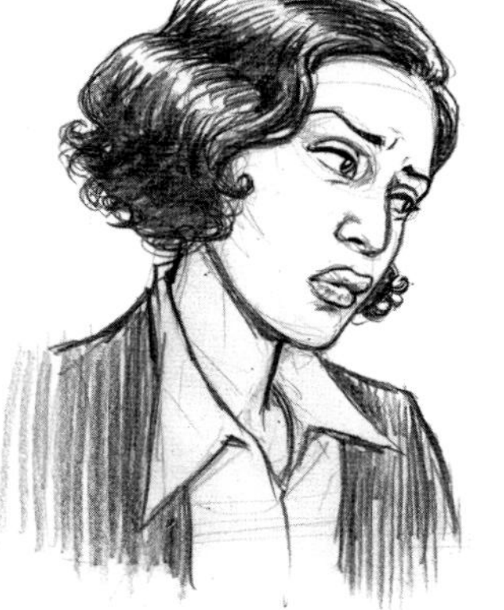

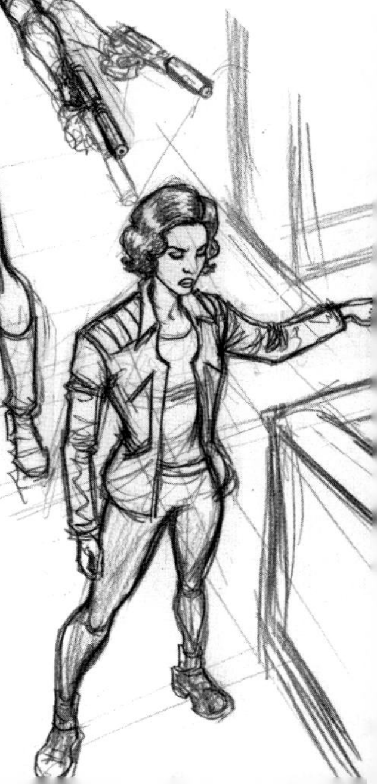

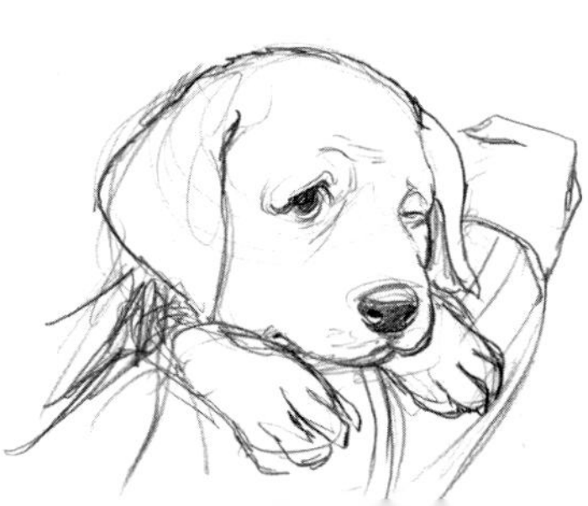

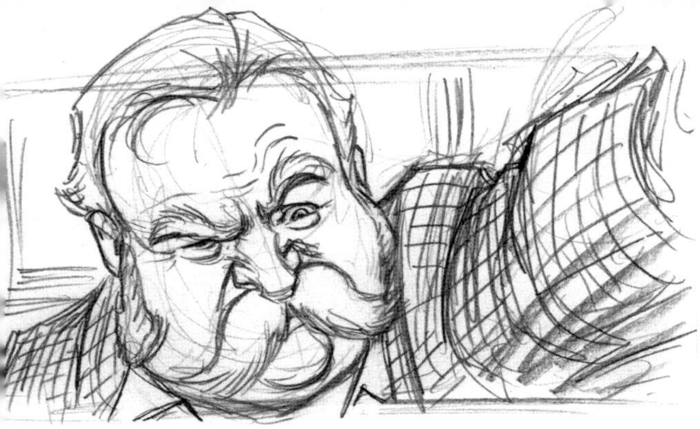

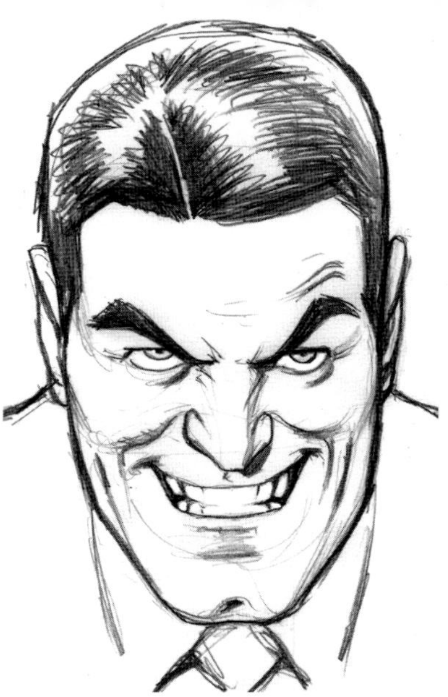

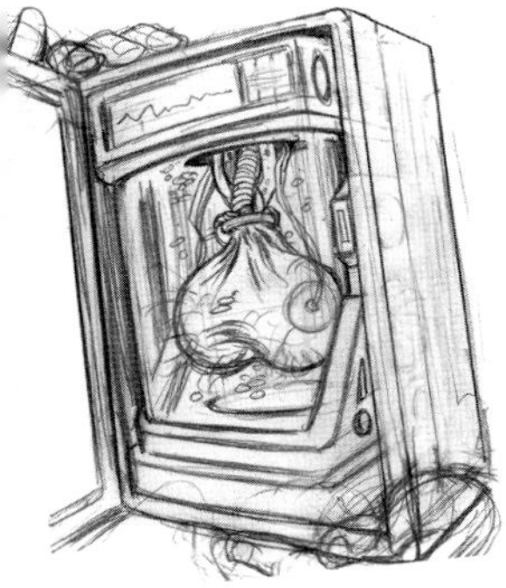

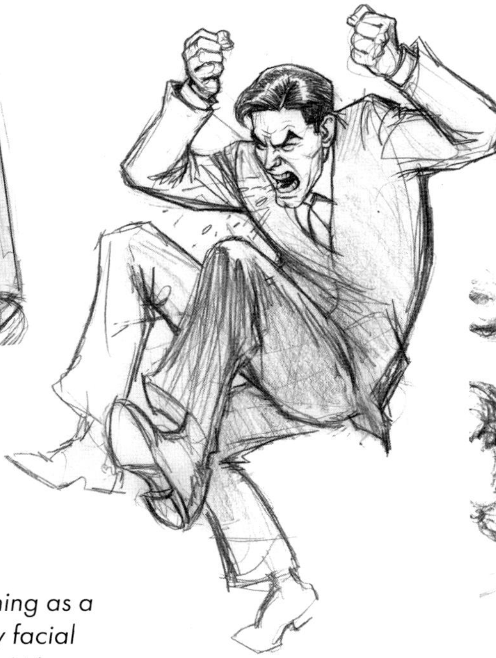

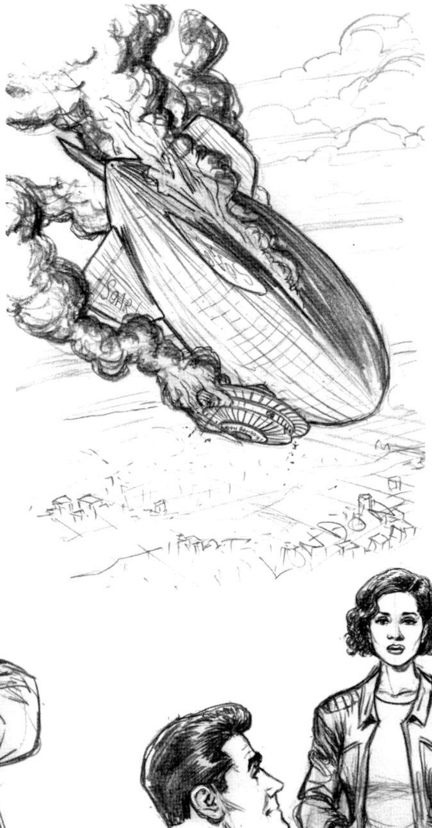

"If I'm known for anything as a comics artist, it's for my facial expressions and acting. It's my favorite aspect of storytelling, and one Garth makes me work hard on, calling for extremes and subtleties, and occasionally asking for warring emotions on one face." — RB

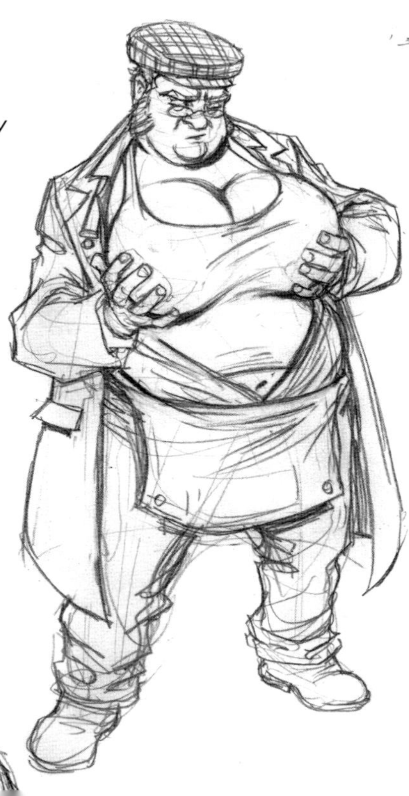

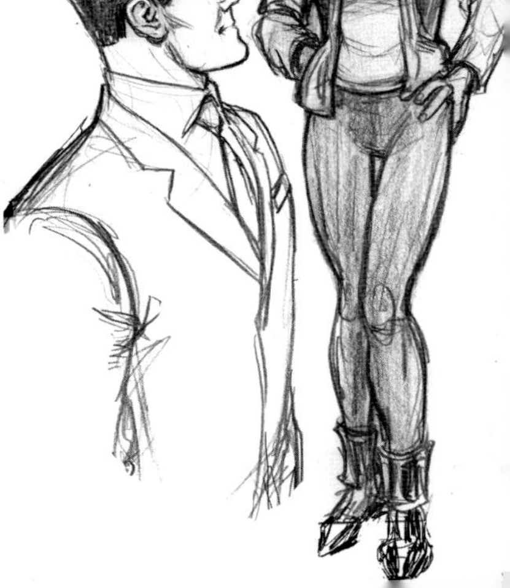

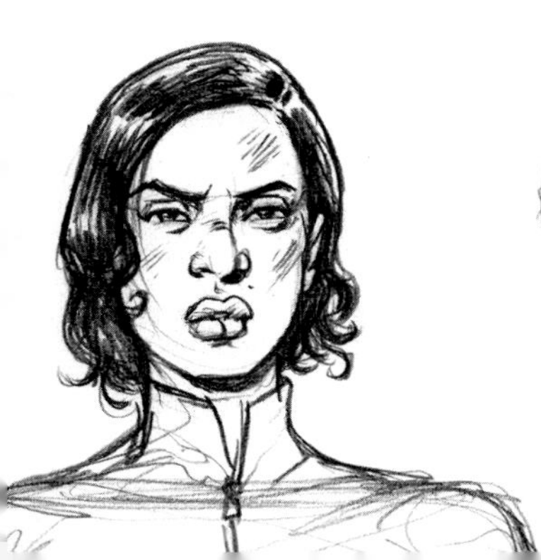

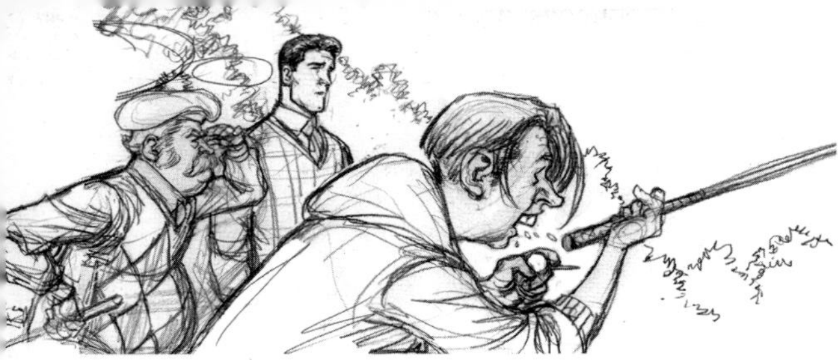

"One aspect I'm not as keen on, but is just as important to the story, is world building. In this case, we're adapting a real-world London to our story, with lots of research and lots of artistic license taken. A couple hundred bastards inside St. Paul's Cathedral is a visual that's key to the story, as is a mass of the same bastards being slaughtered on a spiral staircase, a giant statue of Bobo built into a fortress on a rocky isle, a bevy of gender swapped folks having at it in Trafalgar Square...you get the point—not easy, but crucial to the story." — RB

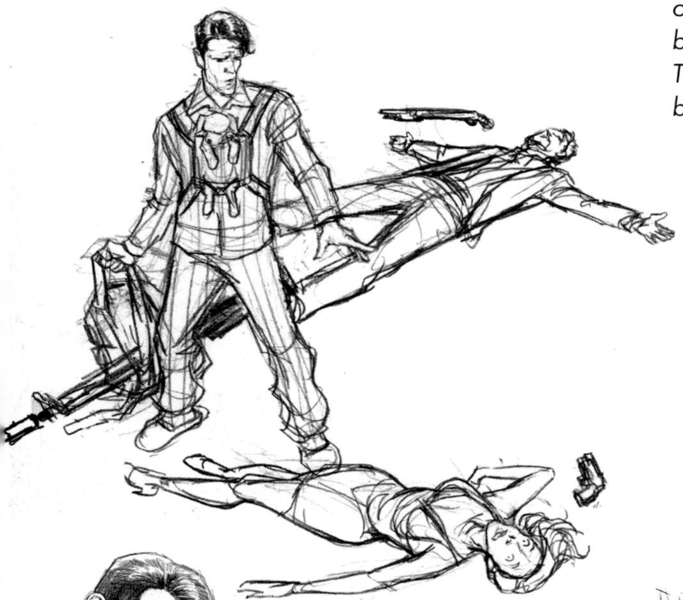

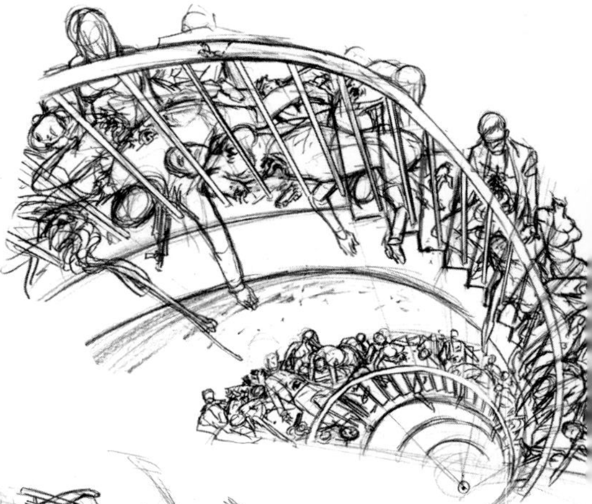

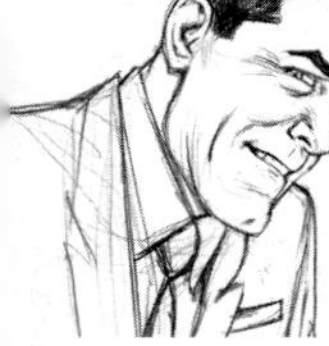

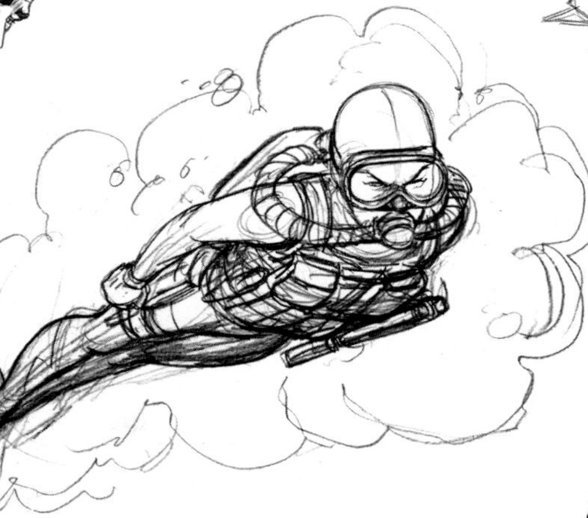

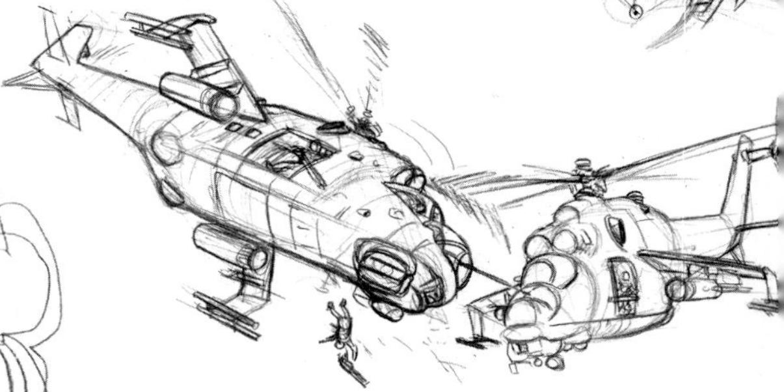

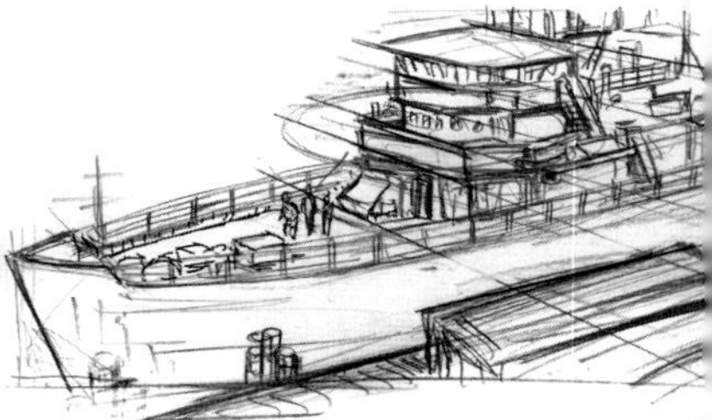

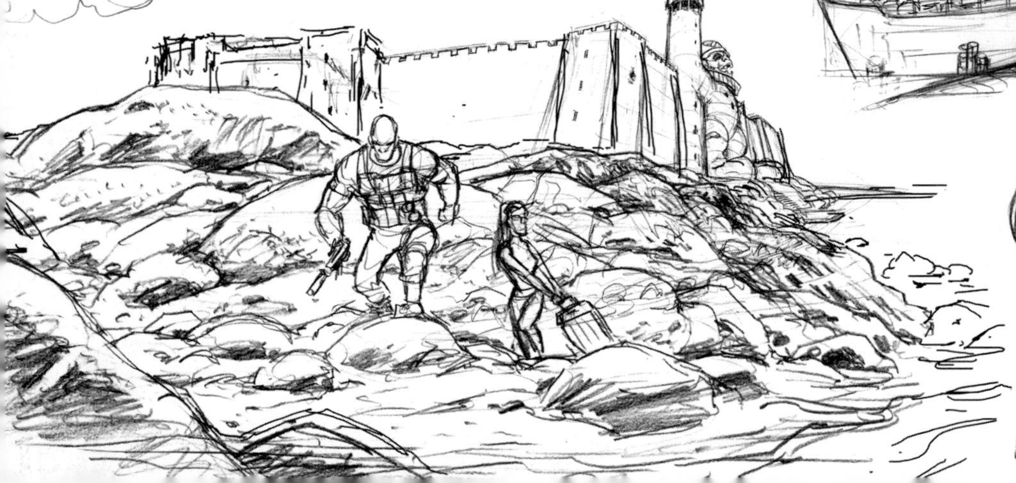

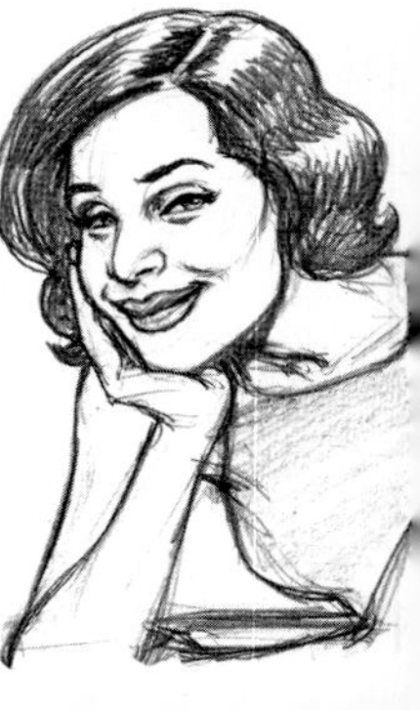

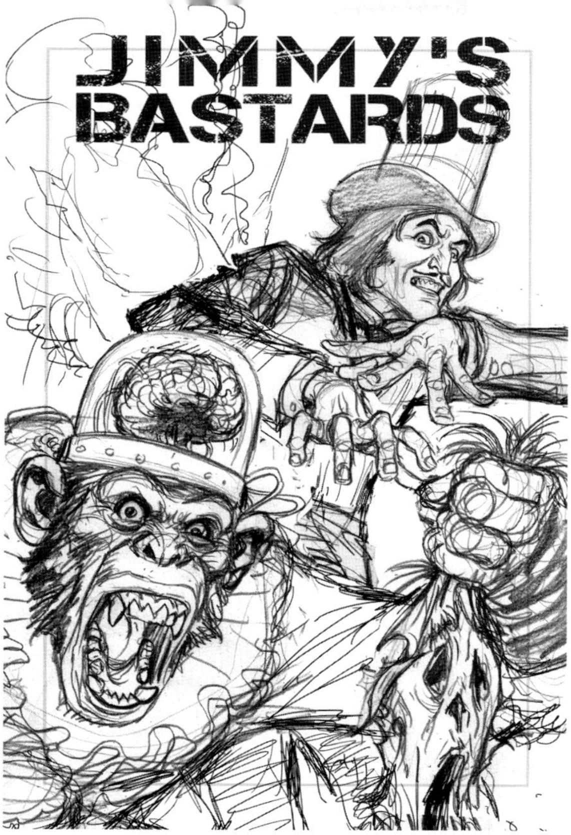
JIMMY'S
BASTARDS

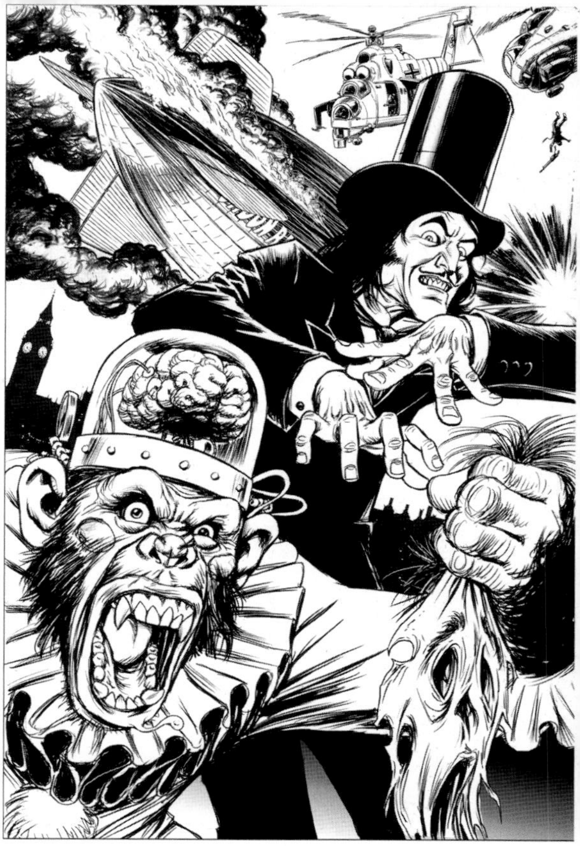

"The way I work out a page is odd, I suppose. I do little scribbled thumbnails of the basic page shape and then go right into the sketchbook, where I'm most comfortable, to figure things out. Lots of individual drawings working in the same direction." — RB

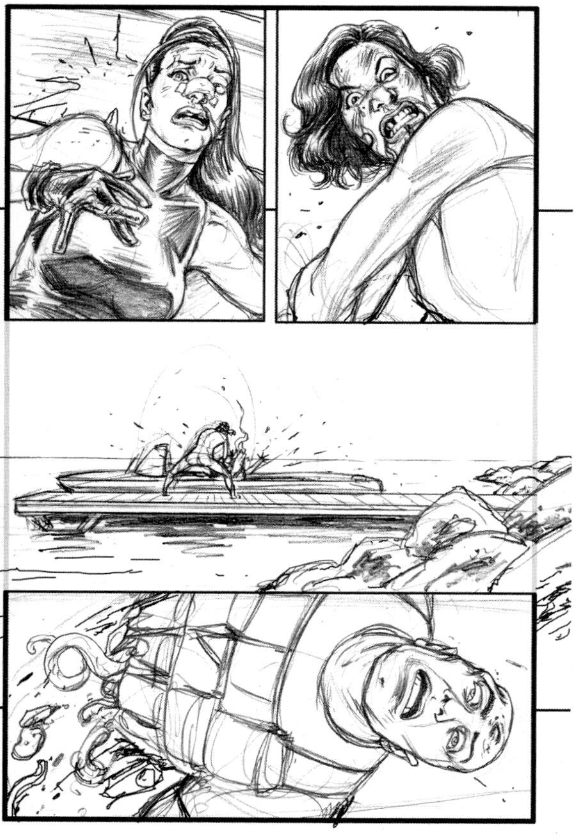

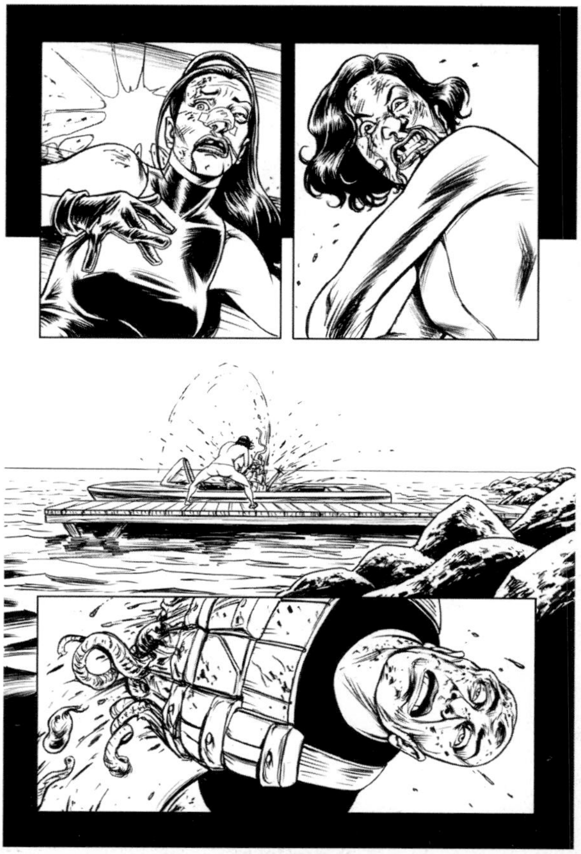

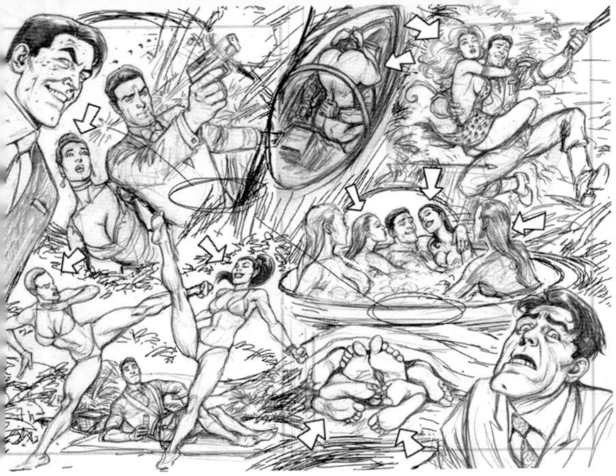

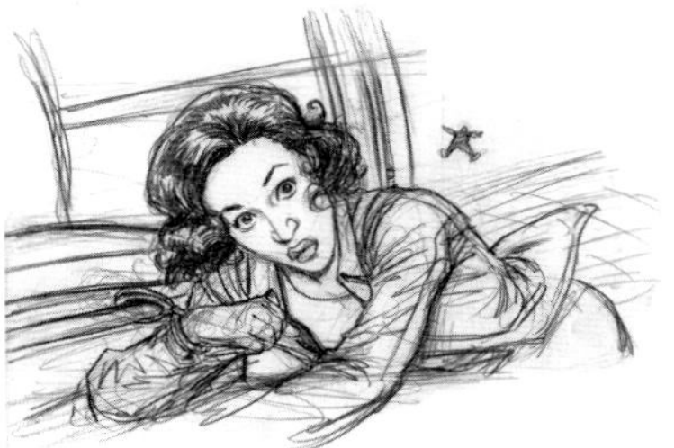

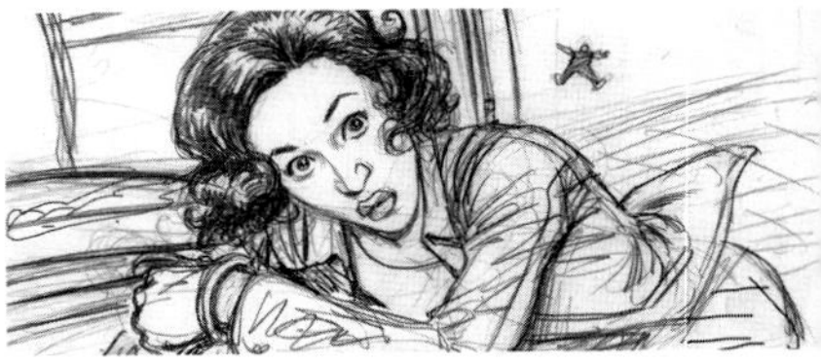

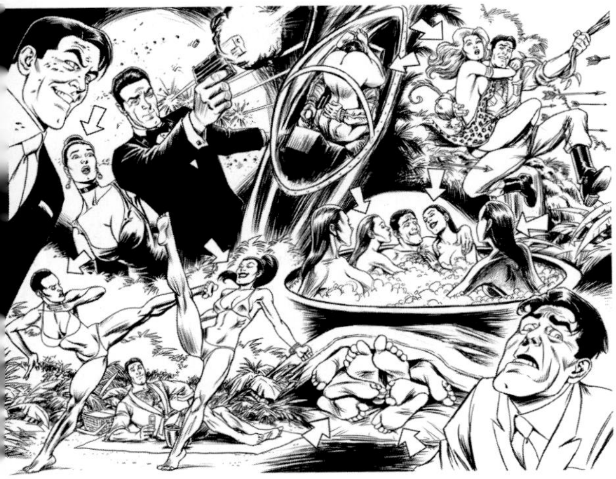

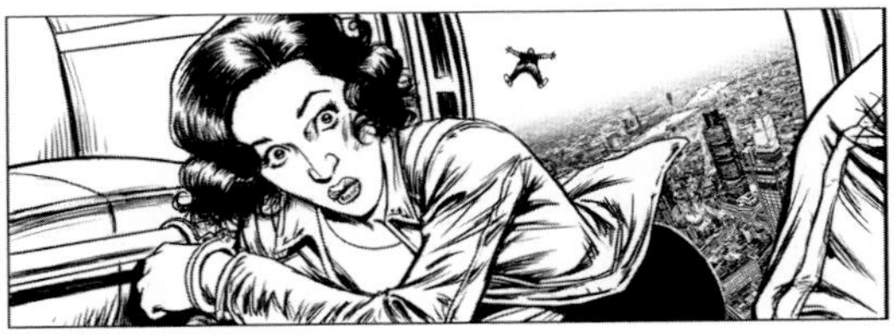

"The next step is to scan everything in...take all of those ingredients and make them into a carefully assembled layout, zooming in or out, tilting or even flopping an image to get the storytelling right." — RB

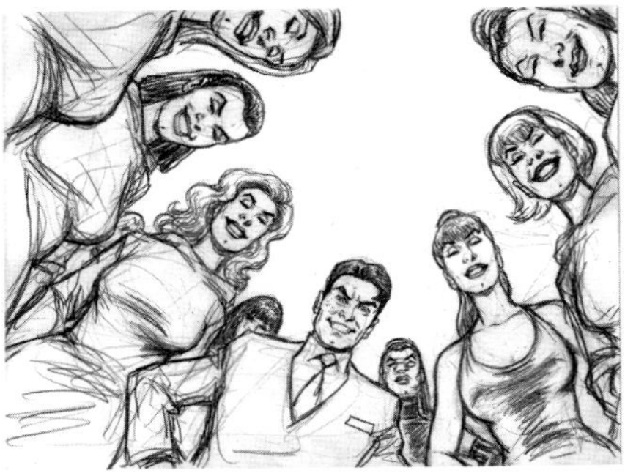

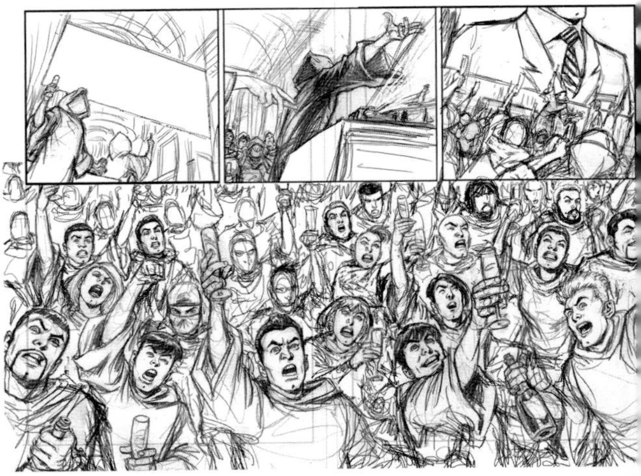

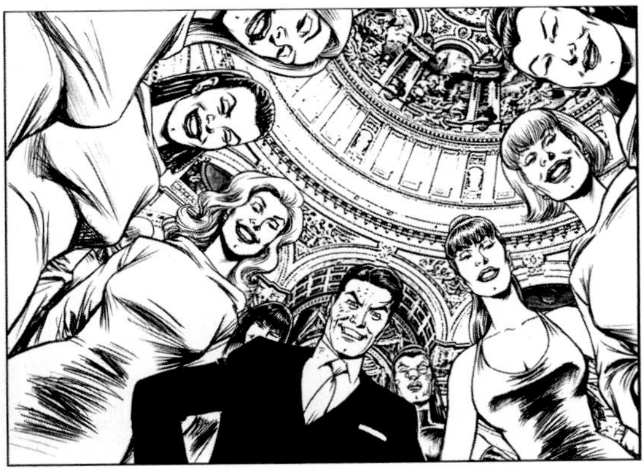

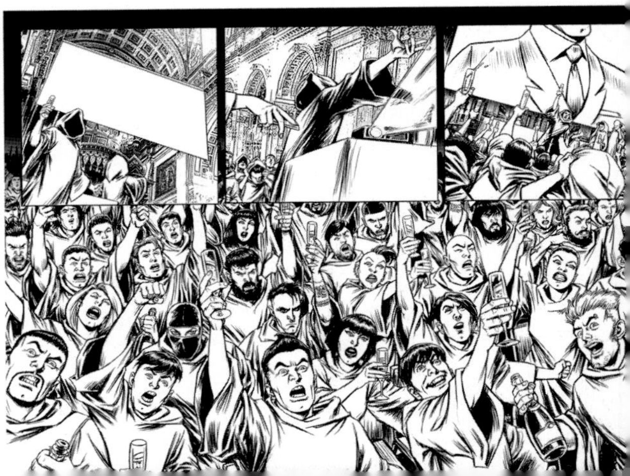

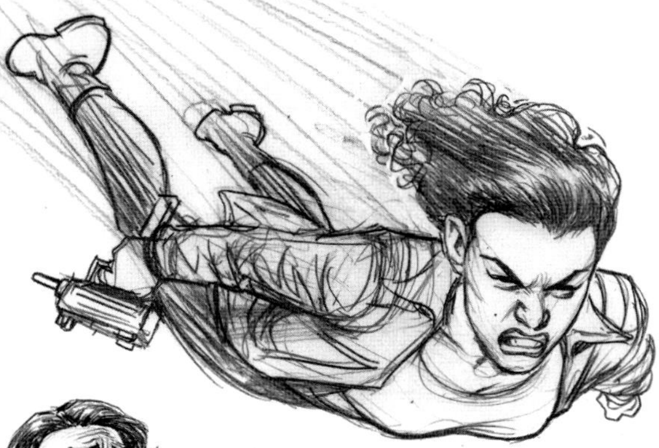

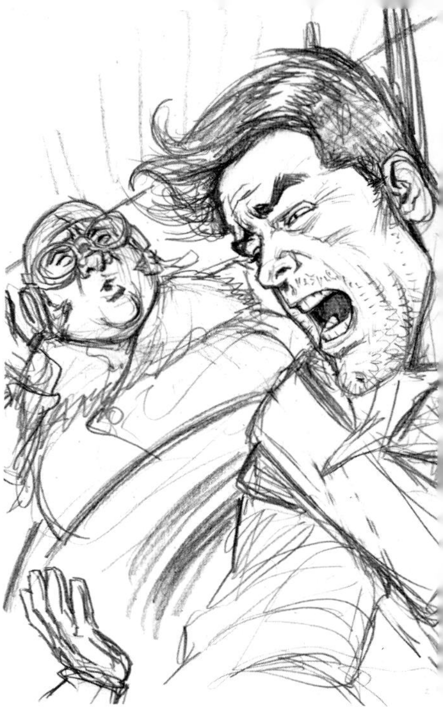

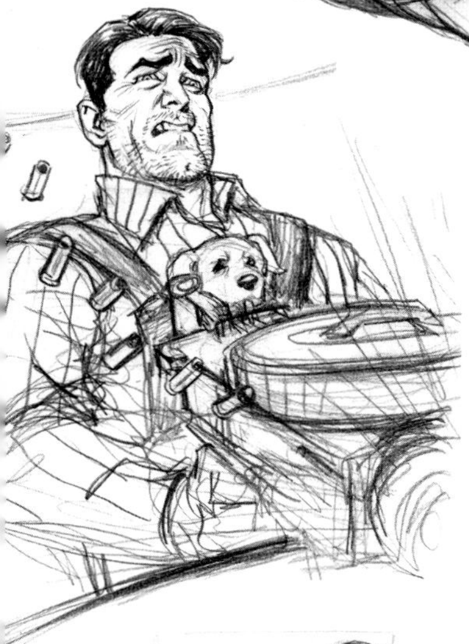

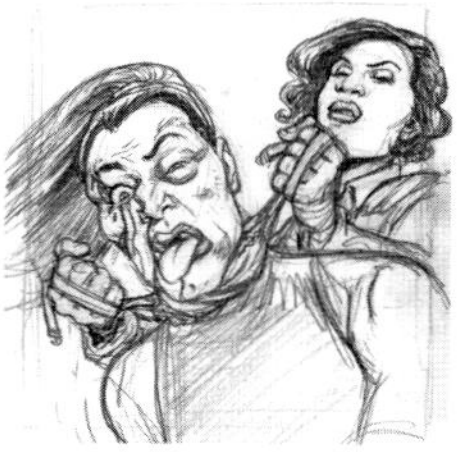

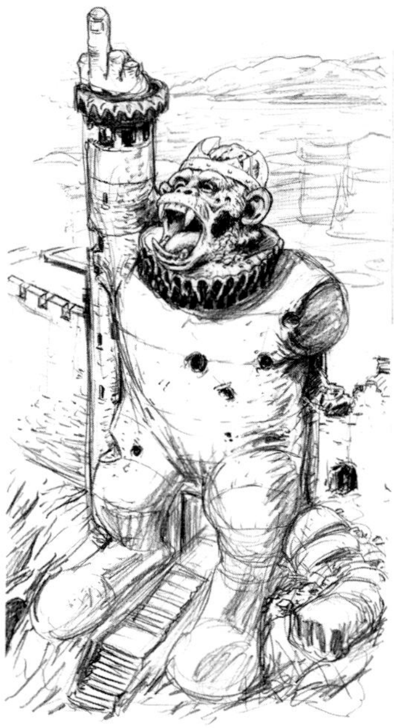

"I print out the layout to page size and do a finished, rendered pencil to unify it all into one coherent world. My finishes are those rendered pencil pages scanned in, darkened and cleaned up in Photoshop. At that stage, I can drop in background elements, textures, etc.—things like posters and framed artwork, details that give the environment a history and a little life." — RB

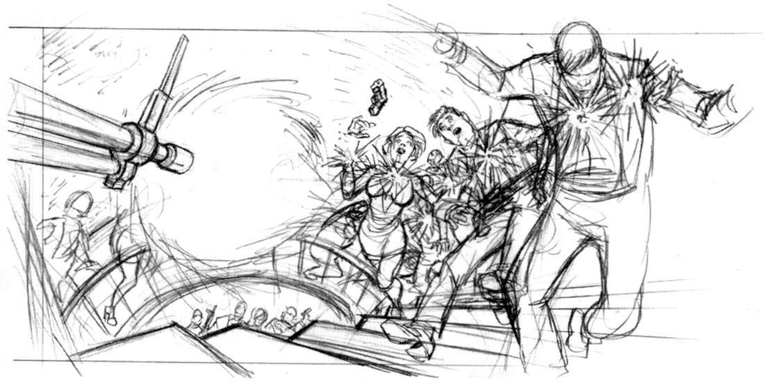

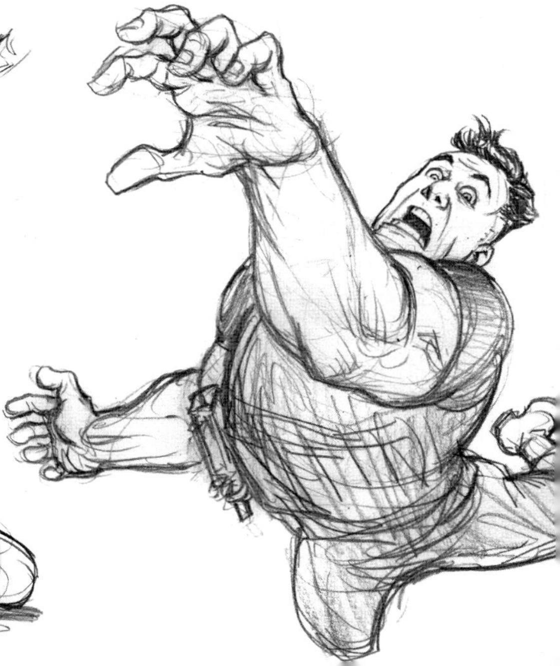

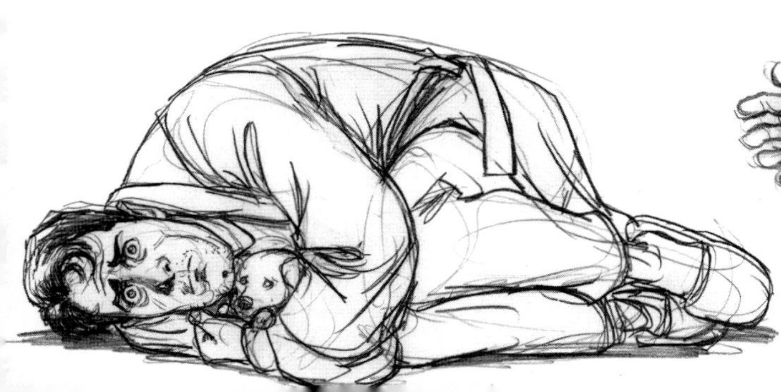

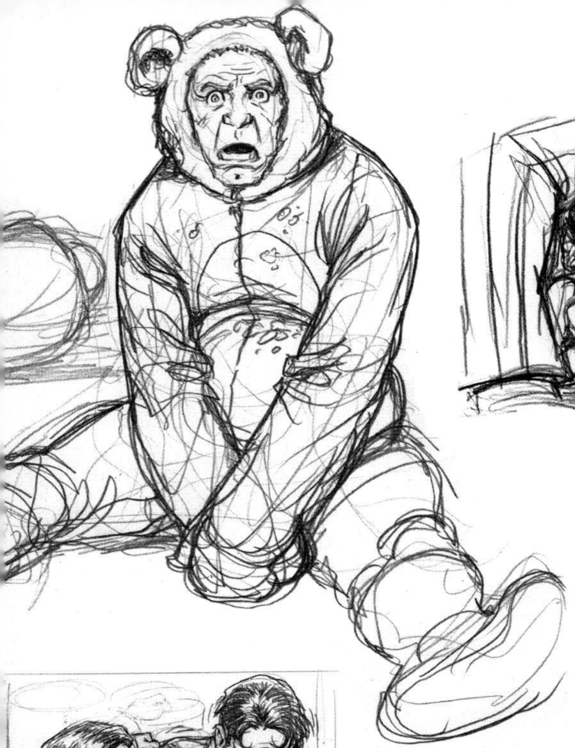

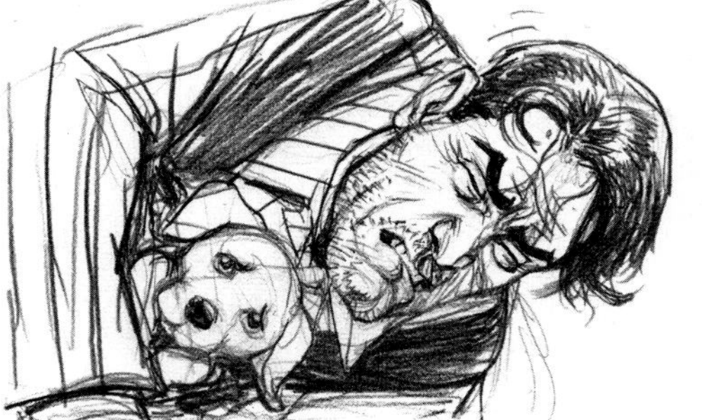

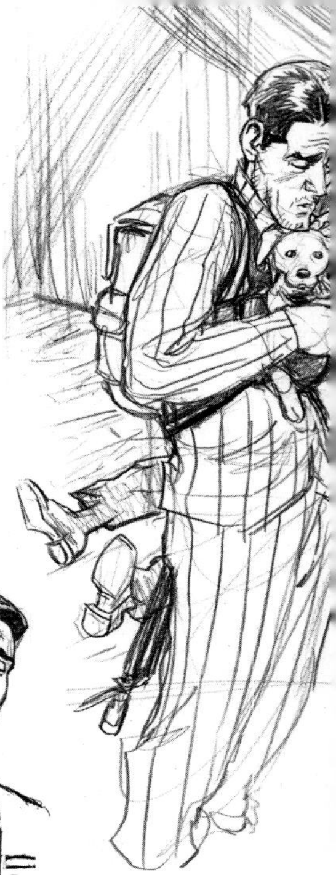

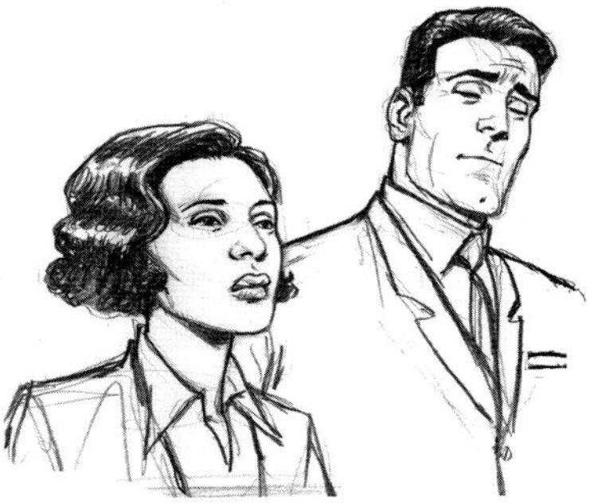

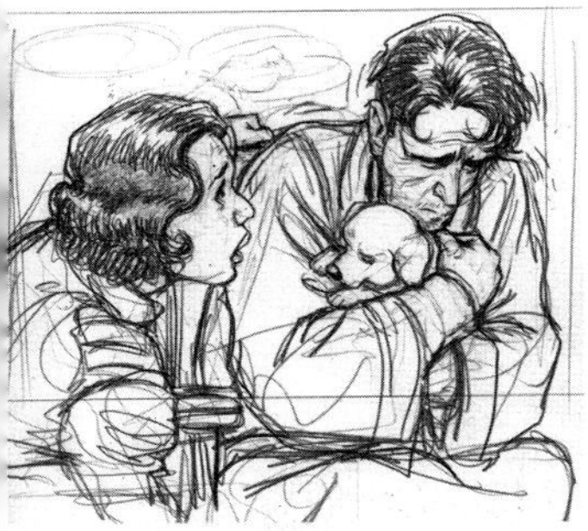

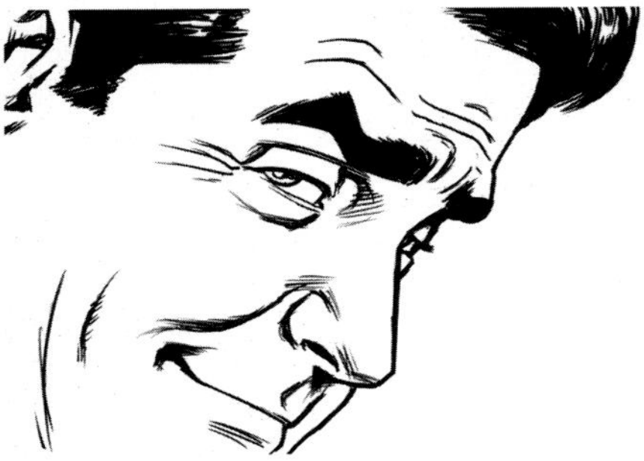

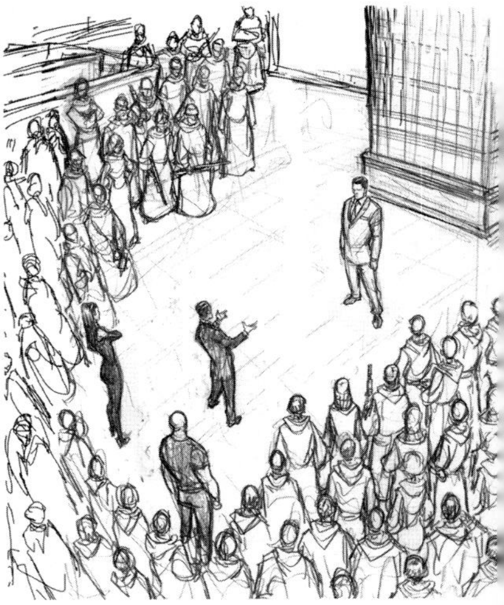

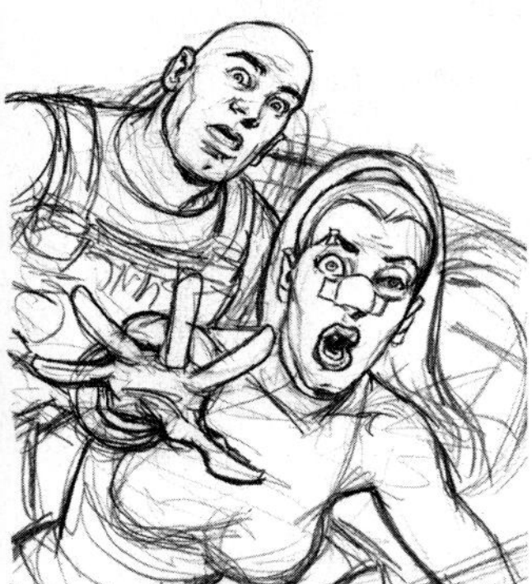

"Lots of action in JIMMY'S BASTARDS. A good deal of the old "Ultra-vi", blood and guts for good measure. All carried out in a, hopefully, darkly humorous way."
— RB

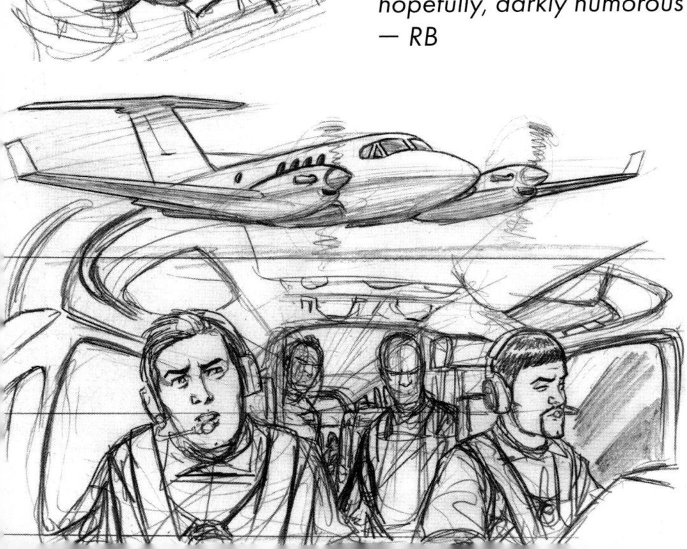

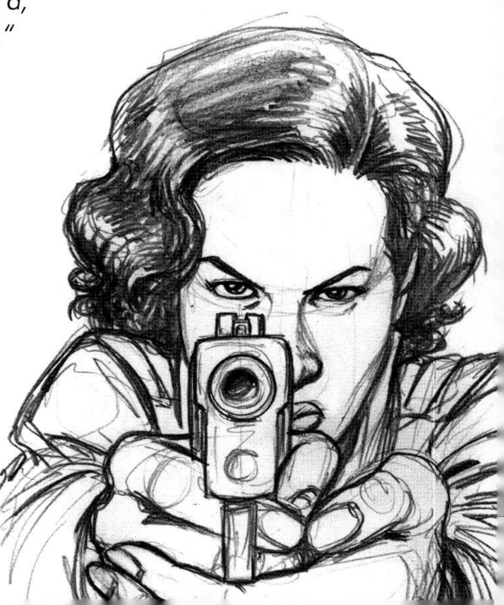

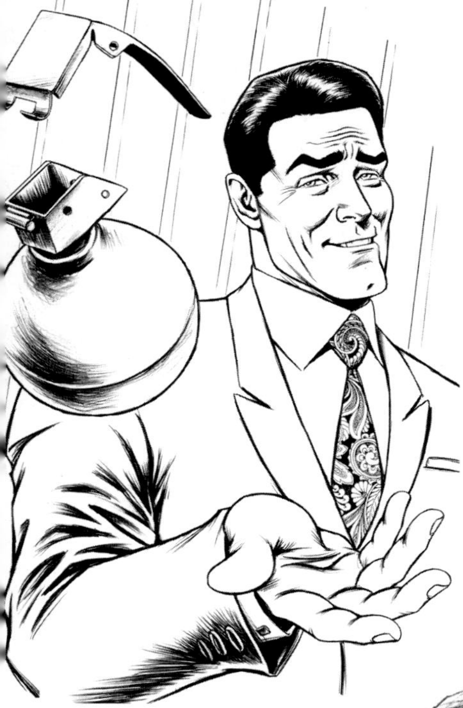

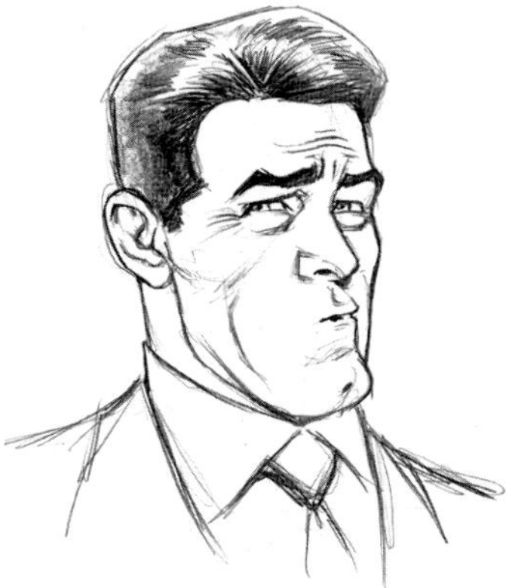

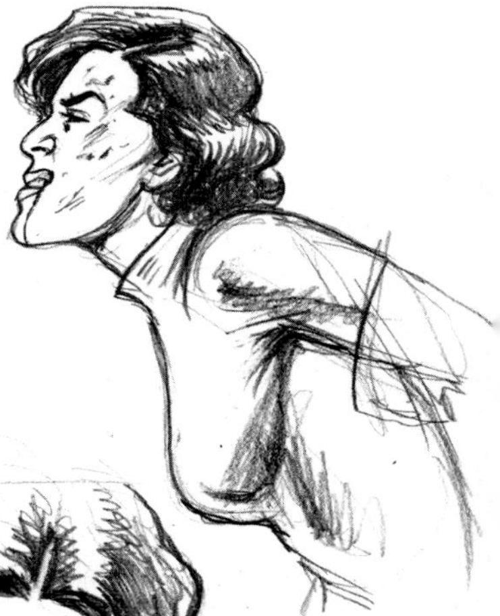

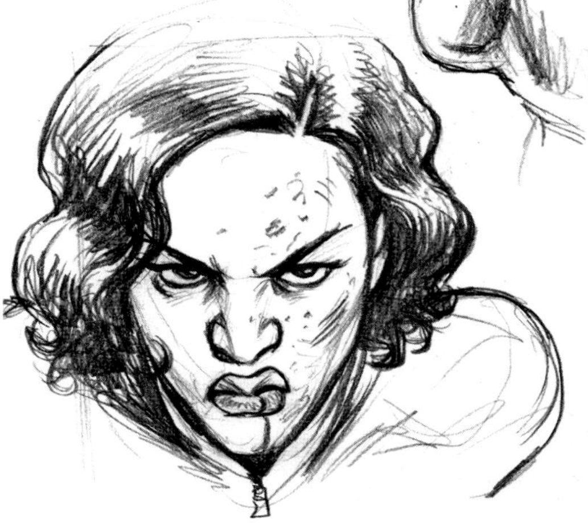

"The main relationship in the book is the Jimmy/ Nancy dynamic that grows and changes several times, but relies on a slightly tense camaraderie at every point. "Nancy's not having it," is pretty much true at every stage--rightly so." — *RB*

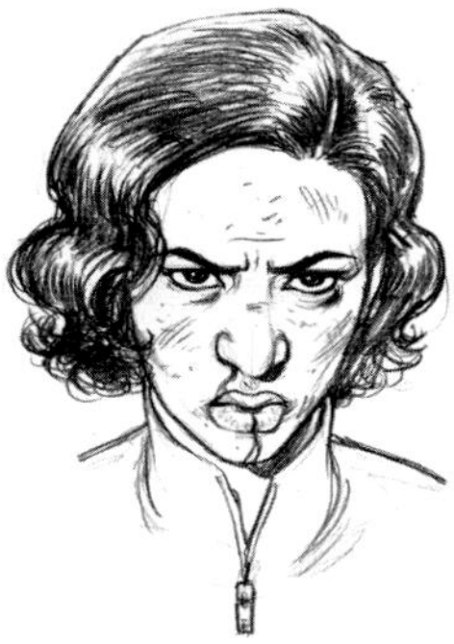

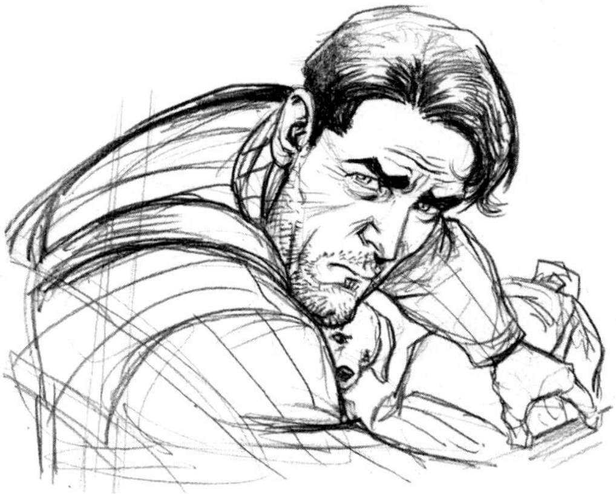

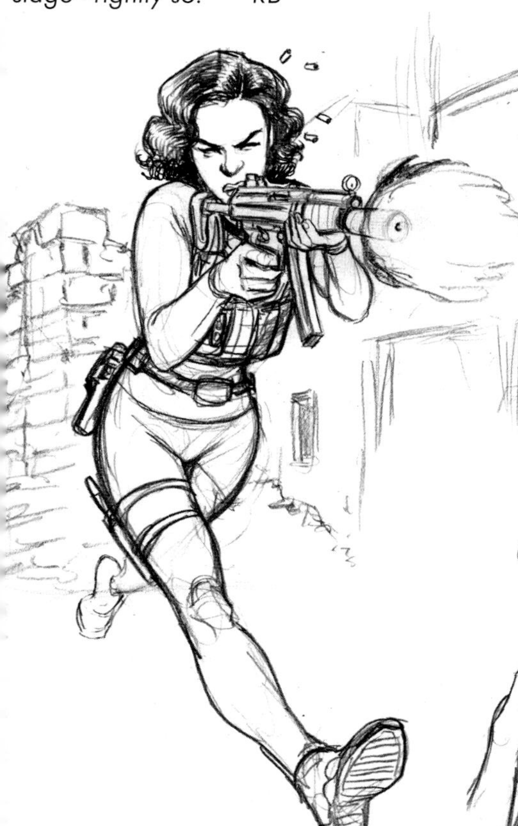

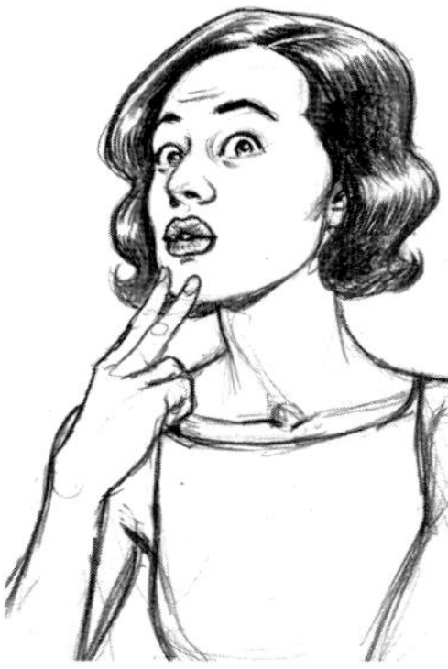

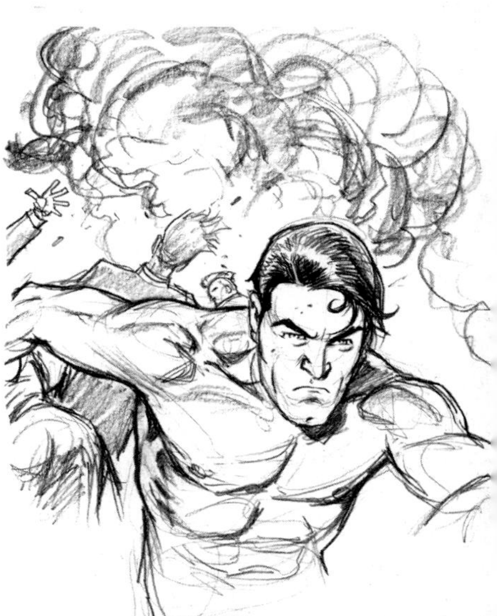

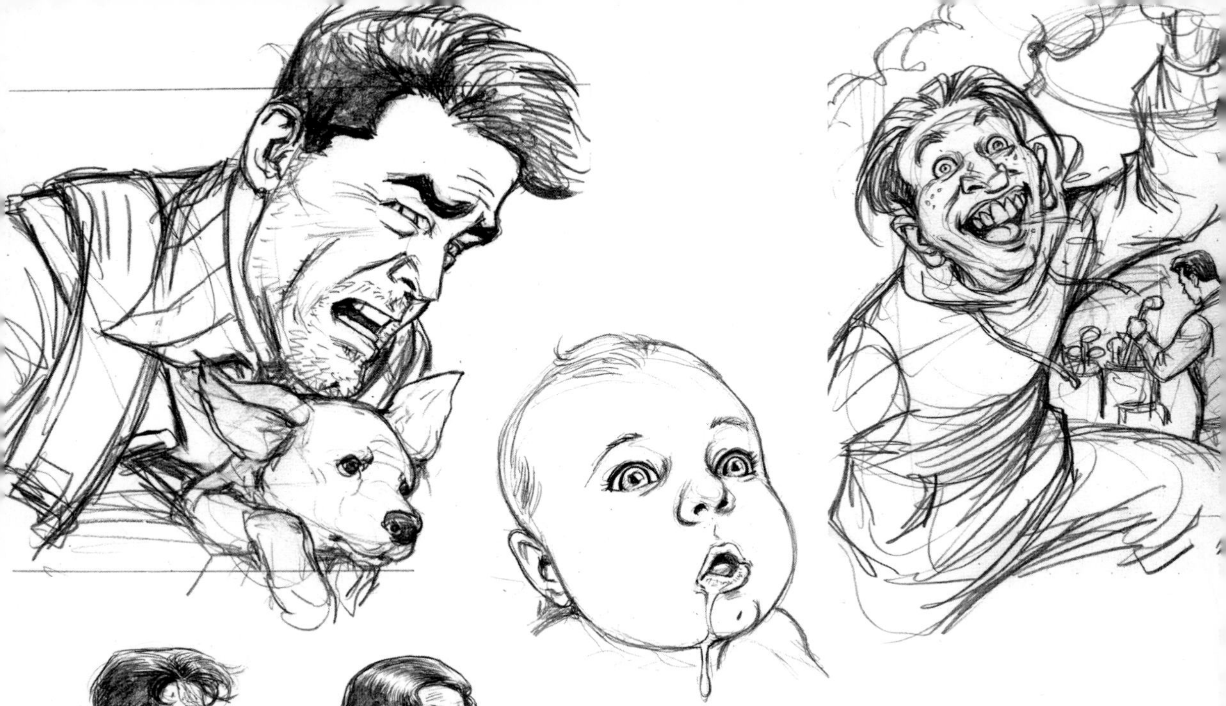

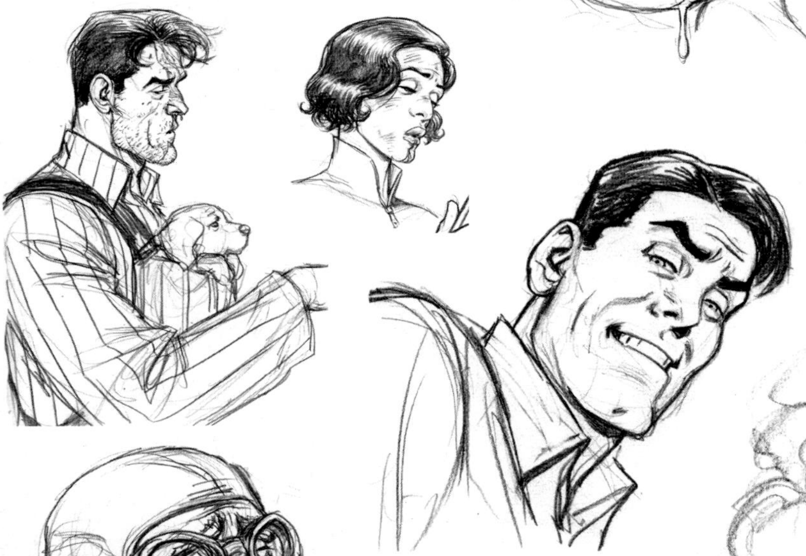

“I believe we’re an equal-opportunity offender on this one...a nudge and a wink to those who get it, a shrug to anyone who doesn’t.” — RB

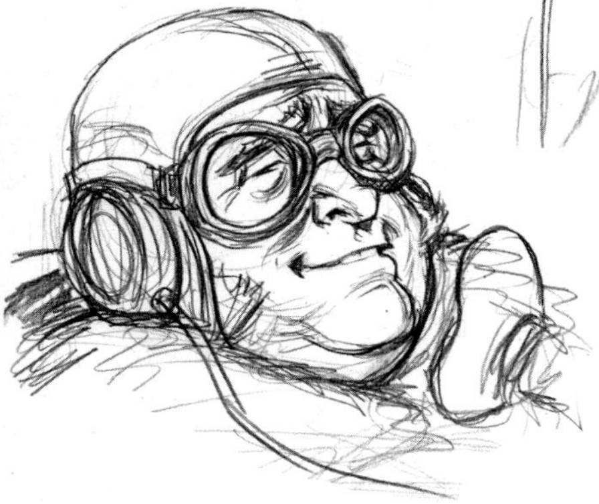

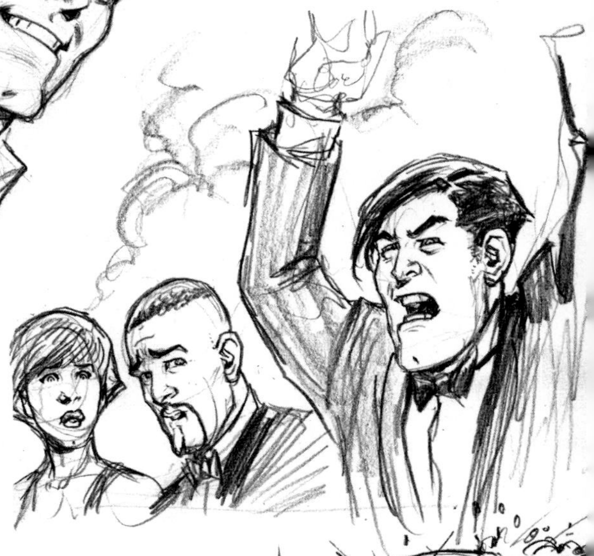

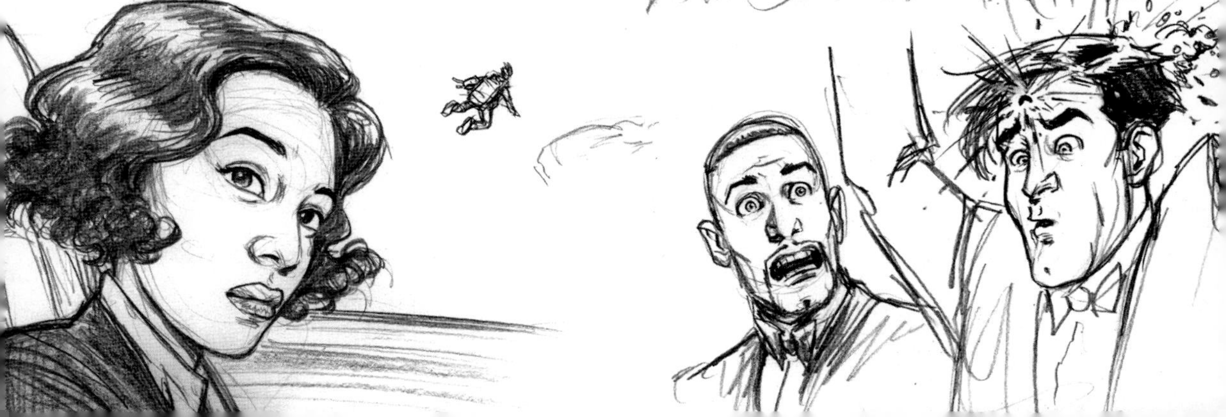

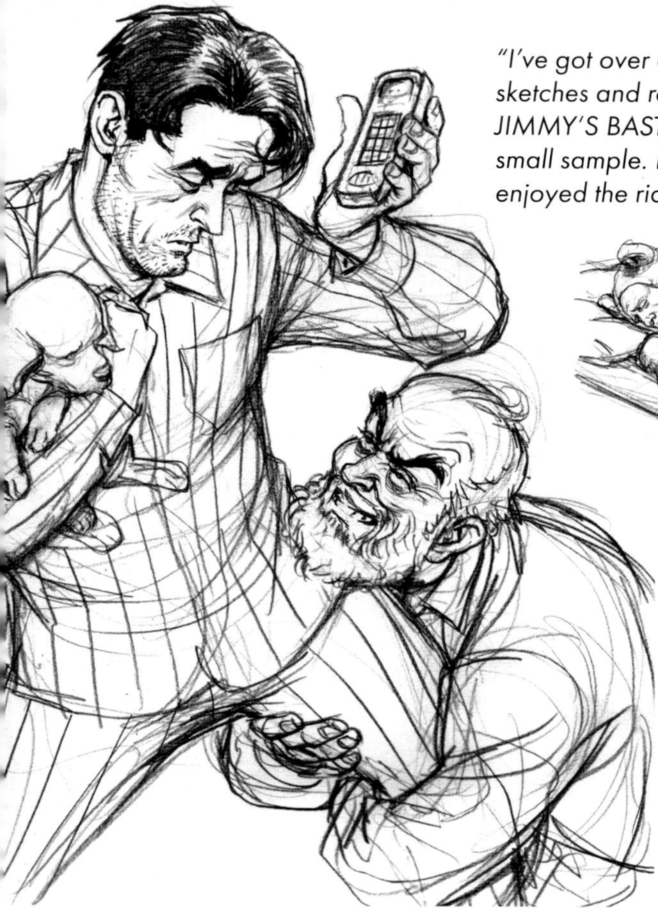

"I've got over a year's worth of sketches and roughs and pages of JIMMY'S BASTARDS...this is just a small sample. Hope you've enjoyed the ride!" — RB

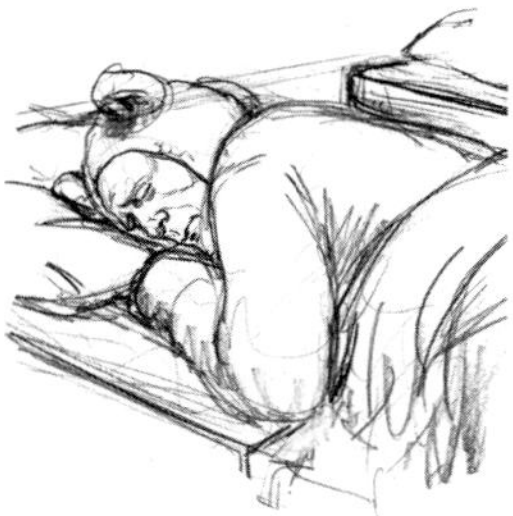

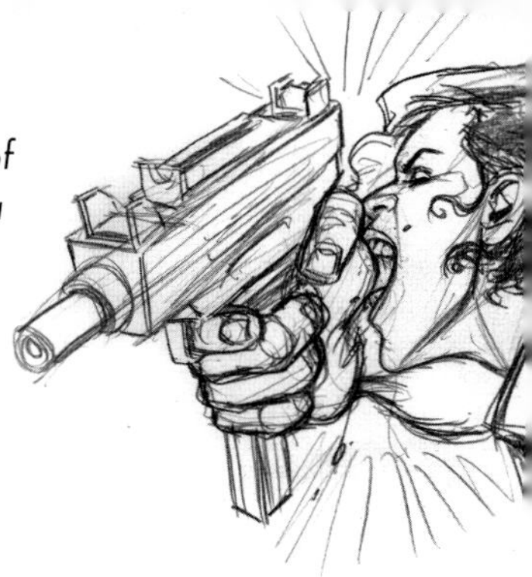

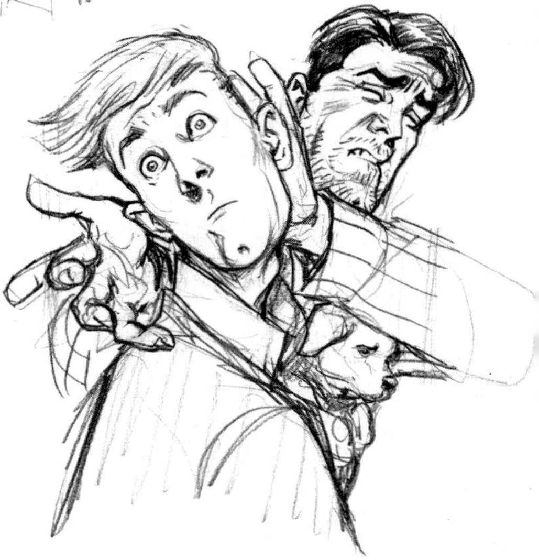

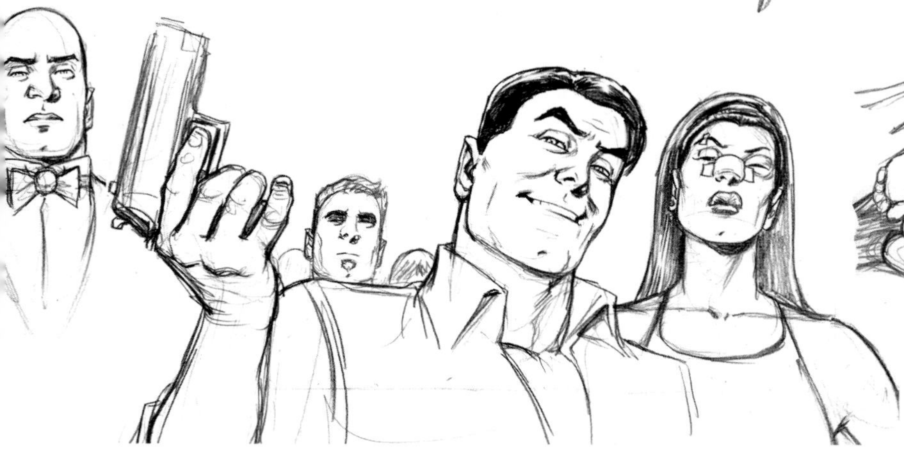

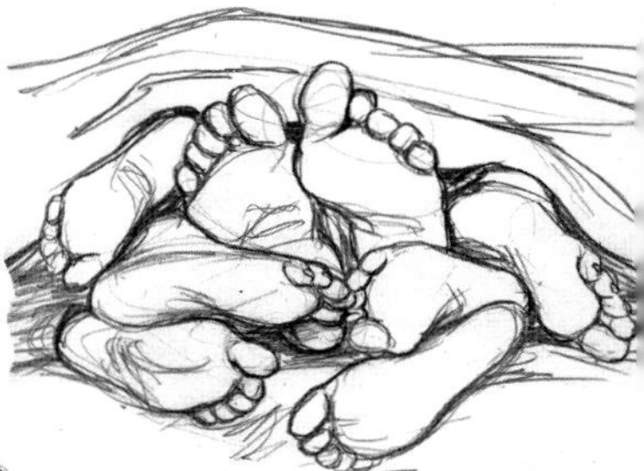

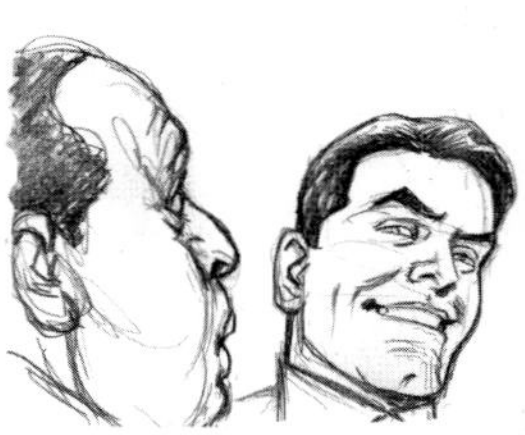

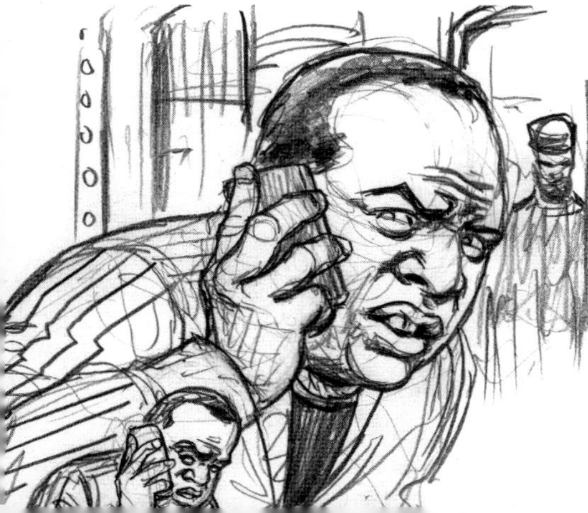

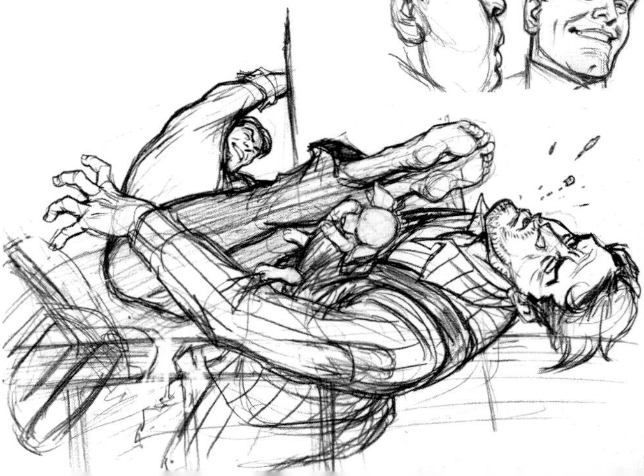

ABOUT THE CREATORS OF JIMMY'S BASTARDS™

GARTH ENNIS writer

Garth Ennis has been writing comics since 1989. His credits include *Preacher, The Boys, Crossed, Battlefields* and *War Stories*, and successful runs on *The Punisher* and *Fury* for Marvel Comics. Originally from Belfast, Northern Ireland, he now lives in New York City with his wife, Ruth.

RUSS BRAUN artist

Russ has been drawing comics for over twenty-five years, with a seven-year break for a stint with Walt Disney Feature Animation. Known for his expressive characters and storytelling, readers have enjoyed Russ' work on numerous titles, including *Batman, Animal Man* and *Swamp Thing* for DC, *Fables, Fairest* and *Jack of Fables* for Vertigo, and *Son of Satan* and *Where Monsters Dwell* for Marvel. Russ is best known, however, for his frequent collaborations with Garth Ennis on *The Boys, Battlefields,* and most recently, *Sixpack & Dogwelder.*

JOHN KALISZ colorist
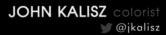 @jkalisz

John Kalisz has been coloring comics for over twenty years, working on just about every major character or book in comics at one point or another...from *Avengers* to *Zatanna* and everything in between.

ROB STEEN letterer

Rob Steen is the illustrator of the *Flanimals* series of children's books written by Ricky Gervais, and the Garth Ennis children's book, *Erf.* He is also the colorist of David Hine's graphic novel, *Strange Embrace,* and letterer of comic books for AfterShock, Marvel, Dynamite, Image and First Second.